Let's Pretend we're Sisters

Let's Pretend we're Sisters

PAULINE MONTOYA SOLIZ

LEONINE PUBLISHERS
PHOENIX, ARIZONA

Published by Leonine Publishers LLC
Phoenix, Arizona
USA

ISBN-13: 978-1-942190-26-4

Library of Congress Control Number: 2016954771

Printed in the United States of America
10 9 8 7 6 5 4 3 2 1

Visit us online at www.leoninepublishers.com
For more information: info@leoninepublishers.com

Dedication

To my Lord, Jesus Christ, who comes to me every time I call Him. He has blessed me with the gift of faith and a love for writing.

To my parents, Ignacio and Deluvina (Della), for their love and guidance. They taught me by example to love, praise, and glorify the blessed Trinity: Father, Son, and Holy Spirit, and Mary, the Immaculate Conception and perfect mother of Jesus.

To the love of my life, my husband Clemente (Junior), for patiently waiting for the time I could spend with him and for his encouragement and strength.

To my four daughters: Teresa, Veronica the first, Veronica, and Justine, for they are the reason I want to wake up in the morning; my gifts from God.

To my grandchildren: Roberto, Vincent, Iliana, Samson, Arian, Isabella, Caralena, and Aveleno, for the joy they bring to my life.

To my great-grandchildren; Adeus, Mateo, and Angelina, for the smile they put on my face.

To my sons-in-law: Big Roberto and Dennis.

To my five sisters: Mary Grace, Bessie, Priscilla, Mary Ann, and Debbie, who shared in my childhood adventures; for the closeness, love, and loyalty that only Montoya sisters know how to give.

To my brothers, Joe and Leo, for the love and respect they have always shown for their six sisters.

And last, but not least, to all my nieces and nephews.

Contents

Chapter One

March had come to Monte Vista, Colorado, a small town in the San Luis Valley east of the Rio Grande. It was barely light on the morning of March 5, 1954, and the call of birds could be heard. I raised the white shade just enough to let a ray of light come into the small room I shared with my sisters. I caught a glimpse of willow trees in the distance, their narrow leaves swaying gently.

The yard was large. The green front lawn had a pine tree and an aspen tree, both of which Mother and Father planted. There was a circular driveway to the back of the house. On one corner of the yard stood a one-room shed which housed a nice looking piano left behind by the previous owners. Father tuned it and played for us. Father also stored sacks of potatoes, bushels of apples, and peas in the shack. On the other corner of the yard stood the outhouse that Father hosed down once a month to keep clean. Between the shack and the outhouse was our wood pile, where Father and my brothers sawed and chopped firewood. Facing the front of the house to the left was a white picket fence along which sweet peas and pansies grew. A vegetable garden was to the right of the house. About fifty feet from the circular driveway were two lilac bushes, growing alongside a pebbled creek flowing with crystal-clear water and pollywogs. From the creek we could see Mr. Corlett's farm.

Every now and then Mother would say to Father, "There goes Miss Rita—she's going to the Willows." My sisters and I wondered what Miss Rita did there. The land is marshy, with only a single row of trees forming a windbreak where cows crowded on very windy days. Miss Rita's car was one of only five or six cars that went by in a day on our country road.

Mother would give Father a very slow wink, and say, "Miss Rita is picking wild spinach to sell. This helps her earn a living, now that she has become a widow."

Mother was very attractive and had a beautiful smile. Her light ash-brown hair always shined, and her eyes seemed to light up a room. She was slender and stood about five-foot-two. She carried herself with confidence; she had a fine style. When Father looked at her, we could see that he was very proud that she was his mate.

Bessie and I would give each other a secret look. We'll snoop later for an answer from Mary Grace or Joe, we'd say in our silent sister brain-wave talk. We knew that there was more to what Mother was saying to Father about Miss Rita, but we couldn't read between the lines. Our brother Leo would scold us if we asked him.

"You girls are too curious for your own good! Don't be asking me questions that don't concern you!" That was just his way.

I pulled the shade up a bit more. It took a lot of courage to set foot on the floor of a dark room. I remembered the spooky stories Mother's sister Aunt Dolores told. Closing my eyes, I imagined hands grabbing at my ankles as my feet hung off the bed. I pulled my feet up fast, heart pounding. I promised myself never to listen to ghost tales again. I had heard so many that I never wanted to be alone. Grandmother Genevieve, my mom's mother, was also very superstitious.

Uncle Paul, Mother's youngest brother, would tell us, "You girls have to behave, or The Man with Five Guns will come after you." We believed him because, on April 10, 1940, a sheep man from Monte Vista had murdered our grandfather Manuel Ortega, and five other people: his sister, her unborn child, her teenaged son, the county sheriff, and a witness to an investigation about some stolen sheep.

Uncle Paul was a very young boy when this happened to his father. Grandfather had been born on March 26, 1886, so he was fifty-four when he died.

When Grandmother babysat for Mother, we were told, "It's late, girls! You need to go to bed and stay in bed or the dead will come and pull at your feet!" Mother and Father assured us that this could never happen. But the seed had been planted in our imaginations. The ghost tales ended when Grandmother Genevieve and most of Mother's family moved to California, but the girls and I had already deposited these tales in our memory bank.

The night's fears behind me, I couldn't wait to meet the morning sun.

"Goody! It's Saturday morning!"

My sisters were asleep. I sighed, "Thank you, Jesus, for my sisters! It isn't hard to fall asleep at night with Mary Grace to my left, and Bessie, Priscilla, and Mary Ann to my right." Sometimes I fell asleep curled at the foot of the bed, but the girls were still close. My foot touched their feet until they kicked my foot away.

Father had actually helped to build this house for someone else. My sisters and I would fall asleep on our parents' jackets on weekend evenings when Mother helped Father build the kitchen cabinets.

Father said, "I would have added more bedrooms if I'd known I was going to move my family into this house."

Mother told him, "We'll make do. The girls are still young; they still fit on the bed together. Joe and Leo love sleeping in the big room at the back side of the house, and it has plenty of room for the wringer washer."

Blacky, our seven-year-old dog, had also made himself at home, curling up in front of the potbelly stove in the cold weather. If Mother wasn't with Father, then you could be sure that Blacky would be. Father also called Blacky "Ma Gros' Chien," which is French for "My Fat Dog." My brother Leo had once claimed that poor Blacky got a nervous stomach and gassy when Mother was home from work.

Blacky stood fourteen inches high and he weighed about ten pounds. He was a sweet mutt and he resembled a Border Collie. His black coat was a solid color and he was covered with silky hair. I don't recall that he had a "doggy" odor, for Father kept him well groomed. He would have to be if he was to go on errands with Mother and Father. We loved him and he was friendly and gentle.

Our cousin Jimmy had replied, referring to our mother, "Aunt Della is a very fussy house keeper. I love my aunt; she is very good to me, my brother, and sisters, but she gives me a nervous stomach too!"

Leo had agreed with him, but defended, "With eight children in our home, can you blame her?"

"Why that room was not attached to the big house I'll never understand!" Mother was saying.

"Maybe the builder, Mr. Corlett, couldn't find good help after Buck House called my friend Delfino and me to work in Jasper at the Green Chain Saw Mill," said Father. "Or maybe Mr. Corlett had plans to add another room to connect the big room to the kitchen."

"Hopefully we'll soon have saved enough to purchase our own home," said Mother.

"It's too bad my crew got laid off. Working at the lumber saw mill sure paid good money. But there's always work in farming; thank the Good Lord for that!"

Mr. Delfino and his family had been our neighbors for a short time, and he and Father had become friends when they both went to work in Jasper, Colorado, which has an elevation of about 8,000 feet.

The sound of my parents' voices in the next room made me feel secure. I felt joyful, safe and loved. Father was loving, but firm. We were daddy's girls. Mother was the center of our universe. She worked endless hours to make and keep our home comfortable. On this spring morning, I thought I'd jump out of bed, join them in the kitchen and have them all to myself. But I had to leave the room very quietly so as not to awaken my competition.

Our kitchen was warm and toasty in the winter months. The aroma of homemade bread lingered throughout. During the summer months, there was the smell of fresh vegetables coming from a large bowl on the counter in front of the country window. The kitchen had bottom cabinets but none on the top. A bushel of apples, or at times a bushel of fresh peas in pods, were held by a large basket made of woven wood strips. This basket sat between the counter and the wood stove. The stove often held hostage the aroma of cinnamon rolls for days. Behind the stove sat a firewood box. The kitchen also had brand new linoleum flooring. My sisters and I loved to slide on our bottoms across the slick linoleum. Father had installed a wood railing on the wall and beneath it he glued a square pattern of tea rose linoleum that looked like tile which stopped at the baseboard. In front of this wall sat a large oak table, holding two wash basins.

Joe, my oldest brother, was already a Don Juan at eighteen. He was quite good-looking, with a fair complexion, big brown eyes, and black hair that he thought required a lot of care. He liked hunting jackrabbits, and claimed that the meat didn't have a wild taste. He took great pride in keeping his car clean. Right after high school, he went to work at Monte Vista's biggest grocery store. My brother Joe purchased his two-door car for 1,500 dollars. His 1950 Fleetwood was his pride and joy. He kept the white interior and whitewall tires spotless. The car's green metallic paint shined and was free of nicks. The scent of Doublemint, Spearmint, and Juicy Fruit gum lingered throughout. If his metallic-green car was parked in the market parking lot, you could be sure there would be a few girls checking him out, hoping he would notice them. Once he started dating girls, we didn't see very much of him. We liked to see him drive up with our cousin Phil, because Phil got Joe to play Father's guitar, accordion and harmonica, and sing country music. I especially liked the song Jambalaya. He taught himself to play by watching Father at family weddings. On winter weekends, he chopped wood and shoveled snow, doing Leo's chores so that Leo could spend the morning hours checking his muskrat traps. Joe was a sleepy head: he wasn't eager to jump out of bed like Leo. Father's nickname for Joe was "Mon Acito." Mon is the masculine French word for My, and Acito is the Spanish short word for Ignacio. Ignacio being Joe and Father's middle name.

Mary Grace, the second eldest, was plump and very pretty with large brown eyes like all of us girls. She loved to dance with energy and show off her pretty long nails. She and Joe danced the Jitterbug so well together that at dances they were left alone on the floor. Mother worked for our family doctor, cleaning his medical office and doing housekeeping for his wife Mrs. Roth. Mother depended on Mary Grace to help care for Bessie, Priscilla, Mary Ann, Debbie, and me: Pauline. Mary Grace took charge with confidence. She combed our hair every morning and watched over us after school. She started dinner before Mother and Father got home from work. She was very popular in school, well-liked by the students and teachers. She always brought home good grades, and played a little accordion. She was very close to Father. She was also a sleepy-head. She'd fall asleep after school without even removing her jacket.

Mother showed some concern, but Dr. Roth assured her that Mary Grace was fine.

"Della, you must realize that Mary Grace, at sixteen, is on the cusp of becoming an adult."

Father used to say, "I do believe Joe and Mary Grace are part whippoorwill: only active at night! Only time will tell if the rest of my little girls are part whippoorwill."

Mother would laugh at Father's comment and say, "It's just the change in the season. The weather is perfect for sleeping. On weekends Joe and Mary Grace practice dancing late into the night, especially if they have Cousin Phil for an audience. In the morning they have a hard time waking up."

Leo was two years younger than Mary Grace. He was quiet, fair, very cute, and looked more like Mother than Joe did. Leo loved and respected Father, as we all did, but anyone could see how close he was to Mother. When Father was away up in the mountains, working as a lumberjack, he could depend on Leo to help Mother with the outside chores. He made sure the firewood box was full at all times. He made sure the hogs and chickens were fed. He kept the driveway clear of snow so that Mother and Joe could leave for work on time. In the summer months he made sure the lawn and vegetable garden were watered. We never heard him complain. He liked to joke and tease, but he didn't like it when Joe teased him. Leo would work alongside Mother for hours. He loved riding his bike, and would jump on it to run errands for Mother. When Mary Ann was in kindergarten, he would drop her off and pick her up on his bike, and then drop her off at Mrs. Roth's house.

Grandmother told us, "When Leo was an infant he was very ill: on the brink of death. Your father took him in his arms and asked out loud with much emotion, 'Lord Jesus Christ, please don't take him from his mother! Please, lend my son Leo to his mother for many more years!'"

Grandmother claimed that she had witnessed other infant deaths in her life, and that she believed Jesus Christ heard Father's prayer.

"Your mother Della couldn't have taken another loss. She had lost her father, who died horrendously just nineteen days prior to Leo's birth. There is a very special bond between my daughter and her baby boy Leo: a gift given to her for the second time. And Jesus knows what a good man your father Ignacio is."

Leo loved the outdoors. He went out very early every weekend to trap muskrats and collect scrap iron to sell. He also helped Mother and Father raise chickens. He hated going to school; he'd rather be at home doing chores. He was very energetic and didn't have a lazy bone in his body.

Bessie was two years younger than Leo: pretty and slender, with a quiet and shy manner. Her eyes seemed to say, "Don't worry, I'll fix everything." But at times she seemed frail. She had the ability to form a special relationship with each member of the family. She was special to Mother and Father; they called her "Le Blanc": our father's mother's maiden name. She didn't make decisions quickly; she was a thinker. There were times when I became impatient and wanted to light a fire under her. She liked to bargain. "Let's make a deal" were her four favorite words. For example, she'd say, "Sure, Pauline, you may wear my top to school, but only if you'll do my turn for the dinner dishes for two nights." Priscilla, Mary Ann and I made note of it, and hoped the time would come when she would have a need, and then we could strike a bargain with her.

I, Pauline, was two years younger than Bessie. I believe I was named after my father's aunt. Pictures show her as an elegant French lady. I was also named after my godfather, Uncle Paul. I found it delightful hearing about the events of my Baptism. Uncle Paul was only eleven when I was born. Soon after, mother and father were making plans for my Baptismal day. Paul joined in the conversation.

He asked father, "Tachito (Ignacio), would you like to have me as your compadre? I would be proud to be the baby's godfather."

"Being a godfather comes with responsibility. The godfather has to make the arrangements with the priest at church."

A couple of days went by; then, to mother and father's surprise, their little brother announced that the special day was set for September 4.

Paul explained that Father Paves told him, "A date can only be set if and when the godfather comes in to talk with me."

Paul continued, "I ran two miles to get there. 'I'm here! I'm the godfather to be!' I even stopped at the store and bought these shoes for the baby. I lost the bag on the way while running!"

Father Paves, mother, and father could not refuse him.

Paul's determination to stand next to his mother, Genoveva, as godparents to the now two-month-old Pauline was not to be denied.

I saw myself as tough, if I felt that my sisters were threatened. When Father was annoyed with me, he called me "Apache," which I don't think suited me in the least. I carried myself like a lady at ten years old, mindful of my manners. Sister Amelia, my favorite nun at school said, "Pauline has big expressive eyes, and is such a sweetheart." A lot of people said this about me, but then Mary Grace would say, "That's only because they don't live with you every day!"

My other nickname was "Pockets," a name given to me by Uncle Tony, Mother's brother-in-law. It made me feel special. Apache was a hurtful name, even though I must have acted at times like one—stubborn—because it took a lot for Father to show disapproval of his children. If I wasn't with my sisters, I was sitting close to a radio. I especially liked country music at that age, and took pride in knowing the words to many songs.

Priscilla was two years younger than me. She was the prettiest of all the girls, fair, with large eyes that seemed to say, "I can do anything you can do!" Mother and Father tried to serve her first at mealtime because she was so thin. They always took Priscilla with them when they went far from home. Grandmother had warned Mother, "Never leave her behind. I had a dream that she was stolen from you!"

Mother concluded that she didn't gain weight because she was very active. Priscilla seemed to think it was her job to watch over the "baby"—two years younger than herself. She took pride in her self-assigned duty to watch over Mary Ann. Father's nickname for Priscilla was "Te`re`mo`te." He told us that this was the Spanish word for tornado. She was always on the move, whirling quickly so as not to get caught, especially if she suspected she was going to be spanked. Leo commented once, "Boy, can Priscilla twist! She has perfected the crocodile death roll. She always manages to get away." Mary Grace told Mother, "Priscilla is a handful; she is always into something. I'm surprised she hasn't hurt herself by now! I don't know where she gets her ideas, but I must admit she is creative."

The youngest was Mary Ann, the pretty, sweet and somewhat spoiled pet of the family. Everyone addressed her as "Baby." She was two years younger than Priscilla. Her long black hair was always beautifully braided, and her eyes seemed to say, "I'm a very important member of this family, and don't you forget it!" Father's nickname for Mary Ann was "Revilion"—Spanish for hurricane—because she wanted to have a nickname like the rest of us. She was a good listener; she didn't give her opinion very often, but when she did, it was very direct. She was very attached to Bessie. She enjoyed spending time at Mrs. Roth's house, where she learned to use a napkin at the table, with fork to the left, knife on the right, and napkin on lap. She learned to be very neat, never soiling her clothes at mealtime. Mother taught all of her children to be tidy; we liked it that way and it made her job of running her home much smoother.

Mother allowed Mary Grace to pick the youngest child's name: Debra May. She was born seven years after Mary Ann. What joy her appearance brought to our world! She brought new enjoyable experiences to Bessie, Priscilla, Mary Ann and me. The four of us were so close in age that we had no memory of baby announcements. The whys began: "Why is Mother sitting so far from the table? Why is Mother getting so fully packed around the middle of her body? Why does Mother dress in those big, but very pretty new tops? Why does she stay home from work once a month to go to the doctor?"

Mother never complained of being sick. She looked so beautiful when she explained all our whys.

"We are going to have a brand new baby in the family after Christmas."

Mother showed the prettiest smile when we asked questions about the baby. Words can't explain the joy that filled our home the day Father brought Mother and Debra May home from the hospital. She seemed like a real life baby doll from Santa Claus, and everyone had their time to hold, feed, and play with her. Darling as she was, and as much as I loved her, she was still "competition number eight."

Being raised in a large family meant never being alone. I always had someone to play with, laugh and cry with, go to school or work with, fight with, and get into mischief with. Yes, we shared everything, but sharing was the furthest thing on my mind this Saturday morning. I was the first out of bed, so I was the lucky one who could spend time alone with Mother and Father

As I stepped onto the warm wooden kitchen floor, a sunbeam reflecting off the bucket of drinking water blinded me. I rubbed my eyes and reached for the ladle. I spilled cold water on my face as I tried to scoop it out of the bucket, high on the counter. Mother and Father were at the back door talking with Mr. Corlett, Father's boss and a local small-town lawyer. He was our landlord, and Father also worked his small farm.

I stood on a chair to reach the bucket; the first drink was fresh and cool. Father must have brought it in early this morning from the well. I looked out the window and saw the creek that ran behind our house and separated our house from the neighbor. I wondered if the ice had melted by now. Mother couldn't afford to buy ice skates for all of us girls, but it was great fun to pretend.

Father would be furious—actually he would be disappointed. Father didn't know how to be furious: it wasn't in his nature.

"Don't set one foot on that wooden plank running across the creek," he'd warn. "The ice that forms on it can be very dangerous."

We weren't swimmers, and if we ran across, we could slip and fall in. Mother would say, "You girls have no business going across to the neighbor's. You girls have each other. Stay together; there is safety in numbers."

The neighbors were seldom at home. We often saw them pack their suitcases in the car, but we never saw any children.

"The plank is there for the goat," Dad told us. "The neighbors don't mind him in their yard, keeping down the weeds."

I wondered where that billy goat could be. He was mean, so ever since another farmer had given him to Father, we had to be on the lookout.

One day Bessie, Priscilla and I were playing on the haystack. We didn't see the goat so we merrily climbed down. Coming out of nowhere, he charged us. Bessie started to run toward the house, with me following. My heart was pounding and the house seemed to move further away as we ran. I kept looking back for Priscilla, far behind me. I could see her little legs with drooping socks exposing her ankles, and her long golden braids flopping. She was trying hard to keep up with Bessie and me.

She looked terrified.

"He's gonna get me! He's gonna get me!" she cried.

Next I saw him bump her to the ground. I stopped running and called to Bessie. We both stood frozen with fear. Priscilla was face down, but the goat unexpectedly turned and ran away. We ran back to Priscilla and told her he was gone.

"Jesus must have told him to leave!"

Priscilla looked up at us, relief written all over her face. Her eyes were still wide. She had dirt on her nose, and straw in her hair.

"Yes! Jesus made him go away!" I said. I helped her up, and Bessie checked to see if she was hurt.

"I just fell!" cried Priscilla. She bravely tried to convince us, but we had witnessed the frightful attack.

"Do you want me to carry you back to the house?" Bessie asked.

Mary Grace was at the door to call us. We explained why Priscilla's dress was dirty. Mary Grace gave her water and cleaned her up, and we never mentioned the incident to Mother and Father. He would have been upset to know we had played on the haystack after he had forbidden it. Father was afraid we would accidentally fall between the loose bales of hay.

I heard Mr. Corlett cough at the back door as I sang quietly, "Oh, where have you been, billy goat, billy goat? Oh, where have you been? You bully!" That billy goat had no business being so mean. Long after that, we would look for him before we'd go outdoors.

I didn't see that darn goat, but I saw smoke! I leaned closer to the window for a better look.

"Oh my! It's smoke! Daddy, Daddy!" I called.

"What is it, Pockets? Keep your voice down."

"Is this the one you call Pockets? She sure has full round cheeks," said Mr. Corlett.

"Yes, this is Pauline."

I smiled at him.

"But look, Mother!" I pointed.

Smoke was definitely coming from the neighbor's house.

"It is smoke!" exclaimed Mother. Mister Corlett held the door open for us with his half an arm. Somehow I did not like the word "stump," which is what my cousin Jimmy called it. I wondered how he lost his left arm, and how he was able to drive.

"Ignacio, that house must be on fire!" said Mother, grabbing the receiver off the magneto telephone. "Operator!" she exclaimed. "Give me 12333 and hurry, please!"

Father and Mr. Corlett walked quickly toward the plank to cross over to the neighbor's yard. I followed. Father stopped, bent his knees, and tilted his shoulder so I could climb on his back. I hugged his neck. The piggyback ride didn't last long, but I felt special for those few moments.

We circled around to the front of the house where the smoke originated, and Father helped me down.

"Luckily, there is no wind this morning," he said.

"You're right, Ignacio. It wouldn't take much for it to go up in flames," said Mr. Corlett. "If the fire engine gets here quickly, they may be able to save it."

"It looks like it's just smoldering," said Father.

"Are they smokers?"

"Don't know much about them. They spend a lot of time away from home."

I decided these people must be rich, to come and go as they did. I'll bet they've even taken a trip to Hollywood, I thought. They've probably set eyes on Mr. Jimmy Durante and maybe even Debbie Reynolds and Eddie Fisher! I hoped one day to visit Grandmother in California and meet a movie star.

Mother's hands on my shoulders broke my train of thought.

"No school today, Pauline, it's Saturday. Why are you up so early?"

I looked up at her, smiled, and shrugged my shoulders. She pulled me close to her and I thought she must be the prettiest mother in the whole world.

The fire engine pulled onto the circular driveway, and the firefighters jumped off. The fire had started in the front room. The breaking glass and shooting flames frightened me. Father sensed my apprehension. He pulled his fingers from my grip, and lowered his shoulders again so I could climb on his back.

"It's okay, Pockets," he said. "The firemen are just doing their job." Father lowered me back to the ground.

The fire captain walked up, shook Father's hand, and winked at me.

Father told him that the people who lived in the burning house had left earlier that morning.

"My daughter here was the first to see the smoke," he added.

The captain smiled at me. "Well, young lady, you probably saved this house from burning down completely! What is your name?"

"Pauline." I glanced up at Father, who smiled at me.

"Lucky for these people that you were up early this morning," said the captain. He patted my head, and then pulled some balloons out of his pocket and handed them to me.

"Thank you!" I counted one…two…three…four…five! Just enough for us girls!

After about two hours, the firefighters were sure that the fire was completely out. Two of them started to board up the doors and windows. Mother, Father and Mr. Corlett walked to the side of the house. I watched as the men hammered away.

The words of a song came to me, "Ain't a-gonna need this house no longer, ain't a-gonna need this house no more. Ain't got time to fix the shingles, ain't got time to fix the floor…"

"Pauline," called Mother as they started back to our house. Mister Corlett headed for his car.

"Would you like to come in for a cup of coffee?" asked my father.

"Not this morning, thank you. I need to get back to my office. But I do need to know: do you plan to place salt blocks out for the cows on Monday?"

"Yes, I do. The snow is almost completely gone, and my boys will help me. Leo looks for little side jobs, so he can make extra money to make changes to his bike. He wants to rig something so he can carry home the scrap metal, instead of using a gunny sack. And Joe can always use gas money."

"Okay then, have a safe weekend." He waved as he drove away.

When we walked into the house, Mary Grace cried, "Mother! You didn't tell me you were leaving and taking Pauline with you! I was concerned. I didn't realize you were outdoors. I didn't see the truck—it must be parked on the side of the house. I kept thinking Pauline must have gone somewhere with them; where else could she be? I was sure you wouldn't leave without telling me she'd be going with you, but I looked out and didn't see any of you! I'm too young to have these worries!"

"I'm sorry, honey; I didn't think to tell you. You were asleep."

Mother and Father explained what had happened, and everyone ran to the window.

"It's a good thing Pauline was at that very window earlier," said Father. "She alerted us, and your mother called the fire department."

"Father, will you take Mary Ann and me to see?" asked Priscilla. "After you have your breakfast?"

"Your father and I have had our breakfast," said Mother. "Girls, take your places at the table and I'll serve you some pancakes."

"Mother, may I have some warm syrup on mine?" asked Mary Ann.

"Mine too?" asked Bessie. "I've never been up close to a fire engine! Was the siren loud, Pauline?"

"Not really," I answered. "But it sure was neat watching the men in their uniforms. One of them looked like a movie star! He looked like that actor that played in 'Seven Brides for Seven Brothers'!"

"Really? You mean Howard Keel?"

"Yeah, that's the one! He sure was dreamy," I whispered to Bessie.

"Mother, may we go to the movies?" asked Priscilla.

"Not this Saturday," answered Mother.

"Guess why!" said Mary Grace. She twirled around the kitchen table, then bent down and kissed Priscilla on the cheek.

"Why?"

"Because I can't take you girls. Phyllis is coming over today to help plan my sixteenth birthday party next Saturday!" exclaimed Mary Grace.

"Really, Mother? Does she get to have a party?" asked Bessie.

"Yes, her very first!" said Mother.

"Did you hear that, Pauline?"

"I sure did, Bessie! One day we will get a birthday party too! If we are lucky, we may get to see how that game 'spin the bottle' is played!"

I poured warm syrup over my pancakes. I had never been to a birthday party, but I'd heard about them from friends at school.

"To hear Mary Grace tell it, she has very special plans for her party," said Leo, entering the kitchen with an armful of firewood. "It includes cake, ice cream, potato chips, Royal Crown cola, Bobby Allen, and Ernest Samara!"

"A little breeze is pulling the smell of burnt wood this way," he continued. "It will be in the air for a couple of days no doubt, because of the dampness. Those people are in for a big surprise when they see their windows boarded up."

He put the wood in the wood box.

"I'll let you go back to your birthday planning, party girl!" he said, winking at Mother and heading out to chop more wood.

"I have to invite some of Joe's friends," said Mary Grace defensively. "After all, Bobby and Earnest are in my class, you know!"

"It's okay, Mary. Leo just likes to tease," said Mother.

"What are we gonna wear to the party?" asked Mary Ann.

"I don't think you and your sisters are on the guest list," said Father.

"Is that true, Mother? We can't be here for the birthday party?" asked Mary Ann. She ran out of the kitchen crying. Priscilla went after her.

"If we have to help clean the house, we should be able to stay for the party," said Bessie. "Besides that, where would we go? The drive-in is still closed. If you let us stay, I promise to keep the girls occupied and out of the way."

"That sounds like a good plan," said Mother. "What do you think, Mary?"

Priscilla came back into the kitchen with her arm around Mary Ann, who was still pouting. "Don't cry, Baby, it's okay," she said.

"They can stay; they will fall asleep early."

I leaned over and whispered to Bessie, "That's what she thinks! No, we won't!" I giggled.

"Quit, Pauline! Do you want Mary Grace to hear you?"

A truck pulled up in the front yard. Mother went to the door.

"Hello, Phyllis!"

"Hello, Mrs. Montoya."

"Come in. You may call me Della."

"I'd like that," said Phyllis. She smiled at Mary Grace.

"I'm so glad you're finally here! We have so much planning to do," said Mary Grace.

"Are those your brothers in the truck, driving away with your dad?" asked Priscilla.

"They sure are. My dad's taking them fishing," answered Phyllis.

"How are you all doing?" asked Mother. "Have the boys adjusted to the new school? It can't be easy moving to a new town."

"We are all doing well. Meeting Mary Grace has made a world of difference for me. She makes me feel as though we've known each other forever. Our brothers have become best friends too."

"Do you have any sisters?" asked Priscilla.

"Yes, but they're back in Durango with our grandparents. My parents wanted to settle here first and be sure we like it, before disrupting the lives of my three sisters. They're much younger than the boys. I brought pictures to share…"

"Later," said Mary Grace. "Right now we have plans to make. Come, Phyllis. Shall we go to the front room?"

Priscilla and Mary Ann followed them. Mother had placed two big pans of water to heat early that morning so Bessie and I could do the breakfast dishes, and for bathing. We'd have to heat more for all of us girls to bathe. Mary Grace had to make the beds and sweep the floors. Bessie and I worked well together; even if we disagreed, we quickly found a solution.

"You wash, I dry. Is that alright, Pauline?"

"That's fine," I said. "You washed the last two times. If Mother goes shopping today, we need to remember hand lotion, comic books, and shelled Spanish peanuts."

"I don't believe we'll be going to the Boy's Market today," said Bessie. "Mother mentioned that Uncle Manuel, Aunt Elsie, Robert, Ruth, Virginia and Andy are coming to dinner."

"That reminds me! Did I tell you what Priscilla and I did for baby Andy?"

"No, you didn't, but you can tell me as you start washing so I can start drying!"

I put my hands in the soapy water and began. I was proud that I'd done something for my Catholic Faith.

"We've been working on our catechism, and the last lesson was about being baptized a Catholic. Sister Alquin explained the importance of Baptism and how crucial it is to baptize a newborn right away. An infant who dies without Baptism is unable to reach Heaven, and he goes to a place of natural happiness, called Limbo. Parents have a serious obligation to see that their children are baptized soon after birth, to be rid of original sin. If a baby dies without Baptism, he will never see the face of God! I couldn't let that happen to that sweet baby boy. I asked Priscilla to help me and she agreed."

"What did you do?"

I was pleased that Bessie was so interested. I told how, while our parents and aunt and uncle were outside visiting, I told Priscilla to get the salt shaker, and I got half a cup of water. I picked up the baby who was fast asleep. I brought him to the kitchen table and told Priscilla to put a little salt on the tip of her freshly washed finger. I instructed her to put it on Andy's tongue as I poured water over his head. As I poured, I said, "I baptize thee in the name of the Father and the Son and the Holy Ghost."

"You girls really did this?"

"Yes, we did! If anything should happen to Andy, we know that he has received the Holy Spirit, and will see the face of God!"

"Did he wake up when you poured the water over his head?"

"He woke up when Priscilla put her finger on his tongue, but he just made a funny face. I dried his hair quickly and he went back to sleep. We smiled, because we knew that we must have earned a couple of feathers or maybe even an angel wing! We'll tell Mom and Dad, but not right away. If they tell Uncle Manuel and Aunt Elsie, they may try to undo the Baptism because they are not Catholic!"

Bessie laughed. "I don't believe anyone could change it. You and Priscilla did a good thing! I'm sure you did earn a step into heaven! You could have been caught, if Andy had started crying. Uncle Manuel is studying to be a minister for his religion. I think all religions believe in Baptism, though they don't call it a sacrament, like the Catholic Church does."

"You sure have learned a lot about Church teachings, Bessie. You're so smart!"

"Not really. I'm just two years older than you and I've studied further along in my catechism book. There are seven sacraments and Baptism is the first. Baptism is the sacrament of rebirth through which Jesus Christ gives us divine life and joins us to His Mystical Body."

"I know, I read that, but I really can't pretend to understand what it means. When we get older and study more we will understand."

"By the end of the school year, you'll have learned so much about the Church and her teachings."

"Gosh, there is so much to learn!"

"We need to finish up," said Bessie. "Mother wants to mop the floor the minute we are done."

Mother came into the kitchen. "If you girls are done with the dishes, toss the dirty dishwater out, but not too close to the front door, or the boys will track in mud."

Bessie and I each grabbed our dish pans and walked out very carefully. We went a little ways from the house. We counted one… two…three! and tossed the water to see whose water would go out the furthest. The margin was even! The very first time ever!

"I bet we couldn't do that again!"

"You think so, Pauline?"

"I think it was a very lucky throw. It will be a very, very long time before we throw evenly again."

When we returned to the kitchen, Mother had mop and pail in hand.

"Okay, Girls, out of the kitchen!" she said.

We found our sisters in the front room. Priscilla and Mary Ann were listening intensely to Mary Grace and Phyllis making plans for the party.

Phyllis never made us feel like we were in the way. Sometimes she'd wink at us. We couldn't get over her very small waistline, and someday we wanted to wear Levi jeans like she did.

"Are you going to play games like 'Spin the Bottle'?" I asked.

Mary Grace and Phyllis looked at each other and giggled.

"What do you know of 'Spin the Bottle,' Pauline?" asked Phyllis.

"My friend Julia told me her sister and her friends play games at their parties. She said that they play 'Spin the Bottle' the most."

"Why would anyone want to spin a bottle?" asked Mary Ann.

"You spin a bottle and when it stops spinning, the neck of it points at one of the boys sitting in a circle," explained Phyllis.

"Then what?" asked Priscilla.

"You girls are just full of questions, aren't you?" said Mary Grace.

Bessie smirked. "Sister Devota tells the class, 'You can't learn if you don't ask questions.'"

I realized that Bessie must know about the game. Later I will corner her and bargain for answers, I thought.

"Oh, really? Is that what Sister Devota tells her class?" said Mary Grace. "Far be it from us to keep you girls from learning." She and Phyllis looked at each other and giggled again, then she changed the subject.

"Come on, Phyllis, let's find my mom and run our plans by her," said Mary Grace.

Leo passed by the window and waved as he headed for the back yard, with a gunny sack in one hand and traps in the other.

Priscilla jumped up. "Let's go watch Leo skin the muskrats he caught!" Bessie, Mary Ann and I ran after her.

"Leo, will you buy us some penny candy with money from the sale of the furs?" asked Priscilla.

Mary Ann motioned to Leo to bend down so she could whisper in his ear. She put her arm around his neck and pressed his ear against her ear instead of her lips.

"Leo, will you buy us some lipstick candy? We'll love you forever and ever!"

Leo teased, "Isn't that what you promised last time?"

"Yes, but we will love you more! Forever and ever!"

"More? Well, in that case, you've got it! Lipstick candy it will be!"

"Thank you, Leo! You're the best!" Mary Ann looked at us proudly.

"Thank you, Leo!" echoed Priscilla. "When will you go to the candy store?"

"Maybe this afternoon. Do you suppose that's soon enough, dear little one?"

Priscilla looked sheepish, realizing how it had sounded. But Leo smiled, and she beamed back at him.

"Did all the traps go off today?" I asked. But before he could answer, I screamed. Then Priscilla and Mary Ann screamed too.

"What in the world is going on with you girls?" said Leo.

"Look!" I pointed at a black salamander crawling away toward the muddy ground near the cows' round water tank.

"Oh, they're harmless," said Leo.

"But they are so ugly and slimy!" said Bessie.

"Just the same, they are God's creatures. It looks like a lizard, but it's related to the frog," said Leo.

"It gives me goosebumps," said Priscilla.

"It makes my skin crawl!" said Bessie.

"Well, since you girls aren't going to help skin these muskrats, I suggest you go back inside," said Leo.

"Great idea!" said Bessie. "With muskrats, salamanders and worms in the mud, I'm wishing for hot summer days and green lawns!"

Cousin Jimmy knocked at the screen door. "Is Leo back from trapping?"

"Yes," said Bessie. "He was headed for the side of the wood shed."

"Have you a new comic book?" asked Priscilla.

"Yes! Can't wait to read it!" He walked away, pushing the comic book further down into his back pocket to secure his entertainment for the evening. Jimmy didn't care much for our Saturday evening pastime: listening to "Boston Blake" and "Murder at Midnight" on the radio.

Father brought in the long tin bathtub and filled it with water. Mother signaled to Priscilla and Mary Ann to get in, and the rest of us went into the living room.

Dad always helped to untangle the girls' wet hair. Mary Ann's thick hair didn't tangle as much, but Priscilla's hair required special rinsing. Hers was very fine and golden, almost blond.

"Priscilla inherited her light complexion and blond hair from me and my mother Genevieve," Mother had told us. She explained that our grandmother Genevieve was Spanish from her mother's side and Welsh from her father's side. "We know very little about her father, except that his last name was Mason and that he was a tin miner from Wales who had settled in Trinidad, Colorado. Grandmother Genevieve was born there and raised by her grandparents. She married at the tender age of sixteen. Pictures showed her in a wedding dress alongside a tall, good-looking man who was about twenty-three.

"My father Manuel Ortega is Spanish from his father's side and American Indian from his mother's side," we had learned. Some members of the family believe he was part Jewish also.

Together, Genevieve and Manuel had twelve children. Their first child was Mother's brother Louie, the second son passed away at a very young age. Mother was their third child, also born in Trinidad, Colorado.

All the rest of us looked like Father's side of the family, although as Bessie grew older she looked more like Mother. Father had told us that his mother, Vicentia LeBlanc, was a first generation American of French descent. She was a widow with four sons and three daughters when she married our grandfather Pablo Montoya, a Spanish widower who also had children. The Gold Rush in 1858 and 1859 had brought him here from Barcelona, Spain.

"Your Grandmother Vicentia and Grandfather Pablo had three daughters and one son together," he had told us. "I am the youngest and their only son."

Father spoke well of his Martinez half-siblings. "They are very good people," he said. "They accepted the marriage of their mother to my father Pablo after their father Mr. Martinez passed away. I regret that we didn't visit more often with my half-brother Amadio or, as his daughter Anna called him, Papa Mateo. He is now very ill and bed ridden. I will make time to go and visit more! They treated me like a real brother always. I was blessed to have this extended family. I also learned to love my father's first family: the other Montoyas. My other half-brothers are Georgoria, Manuel, and Salistino Montoya, sons from my father Pablo's first wife."

Father opened the door for Leo, returning to grab his jacket. "Della, I'm going out to feed the hogs," said Father. "I'll be back in a little while to help with the girls' hair."

"No need to help with my hair, Dad," said Bessie.

"Are you sure?" asked Mother. "Your hair is long and tangles as much as your sister."

"Mother, I'm older now. I need to do some things for myself. Mrs. Roth puts something in her hair: I believe she calls it 'conditioner.' It seems to take the tangles right out!"

"I'll ask Mrs. Roth where to find the solution when I go in to work on Monday. It sure would save time. Bessie, Pauline—you need to share the same bath, we've run out of hot water."

As Mother poured an egg mixture over Priscilla's hair, Priscilla asked, "Are we going shopping today?"

"Not today, Sweetheart. I need to finish baking my bread and your father has planned to go over to Mrs. Chain's to pick up a few gunny sacks of potatoes."

"Is she that nice lady that lives next door to Dr. and Mrs. Roth?" I asked.

"Yes," said Mother. "When your father and Mr. Catalino went out to plant that tree for Mrs. Roth, Mrs. Chain offered the potatoes. Her son isn't able to come from out of town to visit her, and she can't use all those potatoes. She'll buy fresh ones in the next potato harvest, six or seven months from now."

Mother rinsed our hair and wrapped our heads in towels.

"Now step out of the tub on to the rug and finish drying yourselves."

The door suddenly opened, and Leo, Cousin Jimmy and Billy McCoy came in through the kitchen door. Bessie and I flew into the bedroom.

Father walked in and heard the commotion.

Mother said, "Leo, I think it would be a good idea to knock when water is being heated for bathing."

"I'm sorry, Mother! Here are some eggs from Mrs. McCoy."

"It's okay, Honey. It isn't your fault that we have to place the tub in the kitchen."

"Aunt Della, I'll mop up the water on the floor. Where's the mop?"

"That's okay, Jimmy, you run along with Leo and Bill."

The boys sprinted out the door, as Mary Grace and Phyllis came in and saw the water on the floor. Mother explained to them what had happened.

"If you ask me, the girls would have been better off if they'd just stayed in the tub," said Mary Grace. "What do you think of my sisters now, Phyllis?" She laughed. "The poor sweethearts will remember this for a long time."

Phyllis laughed. "You must realize, Mary, they were embarrassed!"

Bessie and I stayed in the bedroom. She helped me take the tangles out of my hair.

"I'll never be able to face Billy again!" I wailed. "He'll probably never want to take me horseback riding around the farm again! I do enjoy those rides!"

"Yeah, I know! I've seen how you exaggerate the movement of your head when you ride."

"Doesn't it look cool when my ponytail bounces up and down? I hope Jimmy doesn't tease Billy."

"I don't think he would. He'd have to answer to Leo, and Leo is very protective of us."

"Oh, my goodness! If Sister Alquin heard about this, she would say there is no excuse for that kind of behavior!"

"Pauline, you're driving me crazy. First you worry about Billy, then Jimmy and now Sister Alquin!"

"You just better pray that you don't get Sister Alquin next year!"

Bessie chuckled. "If you say so; but you have to admit, sometimes you can be so—dramatic!"

"Sister Alquin always says, 'Explanations are just a person's way of making excuses!'"

Mother stepped into the room. "Now girls, that's enough funning for today. Finish dressing and go outside. Please keep an eye on Priscilla and Mary Ann."

"Do you want to play baseball?" I asked, as we walked out into the yard. "Or we could put flowers in our hair. The lilac bushes are blooming so pretty and full; I can find us some bobby pins."

Bessie rubbed the fold of her elbow. "I don't know. What do you want to do?"

"Let me know when you've made up your mind!"

I picked up a stick from the ground and skipped away toward the deserted hay wagon that Mr. Corlett didn't use anymore. I climbed into it and began singing the ballad "Secret Love" from the movie *Calamity Jane* as I remembered it.

I stood on the front of the wagon and reached for the leather strap that we had tied to it. I pretended to have control of our make-believe horses and called out, "Yippee-I-O-Yippee-I-A!"

"Hey, Dale Evans!" Priscilla called, as she, Bessie and Mary Ann came running. "Draw in the reins, Cowgirl, we want to jump on!"

"Slow down them there horses!" yelled Bessie. "Mary Ann wants to pretend we are pulling hay."

"Okay, but only if you sing along with me!"

"Here we go again," said Mary Ann. "We can't hear ourselves over your voice!"

"Okay, Baby! I'll try to keep it down, but you girls don't always know all the words!"

"She has a point there," said Priscilla. "Let's jump on the wagon and sing country songs. We all know Eddy Arnold's 'Cattle Call.'"

"We need to learn more words to that one!" said Bessie.

We repeated the verse a few more times, sitting on the wagon with our legs dangling.

"There is a new boy in my class," I said. "He is the cutest I've ever seen. His name is Albert Sanchez."

"I have a new boy in my class too," said Bessie. "Sister Devota assigned him the desk in front of me. I didn't mind in the least when he turned around and said, 'Bessie, do you have an extra pencil I may borrow? I'll return it to you when the bell rings.' I smiled and handed him one. He didn't smile back, but that's alright—he remembered my name! He parts his hair in the middle!"

"Why would any boy want to part his hair in the middle like Bob Hope?" asked Mary Ann.

"I wondered that too, but he's shy and he's cute."

"I know!" exclaimed Priscilla. "Maybe a cow licked his hair! Joe once told me, 'You have a cow lick in your bangs.'"

Bessie giggled, but then gave me a secret look. She didn't want Priscilla's feelings to be hurt or for her to feel foolish.

Priscilla looked puzzled. "Think about it," she said. "There are a lot of cows around; one could have licked my hair."

Bessie explained what a cowlick was. Priscilla jumped off the wagon with a sheepish grin.

"Come on, Mary Ann, let's find Leo, and ask him to make slingshots."

She helped Mary Ann down and they skipped away with their arms entwined. Their hands slid off their shoulders as they bounced up and down. Bessie and I watched until they found Leo.

"What's the new boy's name?" I asked.

"Raymond Sanchez."

"How lucky can we get! They're brothers! I wonder where they live. They don't ride the bus; I looked for Albert on Thursday and Friday."

"They must live on Sunny Side or Lariat."

"Oh no! Not Lariat. That is where the Ratenias live."

"We don't know for sure. Besides, even if they do, it doesn't mean that they will behave like the girls we call 'Ratenias.' Joe's girlfriend lives there and so does Aunt Louise, but they own their own homes. Most of the homes in Lariat are run-down rentals. Some are even made of adobe. Most of the people that live on Sunny Side are homeowners, with nice homes and wonderful yards."

"Wouldn't you like to be a homeowner when you grow up?"

"Very much!"

"We will when we grow up. But we don't own our home now. Father rents from Mr. Corlett."

"But ours is a farmhouse. It's almost as nice as some of the houses on Sunny Side. And someday, Mother and Father will be homeowners."

"Just the same," I said. "I hope Albert and Raymond don't live in Lariat."

"I agree those Ratenias are different. The tall dark one looks really mean. They act like they hate us, but, why?"

"Do you remember the first time we ever laid eyes on them? We were getting on the bus and they pushed us from behind, almost knocking us down! They yelled, 'We're gonna get you all! Just you wait!'"

"I don't understand. What did we ever do to them? It's scary and unfair. We're always looking over our shoulders and taking detours after school just to avoid them."

"I get really scared when I see them coming," I said. "But what I hate most is seeing Mary Ann and Priscilla frightened. If I wasn't so scared, I'd stop and ask what problem they have with us. It could be a case of mistaken identity."

"Oh Pauline, you're too funny! You sound like the policeman on that radio program: 'Murder at Midnight.' You are forgetting there are four of us!"

"Well then maybe they are after you."

"Why would they be after me?"

"Because you are older and wiser."

"Pauline, you get funnier by the minute! I've never heard of such a thing. Let's drop the subject for today. We don't have to think about it until Monday after school."

Mary Ann called to us. "Mother wants you girls to come play closer to the house."

"We just have to pray to God in Heaven to bless those Ratenias, and to soften their hearts," said Bessie as we walked back toward the house. "Sister Mary Joseph says that about people who want to harm us, like the Russians. She says they need our prayers so that they will be converted and bring down the Iron Curtain."

"What iron curtain?"

"Oh, some curtain they have. I don't know much about it, except that Sister Mary Joseph has said time and time again that our Blessed Mother wants us to pray a rosary every day. The Russian people will be converted. With prayer, the Ratenias will too, and they'll let us be."

"Do you think the name 'Ratenias' came from the word 'rats'?"

Bessie giggled. "You could be right!"

We watched Priscilla chasing a chicken, while Mary Ann watched and laughed.

"Did Leo make sling shots for you?" asked Bessie.

"No," answered Mary Ann. "He didn't have an old tire tube, and he and Jimmy were getting ready to leave for the dump to search for scrap iron and metal to sell."

Mother and Father came out of the house; Mother was carrying her purse.

"One of the lambs has an infected leg," she said. "He may have been bitten by a dog. One of the ranchers recommended turpentine to kill bacteria, so we're going to pick some up. Mary and Phyllis are in the house. Would you like to stay home or come with us?"

"Will you treat us to a Coke at the drugstore or an ice cream from Dairy Queen?" asked Priscilla.

"I suppose we could stop at Dairy Queen on our way home."

We all climbed into the car and headed for the lumberyard.

"Hello, Della! Hello, Ignacio!" the saleslady greeted our parents. "My, but your little girls sure have grown! I wanted at least two girls and two boys, but the good Lord only blessed me with three boys. I guess it's for the best."

She was interrupted by someone I hated to see—Mr. Delfino!

"Yes, the girls have grown. How they frolic about!" he said, as he offered Father a handshake. He put his other hand on Mother's shoulder, and soon his whole arm was around her shoulder. I did not approve. He was way too friendly!

"Come on Bessie, Pauline," said Priscilla. "Let's find where they keep all the different kinds of rock for gardens."

"No! I'm gonna stay right here with Mother!" I said.

Mary Ann and Priscilla walked away to look at the displays. Bessie knelt a few feet away, pushing sawdust that lay under a table saw, dipping and dropping it from one hand to the other.

I stood by Mother as she carried on a conversation with Mr. Delfino. Father had walked away looking for the turpentine. Why aren't you over there showing Father where to find it? I thought angrily. I'm staying right here! Why do you need to put your arm around Mother? Why don't you save that arm for your wife? Your wife Nancy is a very pretty lady; so why do you need to be so friendly with our mother? She belongs to us and to Father!

Bessie rescued me from my tormented thoughts. "Pauline, why do you look so annoyed?"

I wondered if I was misjudging Mr. Delfino. I felt a twinge of guilt.

"What is it? You look like you want to cry!"

"I hate every minute we spend at this yard! I should have stayed home with Mary Grace."

"I think I know what is bothering you."

I could feel the frown leaving my face.

"Is it Mr. Delfino?"

I felt instant relief. She shared my pain.

"Please don't fret about things you can't change. For the longest time, I felt the way you do. I think it's his job to be friendly, to bring in customers. He looks like a happily married man. When I see him with his wife they look very happy together. And don't forget Mother loves Father very much."

"Why did you not share this with me sooner?"

"You are always so happy, silly and showing off. I didn't want to burden you with annoying thoughts. Jealousy isn't a very nice emotion."

"Yeah, I know!"

"When you feel that kind of anguish, say the Lord's Prayer. The Our Father is the mightiest tool to fight evil thoughts. Sister Devota told this to my class, and it works for me every time!"

"You are so lucky to have Sister Devota for your teacher! I sure hope I get her next year! Thank you, Bessie. I feel a little better."

I soon realized that my feelings of jealousy stemmed from reading too many love stories in comic books. The stories were full of cheating "wolves." I was reading too much into a harmless hug.

Father paid for the turpentine.

"We'll see you folks soon! Have a nice weekend," said Mr. Delfino.

"We will, now that we're getting out of here!" I said under my breath.

Bessie glanced at me sideways and whispered, "I heard that! Mother and Father would be very disappointed if they heard you being disrespectful to anyone. And what would Sister Alquin say?"

"Oh, you would have to remind me!" We both giggled.

On the way home, I hummed while I ate my ice cream. I liked to hum when I didn't know all the words to a song.

When we got home, Mother stopped me and put her hand on my forehead.

"Pauline are you feeling all right? You've been very quiet."

"I feel fine, Mother. I'll just let it be."

Mother looked puzzled.

"Oh, don't mind me. I was just thinking out loud. I'm gonna catch up to the girls."

"Okay, Sweetheart, run along. I love you!"

"I love you too, Mother!"

I ran off, determined to put unsettling thoughts out of my mind. I did not see the girls, so I went back to the kitchen. Mary Grace was telling Mother, "Uncle Manuel called to say they would not be coming over for dinner. Aunt Elsie is having a bad day. She's been crying all day."

"I feel for her, losing her sister in such a horrific way," said Mother.

Mary explained to Phyllis, "About a year and a half ago, Aunt Elsie's eighteen-year-old sister Martha was murdered. She was studying to be a nurse. She was found with stab wounds all over her body. There is still an investigation going on, but they're not any closer to finding who did it. She's buried in the little town of Capelin in a very old cemetery. Her grave is the only one with a headstone; all the rest have crosses, but no names."

"We have a lot of family buried there," added Mother.

Phyllis was stunned. "That's horrible! She was so young!"

Mother looked at me. "Pray for her soul, but try not to think about it too much, Pauline. We hope Martha is in Heaven with Jesus, Mary and Joseph and all the beautiful angels. Think of her happy and smiling. Someday we may understand why bad things happen to good people, but for now we need to pray for Aunt Elsie, so that her pain will heal."

I walked away. I needed to find my sisters, to play, sing, run, laugh, and feel happy again. When I found them sitting on the floor in the front room, I felt my joy return. Bessie was helping Priscilla and Mary Ann with Betsy McCall cutouts. They were cutting out paper dolls from newspapers.

"Come sit with us! I saved pajamas and slippers for you to cut."

"Thank you, Bessie!"

"I'm hungry," said Mary Ann.

"So am I," said Priscilla.

"Mary is adding water to the flour, salt and lard to make tortilla dough," I said. "And Phyllis is helping to peel potatoes. Leo's feeding wood to the stove, but he wasn't in his usually joking mood. He was frowning."

"Where is Cousin Jimmy?"

"He's sitting on the floor behind the stove, reading a comic book."

"That's what's bothering Leo!" said Bessie.

"Why would that bother Leo?"

"Leo is having a hard time at school. Sister Devotee moved my desk next to his, so I could help him with his reading assignments. Sister said she would call Mother to discuss Leo's progress. I think Leo resents that Jimmy enjoys reading so much when he is having such a hard time at school. Jimmy always has a comic book in his back pocket. Last week I heard Leo snap at Jimmy, 'If you don't stop cackling like a chicken, you'll have to go home!'"

"Really? What did Jimmy say to that?"

"He just laughed and went on reading, but quietly."

"You should mention that to Mother," said Priscilla, "He might get teased in class because of his reading."

"I'll tell her, very soon."

It was almost the end of the day and the weekend, with only one more day left before we'd had to go back to school. We hated to see the day end.

Mother hasn't said anything about attending Mass tomorrow morning. I must remind her!

We didn't play long with the paper dolls. The fun was over once we cut out the paper doll and the few outfits in the newspaper. Then we'd wait for next week's addition. We had a shoe box full of cutouts. We appreciated them more on snowy days, when it was too cold to play outdoors.

"I'm done with the scissors," I said. "I'm going to look for Mother."

"What for?"

"Mass tomorrow, or have you forgotten? Sister Alquin will ask on Monday morning what Father McDevitt's sermon was about!"

"Yes, she will! You're right about that. Father said something about the water pump and watering the vegetable garden. Mother may be over by the creek with him."

I went out the front door and circled around to the back. I saw Mother holding a tool for Father.

"What is troubling you, Pauline?" She could always tell. I suppose all mothers can tell when something is troubling their children.

"Mother, we need to attend Mass tomorrow morning. It's humiliating not to know the answer when Sister Alquin asks about the Mass! She quizzes the class about the sermon, and we never know who she will pick on to answer."

"Well, I'll be. Sister Alquin sure knows how to motivate her class to go to church on Sundays!"

"I think the way she does it is mean!"

"Look at it this way, Sweetheart, it is not the nuns' law. It is God's law. The third commandment reads, 'Remember to keep holy the Lord's Day.' Don't worry. Try to enjoy the day."

"Thank you, Mother."

"Tomorrow is the Fourth Sunday of Lent. Remind the other girls that we're going. Mary Grace and Phyllis are practicing for the Easter Sunday program. I need to check for clean socks for you and your sisters right after dinner. Run along and tell Mary Grace that I'll be there in a few minutes to finish making dinner."

Mother and Father both smiled at me, and I ran happily back to the house. Father was working on the water pump. He was setting up this electric machinery that pumps water from the creek to the lawn, vegetable garden, trees and flowers. He had also installed one in the well we had at the back of the house that pumped cold water into a small sink inside the house. As of yet we had no hot running water, but we would have it soon enough.

After delivering my messages, I returned to the front room. Phyllis came in.

"Here are the pictures I mentioned earlier," she said.

Bessie took a few and handed me the rest.

"I don't believe this! Are these your brothers?" The expression on Bessie's face made us sit up and listen.

She held out a picture to me. "Look!"

"Oh, my goodness! It's them!"

"Do you girls know my brothers?"

Priscilla grabbed the pictures from me. Bessie and I sat with the biggest smiles on our faces. Priscilla looked at the pictures closely.

"It's the boy with his hair parted in the middle!"

Mary Ann asked, "Let me see! I want to see that picture! He is very cute!" she added, after she saw it. We all laughed.

"What's all the excitement?" asked Mary Grace.

"Your sisters have already met my brothers," said Phyllis. "You're not the only one. Bessie and Pauline are smitten with love for those boys."

"They were talking earlier today and comparing notes," said Mary Ann.

"Is that right?" said Mary Grace.

"My quiet little sister sure has a lot to say today," said Bessie, rubbing Mary Ann's head. Mary Ann looked embarrassed, and we all laughed.

"We will have to bring the Sanchez boys over to visit! What do you think Phyllis?" asked Mary Grace.

"Oh, I think that can be arranged," answered Phyllis. "And very soon too!"

Bessie and I were embarrassed. Thank goodness Mother called us.

"Dinner is ready, come into the kitchen, Girls!"

"After dinner, I'll do your rag curls. Mass tomorrow, Girls," said Mother.

Bessie and I washed the dinner dishes. Priscilla swept the kitchen floor, and Mary Ann held the dust pan for her. After we were done, we sat at the kitchen table. Bessie read her catechism book and Mary Grace ironed our dresses for church. I watched Phyllis talk to Mary Grace. She looked just like her brothers: light coloring with dirty blond hair.

"Bessie, Pauline!" called Priscilla. "Come here! Hurry!"

We ran into the front room.

"Listen! The radio is playing Mother and Father's favorite song: The Tennessee Waltz!"

"Is that your special song, Mother?" I asked.

"It's a new song by Patty Page," said Mother. "It's a beautiful waltz."

"Daddy, is this your favorite song too?"

Father winked at Mother. "Yes it is. So is Marilyn Monroe!"

"Oh Dad, stop!" said Priscilla, giggling.

"Is it time for Boston Balky and Murder at Midnight?" asked Bessie.

"Ten more minutes," answered Father.

Bessie and I got comfortable, sitting cross-legged on the floor next to the radio. She leaned over and whispered, "Now don't start fretting that we may lose Father to Marilyn Monroe!" I rolled my eyes at her, but secretly I was glad for the reassurance.

"Mother, please wrap that last piece of my hair!" cried Mary Ann. "I don't want to be here when the program starts. The man on the radio scares me when he says 'Murder…at…midnight, the… witching…hour, when the clock strikes twelve for murder…at… midnight!'"

"It's all right, Sweetheart, we'll go into the kitchen with Priscilla and you can hand me the rags for Priscilla's hair," said Mother.

"May I spray wet her hair?"

"Yes, you may."

"Wait a minute! No one asked me! Mary Ann will end up spraying my face, my back, my feet, everything but my hair!"

Mary Ann pouted; and Priscilla, not wanting to see Mary Ann unhappy, quickly changed her tune. "I was only kidding. Of course you may help spray my hair!"

Mother kissed Priscilla on the cheek, and as they got up to leave, she said, "Ignacio, Pauline and Bessie may only listen to one program tonight. I still need to do their hair."

Daddy Ignacio

Mommy Della

Leo, Mary Grace, Mary Ann, and Joe

Priscilla, Bessie, and Pauline

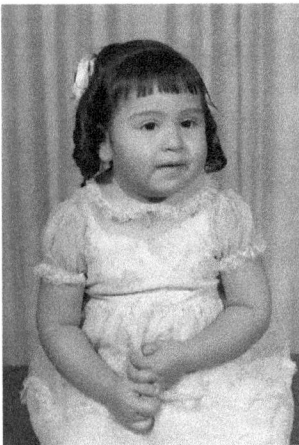

Debbie

Grandfather Manuel

Grandmother Genevieve

Manuel and Genevieve

Della and her brother Jim

Chapter Two

To my great joy, Mother got us up early for Mass. We were excited to go to Mass, and we wanted to be sure Mother would have time to remove the rags from our hair slowly, so as not to disturb the smooth curls.

Father carried Mary Ann into the kitchen, then returned for Priscilla. He sat them at the kitchen table where Mother had prepared oatmeal and toast for them. Bessie and I would be receiving Holy Communion and therefore couldn't have breakfast until after church.

Mother removed the rags from our hair, revealing perfectly rolled, long, smooth curls. We dressed quickly, and Father went out to warm the motor in the new Chevy truck.

At least twice a week, Father had told Mother, "Very soon now, we're gonna need to buy that truck we've been needing for so long. The winters are getting colder and the boys and I are gonna have to make more trips up the mountain to get firewood." Mother had finally given in, and they had purchased the truck.

"It's time to go!" called Father. "Joe has already left in his car with Leo, Mary Grace and Phyllis. They're going to drop Jimmy off at home on the way."

Jimmy and his siblings attended public school. Although they were Catholic, the family didn't attend Mass. I should have asked Sister Alquin to give them a ring!

We climbed into the new truck. I sat next to Father. Bessie sat next to me with Mary Ann on her lap, and Mother sat with Priscilla on her lap.

"I can see for miles!" said Priscilla. "I like our new truck!"

Father smiled and winked at Mother.

"It looks like I'll have to take you deer hunting with me this winter! You'd make a good spotter since you can see for miles!"

"Oh Daddy, you're funny! You never go deer hunting!"

"I will now! With my new Chevy truck and you as my spotter! A friend of mine said, 'If you want a buck, you have to drive a Chevy truck!'"

I was glad we got there early. Father was able to park right in front. Joe's car was parked close by. Bessie had told me that she suspected he had a crush on Phyllis. She flirted with him, but she didn't take him seriously. Phyllis knew he was stuck on his girlfriend Dolly, even though they were taking a break.

As we entered Saint Joseph's Church, Sister Mary Georgia and Sister Mary Julian greeted my parents, but there was no sign of Sister Alquin. Maybe she attended an earlier Mass. I wished she'd been here to see me.

I leaned over and whispered to Bessie, "Look at Priscilla. She's wasting no time at all, she's already leaning back on her knees with her little behind on the pew."

"I know," she whispered back. "Her knees must hurt already."

"Look at her eyeing Mother and Father hoping they don't notice. She looks so funny the way her eyes switch back and forth. In a little bit I'll be doing the same thing. I sure wish the pews were padded."

"We're going to be in trouble for all the whispering we're doing."

I looked up at Jesus Christ on the cross. I thought, Jesus how great Your love is for us! To be born just to grow up to suffer and die on the cross for our sins so that when we die we can join You and your Blessed Mother in Heaven. Gee, the least I can do is sit quietly and listen so I can remember the sermon!

Father James McDevitt sang in Latin, "Lamb of God, Who takes away the sins of the world, have mercy on us and grant us peace." He broke the Host and received his own Communion. A moment later, we prayed silently as the priest said in Latin, "Lord, I am not worthy that Thou should enter under my roof, but only say the word and my soul shall be healed."

I remembered a past Sunday Mass when Father McDevitt told the people, "Jesus Christ was not content even with offering Himself on the cross. Such is His love for us, that on the night before He died, He gave us His greatest gift—Himself in the Eucharist."

The people stood up and Bessie nudged me. It was time to go up to the altar and receive Holy Communion. As Bessie and I made our way across the pew, Mother smiled at us. Priscilla and Mary Ann were sitting comfortably all the way back on the bench.

Father McDevitt placed the Eucharist on my tongue and said in Latin, "May the Body of Our Lord Jesus Christ preserve your soul to life everlasting. Amen."

I walked back to my seat. I didn't chew; I liked closing my eyes and thanking God for everything good in my life as the Holy Eucharist dissolved in my mouth.

When the Mass was almost over, I glanced around to see if I knew anyone. I turned to look toward the back and spotted Sister Alquin. Our eyes met. She motioned for me to face the altar, but she grinned at me. Was it a nice grin? Yes, by George, I think it was! I turned to face forward.

I could see my best friend and her brother sitting up front. They were whispering and giggling—not realizing they were being watched. Julia! Stop! Sister Alquin is watching! You're going to get into trouble. But of course Julia couldn't hear my thoughts. Oh well, sooner or later we all have to face Sister Alquin if we misbehave at Mass or at school.

"Dominus vobiscum," said Father McDevitt, which meant, "The Lord be with you."

"Et cum spiritu tuo," responded the altar boy. "And with your spirit."

Father McDevitt had announced that he wanted everyone to take the time to listen to the choir sing "Forty Days and Forty Nights." The girls and I looked up to see Mary Grace and Phyllis. We were so proud that our sister was up there singing so prettily! They sang, and then Mass was over.

As we exited the church, Father got Joe's attention.

"We're taking a ride up Wolf Creek Pass," he said. "We'll stop on the way up the mountain to visit your Aunt Vittoria. I want to break the truck in. Do you want to come along?"

"Yes, Dad! I'd like to see Cousin Horacio. It's been a while since I've been up there. Mary Grace and I will meet you at the house after we drop Phyllis off."

"Okay, Son. Don't be long."

At home, Mother gave Bessie, Mary Grace and me some oatmeal and toast.

"Pauline, Bessie and I will ride in the bed of the truck with Joe and Leo," announced Mary Grace.

"Pauline can fit up front with Priscilla and Mary Ann, if she'd like," said Mother.

I couldn't answer because my mouth was full of toast.

"Daddy," said Bessie with concern. "I don't want you to drive on that mountain road where only one car fits. It scares me! We might fall off the mountain cliff!"

"But Bessie," said Mary Grace. "We need to go on those roads if you want Father to find Great-grandfather LeBlanc's treasure!"

"What treasure? I don't care about any treasure! I don't want to go if we are going on those scary roads!"

I swallowed. "I don't either! I remember that time when Father had to make a U-turn and the road was so narrow. It gave us such a fright!"

"Now Girls, I would never do anything to endanger your lives," protested Father. "I had plenty of room to make that U-turn. I thought you'd forgotten that ride up to Platoro Reservoir."

"We'll never forget that day!" said Bessie. "I'll ride in the front with you, Mother and the girls!"

"Come on, Bessie! Ride in the back with me and I'll tell you all about the 'Lost Treasure'!" said Mary Grace.

"Don't worry, Girls," said Father. "We will go straight over to my sister Vittoria's house first. If we go on one of our rides, we will leave you girls there to help Aunt Vittoria."

"I want to go on a treasure hunt!" said Priscilla.

"Me too!" said Mary Ann.

"I would rather stay and help Aunt Vittoria milk the cow and make cheese," said Bessie.

"Me too!" said Priscilla.

"Make up your mind, Priscilla!" said Leo. "A treasure hunt or cows and cheese? You can't be here, there and everywhere! But then again Dad does call you 'Tornado' for a reason!"

We all broke into laughter. Leave it to our brother Leo to make us laugh.

Mother threw pillows and blankets into the bed of the truck. Bessie and I ended up riding in the back with Mary Grace, Leo, and Joe. The ride was bumpy, but fun. We asked Mary Grace and Joe to tell us about the treasure.

"Now that's an interesting subject!" said Joe. "It's a long story, and you'll learn more about it from Mother and Father, or Aunt Vittoria. It involves Father's grand-father, some Frenchman named Le Blanc."

"Joe! Le Blanc is our great-grandfather!"

"I know that!"

"Well the way you put it, 'some Frenchman' sounds so detached."

"Sorry! Don't be so touchy!"

"We are talking history here: our history, our family history, and Bessie and Pauline have yet to hear it. I want them to listen well, and be proud of their roots," said Mary Grace seriously.

"You're right. That's why they need to hear the tale of the lost treasure firsthand from Father or Mother."

Leo didn't seem to take any interest in the conversation. He had gathered rocks and brought them along so he could throw them out of the truck while we drove.

When we pulled up the driveway, two of Cousin Horacio's dogs burst out of the enclosed porch, barking and running beside the truck. Uncle Nick, Aunt Vittoria and Horacio followed.

"Ignacio, you finally got your truck! Very nice!" said Uncle Nick. "Have you taken it up higher?"

"No, I just bought it this week."

"Come in! Come in!" invited Aunt Vittoria, as she gave Mother and Father a hug, then turned to hug the rest of us.

Joe and Leo jumped off the bed of the truck and started to walk away with Horacio. Father called, "Boys, what is this? You don't say hello to your aunt and uncle? Get back here!"

They were a little embarrassed, but they smiled and put their arms around Aunt Vittoria and Uncle Nick.

"Okay, Boys, don't go too far. If you want to come along with your uncle and me for that ride up the mountain, we'll go in about fifteen minutes, after my cup of coffee."

Aunt Vittoria served Mother and Father coffee, and offered us girls a glass of cold goat's milk and cookies. She called them "biscochitos." They were the best French cookies in the state of Colorado!

Mary Grace curled up on a rocking chair with a comic book in the corner next to the window. The warm sun rested there just right.

"Come on, Girls," said Aunt Vittoria to the rest of us. I can't recall her ever calling me by name. She always addressed us as "Girls." "You arrived just in time; I haven't yet made cheese. But first I need to go to the well for water. Come along."

We always stayed clear of the little house with the well. When we walked by, we stayed at least five feet away. We were spooked because Aunt Vittoria had told us, "Never, never, set one foot into the little house if you see the lock is off the door. I wouldn't want one of you falling into the well!"

Going in with her this time was a thrill, but I couldn't wait to get out again. We were relieved to be safely back in Aunt Vittoria's kitchen.

Father, Uncle Nick, and the boys were on their way out.

"We'll be back in an hour or two," called Father.

We watched as Aunt Vittoria placed the thin, loosely-woven cheese cloth in a pan with holes in the bottom. She pressed together the curds of soured milk, and the liquid drained off.

"May we have some of that wonderful cheese with syrup poured over the top like you served us last time?" asked Mary Grace.

"Yes, you may!"

"And may we also have some of your wonderful pine nuts?" asked Priscilla.

"Why of course you may, if you all sit around my 'wonderful, wonderful' kitchen table."

We all laughed. Aunt Vittoria was 5'1", her legs bowed outward a little. She had a light complexion and light-brown hair. Her eyes were hazel, like Father's. She had a warm smile. Every once in a while she would surprise us with her light humor. Out of Father's three sisters, she resembled Father the most. It really was 'wonderful' spending time with her. She and Mother were very close sisters-in-law. They enjoyed their long talks.

"Here you go, Girls. These are freshly roasted pine nuts."

We shelled pine nuts, popping one after another into our mouths, never tiring of eating them. After a while, Mother cut apples into quarters and gave each of us a little brown bag to go feed the horses. Across the country road, their horses ran loose. We were scared that they would bite us, so we took turns placing our quartered apples on the fence so the horses could help themselves.

Mary Grace came out and invited us to walk with her to the river, where we threw the biggest rocks we could find. We backed up so the splash of water wouldn't wet us, but Mary Grace wouldn't allow us to get too close to the river anyway.

"Step back!" she'd order. "I don't want to have to fish you out of the Alamosa River!"

Uncle Nick owned about forty acres, with horses, cows, sheep, chickens, two pigs, two dogs, a red rooster, and the goats, of course.

A huge mountain rose up about one-hundred feet from their front door. It looked like nature had dropped a gigantic rock in front of their yard. The Rocky Mountains were all around and the Alamosa River flowed beside the property. Cousin Horacio had shot a big brown bear on that mountain, and another time, my brother Leo shot a bobcat with his .22.

The only time Uncle Nick, Aunt Vittoria, and Horacio came down to Monte Vista was during the Carnival and the Rodeo, which occurred on the same dates. Once a month they went to Capelin for groceries. They enjoyed living up there away from the busy towns.

It was so peaceful up at their farm. Cousin Horacio and some other children attended school in a one-room schoolhouse a few miles away. You could count the students on one hand.

I loved spending time there. You could easily fall asleep listening to the breezes rustling the trees. I especially liked the sound made by water running down the river during the night. Waking up in the morning was even better. The sound of the rooster's cock-a-doodle-doo and the throaty sound made by a male turkey woke all the chickens from their roosts. If you looked out the window, you could see the small head and spreading tail of the turkey. But that was no competition for the beautiful red rooster prancing about, waiting for his hens to emerge from their perches.

Time went by quickly. After about two hours, Father, Uncle Nick, and the boys came back from their ride. Aunt Vittoria and Mother were cooking.

"Boys, come and wash up! Lunch is just about ready," called Aunt Vittoria.

Mary Grace finished setting the table. Mother placed a large pitcher of milk and a basket of homemade bread on the table. We sat down to a leg of lamb, country fried potatoes, and wild spinach fried with onions and red chili seeds. A big bowl of sweet rice pudding sat on the counter, made with fresh cream, sugar, and raisins, and on the stove, a pan loaf of bread pudding cooled.

Uncle Nick led us in prayer. "Bless us, O Lord, and these Thy gifts, which we are about to receive from Thy bounty, through Christ Our Lord. Amen."

The girls and I loved fried potatoes. We could have them three times a day, and never tire of them, especially with homemade tortillas, and freshly grown, steamed, skinned hot green peppers.

Potato harvest time was six or seven months away. We didn't much care for it, but Bessie and I always pitched in and helped pick potatoes. Mary Grace, Leo, and Joe also picked, but Bessie and I were very fast pickers for our age.

After lunch, Uncle Nick and Father went outside for a "smoke." They both smoked Old Gold cigarettes. The boys went out on some adventure, and Mary Grace helped Mother with the dishes. Bessie and I went out to help Aunt Vittoria bring in her wash from the clothesline. It didn't take long to fold the clothes.

Priscilla begged Mary Grace to play jacks with her. She wanted to practice doing "pigs in a blanket" and "half moon," two moves that Mary Grace had taught us.

Mary Grace gave in. "Okay, but remember not to throw the little ball so high."

Mother hung up the wet dish towel and joined the adults at the table for one of their long conversations.

Mary Ann had made herself comfortable on Father's lap and would soon be asleep. If Father was home, and not busy, she never left his side. Mother once told us, "Mary Ann had a very hard time of it when Father went to work for the Forestry. It was hard on all of us, not knowing if he'd be able to come home on weekends. Now she fears he'll leave again."

Aunt Vittoria handed Bessie and me some throw pillows so we could join Mary Grace and Priscilla, playing jacks on the floor.

Priscilla showed improvement. We enjoyed watching Mary Grace play jacks. She could go the longest time without messing up, so losing her turn to one of us was long in coming. At times we'd lose interest and walk away. The conversation at the table caught our interest. We heard the words "El Tesoro": the Lost Treasure.

I'm sure this subject had been discussed dozens of times, but this time the adults had a young, fascinated audience. We listened intently as Father spoke.

"Oh yes! Colorado was a gold mine in the 1700s and 1800s. It brought people from all over the world in search of gold and silver in the mountains. We believe that's what brought Della's grandfather from Wales. He didn't bring family with him. He met Della's grandmother Doloritas in Trinidad, where Della's mother Genevieve was born."

We knew that Grandmother Genevieve had been raised by her grandparents. She had told us, "My grandparents kept me hidden whenever they had company, for fear my father would come and take me away. I was born out of wedlock."

Turning to a discussion of his own family, Father looked at his sister and said, "Our mother Vicentia told us that our father Pablo Montoya was her second husband. He had come from Spain to work the gold mines, and he also farmed. He settled in Taos at a Spanish settlement now known as Taos, New Mexico. On our mother's side, Grandfather Guillermo Le Blanc was grandson to one of only two survivors of the French expedition into the Colorado Rockies."

Bessie and I looked at each other. We were about to hear the tale of Le Blanc and the Lost Treasure, which had been told to Father and his sisters Vittoria, Rosa Bella, and Raquildia by their mother.

"Mama Vicentia was born around 1868. Her father, Guillermo LeBlanc, was born in France in 1844 and went to Nova Scotia in 1865. He was sometimes known in Colorado as Guillermo Blanco. He was the son of Agustin LeBlanc and Margarita Rubéns. He married Maria Alvina Vigil, daughter of Antonio Vigil and Rosa Romero. He came from France in 1865 with a copy of the original map of his grandfather, who had returned to France around 1793.

"'Ignacio, my son,' Mama Vicentia would say, 'You were born to me in 1902. You are the last and only grandson of the man that came from France with a copy of the original map of the buried treasure. It is possible, my son, that you would have been a very rich man today, had it not been for your grandmother Maria Alvina. She lost her temper, out of fear for her husband's safety.

"'A fist fight had broken out after an argument between friends and family members, who were searching for the treasure. She was upset. She grabbed the map from the table and threw it into the fire. "One of these days, someone is going to kill you for that darn map!" she cried. "Besides, you're always away! Your children and I need you home more." But that didn't stop my father Guillermo. Soon after, he made another map from memory. He spent a lot of time looking for the treasure, but had no luck.'"

Mama Vicentia had one sister, Pabla (Pauline) and one brother, Antonio. To my knowledge, they never wed. So Father and his sisters were the only descendants of the man who brought the map. Father finished his mother's account of the lost treasure with the words, "I believe the treasure is lost and buried to us forever." Aunt Vittoria nodded.

Bessie and I were fascinated by the story. I looked at her, and knew she was thinking the same thing I was. If it's buried, we'll just have to find it and dig it up! After all, we are the descendants of the man "Le Blanc"!

Mary Grace called to us, "Come on outside; we are going on a treasure hunt! Want to come along?"

"Really?" I asked. "Are we really going on a treasure hunt? Is Father taking us?" I asked.

"No, Silly. We're going on a treasure hunt for arrowheads."

I was disappointed. "Gold is much better than arrowheads."

"I'll ask Aunt Vittoria for a little bag," said Bessie.

Off we went on our treasure hunt. We passed the boys on the way. Mary Grace asked them to join us, but Horacio declined. He needed to start feeding the animals, and Joe and Leo stayed to help him.

We hadn't gone far when we found some arrowheads that we thought resembled ones in Horacio's collection. We decided to head back and watch the animals being fed.

Mary Grace stopped and inhaled long breaths of fresh mountain air, and we copied her. She began to sing and we joined her.

With heart and song, we pledge, Saint Joseph's School,
we'll be faithful to her every rule!
Come on and cheer Saint Joseph's loud and long!
Come on and join the song!
Saint Joseph, hail!
Ra-Ra, Ra, Ra, Ra, Raaa!

Mary Grace praised us for knowing all the words to the cheer. We listened as she sang a cheer for her new school:

Three cheers for Monte High School!
Stand up and cheer!
Bring forth her spirit;
love her more each year.

She stopped singing as we reached the house.

Father announced that it was time to head for home, so we climbed back into the pickup. Aunt Vittoria handed Mother a bag of pine nuts. We thanked her and Uncle Nick for the wonderful meal and the fun day. We waved goodbye, and the dogs ran alongside the truck barking until Horacio whistled for them to return. Mary Grace, Bessie and I cuddled together with a blanket over our legs. All the way home, Joe and Leo discussed their ride up to Wolf Creek Pass.

"What do you think Monte Vista's elevation is?"

"I think it's about seven-thousand feet."

"What about Wolf Creek Pass?"

"Ten thousand. Horacio said that South Fork is the gateway to Wolf Creek Pass and the Rio Grande National Forest."

"And the Continental Divide is only about half an hour from South Fork."

Bessie asked, "What is a continental divide?"

"It's a point or spot, uh, actually, I need a Colorado map to show you. I'll show you at home."

"The Continental Divide," said Mary Grace, "is an imaginary line that runs along the top of the Rocky Mountains. They rise higher than 14,000 feet."

Nothing was said about the Lost Treasure. The ride home seemed nice and short, because I fell asleep.

At home, Mother told us we could play outside for a while.

"School tomorrow," she reminded.

It would be another week of adventure for us. Actually every day was an adventure. We'd see what adventure tomorrow brought. We'd take the public school bus, then exit it and detour to the Catholic school. Most likely we wouldn't meet up with the Ratenias in the morning, but after school there would be no escape, unless we could outsmart them. We wished the bus would drop us off in front of our school, but Mother said, "The school buses will not transport students to private schools."

I would welcome Monday morning because I could face my morning class and not fear humiliation. I knew Sunday's sermon; I had listened, but would Sister Alquin pick on me to answer questions? She had seen me in church, so she would certainly pick on me! She would want to know if I had been paying attention. I had! I had listened to every word: about a woman who committed a mortal sin. I didn't understand what the sin was, but I knew what Father McDevitt was saying.

Do I really remember? I thought. There were some townspeople that were ready to stone this lady to death. Jesus was walking by and saw. Jesus told them he who has not sinned should throw the first stone. Needless to say they dropped the stones.

Father McDevitt told us how Jesus could see what was in her heart and mind. He saw not only the sin of adultery, but the sorrow for sin as well. His unfailing response was and is, "Thy sins are forgiven thee. Now go and sin no more." There, I hope that covers it. Now I just have to wait and see if Sister calls on me tomorrow morning.

I followed Bessie into the bedroom where she went to put the pillows and blanket from the truck.

"We will be attending school tomorrow, right?" I wanted reassurance.

"I don't foresee any reason why we wouldn't. We have clean socks; you know Sunday's sermon; Mother baked homemade bread so we can make Spam sandwiches for lunch; and it isn't snowing so the buses will be running. Hopefully Priscilla and I won't wet the bed and smell like popcorn in the morning."

"Do you think you and Priscilla could use the bathroom right before we go to bed and sleep with socks on, so you don't get a chill in your sleep and wet the bed? I sure wish I could sleep next to you, Priscilla and Mary Ann." I felt left out because I had to sleep at the foot of the bed with Mary Grace.

"That is your choice. Mary Ann doesn't care if she wakes up wet."

"I don't either, Bessie, but not on a school night! And you know how attached Mary Ann is to you. She either wakes up smelling like popcorn or she has to give up sleeping next to you!"

"I have to get to school one way or another."

"I don't believe any of you suffer as I do!" I mourned. "I have to beg you girls not to miss school, because I don't want to face Sister Alquin the next day!"

"I know this has been a hard year for you, but we only have about three more months of school, and then we'll get summer break. Please take that frown off your face, Pauline! I don't know what else to say. Priscilla and I don't wet the bed intentionally!"

"I know that, but could you try sleeping with socks on, please?"

"Don't worry, we won't miss school tomorrow. Let's go find the other girls and play a little baseball."

We found Priscilla and Mary Ann outside in the garden with Mother and Father. They were checking to see if any flowers had sprouted from the seeds they had buried a couple of weeks ago. If they did bloom, they'd be mixed in with the vegetables, but the girls didn't seem to mind. Mother and Father humored them by allowing them to try their hand at gardening.

Leo was sharpening his knife so he could start the removal of the muskrat fur. Joe was washing his car. He signaled for us to come over.

"You girls want to give me a hand and dry the windows on my car?"

He knew darn well we would help. For some reason, we were shy around him and liked to please him. Maybe it was because he wasn't around much. He had spent a couple of years in California with Grandmother Genevieve, in his early teens. He must have been seventeen when he came back home. We thought he was so good-looking, and that he drove the best-looking car in Monty.

Mary Grace was taking down her skirts and blouses off the clothes line. She called to Bessie, "Come keep me company while I iron my school clothes."

"You girls are good workers," said Joe. "I don't see any streaks. Bessie, look in the glove compartment and you'll find a pack of gum. You and Pauline may each have a piece."

"May we take two extra pieces for Priscilla and Mary Ann?" I asked. Bessie looked at me with widened eyes.

"Go right ahead; take some for the other girls."

I took three pieces, in case Mary Grace wanted one. Joe thanked us again, as we started to walk away.

"I can't believe you dared to ask Joe for extra pieces."

"It doesn't hurt to ask. All he could have said was no. He had just told us what a great job we did on his car windows."

"You're right. We did leave those windows sparkling. It was a very good time to ask."

Mary Grace plugged in the iron. Bessie sat at the kitchen table with her tablet and pencil in front of her. I fetched my catechism book.

"What is it really like attending public school?" Bessie asked Mary Grace.

"Well, Catholic school goes up to eighth grade and public school goes up to twelfth grade." She started to sprinkle her clothes for ironing. "You have men teachers as well as women. Each subject is taught in a different classroom, with a different teacher. Sometimes you get the same teacher for two different subjects; it just depends.

"Another thing that's different is physical education. The course requires one to wear proper clothing for games and sports. Before the class starts you have just enough time to change into shorts and blouse, like the ones I'm pressing right now. In very cold weather, we are allowed to wear sweatpants and sweatshirt. There is one big room, where there are lockers to store the clothes, and on Fridays everyone takes their own clothes home to wash and iron for the following week.

"Another thing that's different is the playground. It is divided into sections to accommodate the different age groups. For me, one of the best things about public school is when I climb out of the bus! I don't have to walk those few blocks to the Catholic school any more. I do miss the nuns though. I only get to see them on Thursday afternoons when I come to church for confession."

"Do you have to undress to get into gym clothes in front of other students?" asked Bessie.

"Yes, but it's just other girls your own age!"

"I don't care! I won't take that class if it's required of us to change clothes in front of other people!"

"Don't worry about it. You still have about a year and a half before you have to deal with it. I adjusted. I had to! It's part of going to public school."

She left the room to put her gym clothes in a bag for tomorrow morning.

Because Bessie and I were very modest, I wondered if she also had plans to miss a lot of school just to avoid going to gym class.

"Does this mean that we will be missing a lot of school when we go to public school?"

"Probably."

Mary Grace popped her head back into the kitchen.

"Oh! And did I happen to mention that after we play sports we also have to shower in front of other girls?" She giggled and disappeared.

Bessie and I just stood there pop-eyed. How could this be? We weren't sure if she was just teasing us. I looked at Bessie; she was deep in thought.

"Maybe when it's time to go to public school, we can ask Mother to let us quit school completely!" I suggested.

"Really! What in the world would make you believe Mother would let us do that?"

"Haven't you heard Leo beg Mother to let him quit school? I've heard him cry and ask, 'But why do I have to go?'"

"You're right, I have heard him beg. It just breaks my heart that he has such a miserable time at school. But Mother keeps giving him reasons why she and Father can't let him quit."

"It makes me feel bad to see Mother's face, when Leo questions her about school. After he walks away, she looks like she is thinking deeply in a sad way!"

"It's because he just turned fourteen in April. Mother tells him, 'Making a living is hard enough, and without an education you don't stand a chance!' But I see it firsthand. He sits right across from me in class, and school is just not for him! I told Mother that Sister Devota wants her to go in so they can discuss Leo's progress in school! It won't be long before Mother and Father are forced to make a decision."

Mother came in and washed her hands.

"My goodness!" she exclaimed. "I forgot about the pan of bread that I left this morning for a second rising! I had worked it up right before I got you girls up for church this morning. But I'm sure it will bake just fine."

"When do you know that it's ready for baking?" I asked.

"Have you ever noticed it running over the pan? When it runs over the pan two or three times, I work it and I can feel that it's ready. I'm going to make small sandwich rolls with this last batch of yeast dough."

The next morning, I could face my class and not fear humiliation. But Ernest Lino, another student in my class had not attended Sunday Mass. He moved quietly to the front of the class when Sister called him up. He hoped not to be noticed, but that was the whole idea. If we got embarrassed, then maybe we would work harder to make it to Mass on Sunday.

He knelt in front of the blackboard with his back to us; I'm sure he was relieved not to have to face the class. I wished I could strangle Naomi, a nasty girl in our class. She couldn't hold back: she gleefully brought to everyone's attention how Ernest's dirty ankles were exposed because he wasn't wearing socks.

Thank you, Jesus, I prayed. You are Ernest's shield today for, because his back is to us, he is not aware of the stares and giggles. After about half an hour, Sister Alquin sent him back to his desk. We knew we needed to either kneel at Mass on Sundays, or do it in front of the class.

The rest of the day went swell. Bessie had found time to prepare a lunch for us girls to share. I didn't see what she put in the little breads Mother had made, but I was sure we'd enjoy them. We were delighted that Priscilla hadn't found time to sneak bites from whatever she managed to lay her little hands on. At times she was tempted to get into our lunch whenever Sister Amelia turned her back. She'd bring up to the edge of the bag, whatever she happened to grab—an apple, a banana, a sandwich on a roll—then sneak little bites. By the time the lunch hour came, you would think there had been a mouse in the lunch bag. In the past, Priscilla had explained how hungry she got. She felt that she had earned the extra bites for she was the only one willing to bring the big brown bag to class with her! We dared to dream that some Christmas, we would each find lunch pails under the tree, like the ones carried by the three pretty blond sisters that rode our school bus.

The end of the school day came. We walked to the public school to catch the bus home. We didn't meet up with those nasty girls: the Ratenias were nowhere to be seen. We climbed on to the bus. Priscilla and I sat behind Bessie and Mary Ann.

We heard a knock at the window. Cousin Phil was at the other side of the bus trying to get our attention.

"Come on, Girls, get off the bus!" he shouted. "Aunt Della and Mary Grace asked me to come get you!"

We looked across the street and saw Mother waving at us from Joe's car. We were off the bus in a flash.

"It's almost Easter! Aunt Della is taking you shopping for Easter clothes and shoes!" announced Phil.

We climbed into the car, and Mother greeted us with her wonderful smile.

"What a nice surprise!" cried Bessie.

"Nothing would make me happier than to be able to do this more often."

We headed for J.C. Penney's. Mother liked shopping there for clothes. She told us that she and Father had decided that we would attend Easter Mass in Capulin, Colorado, a very small town twenty miles from Monte Vista. She added that the most beautiful church she'd ever seen was there, and that all us children had been baptized there.

"Your father and I like to attend Mass there whenever possible," she said. "And we get to visit with relatives we don't see very often. J.C. Penney's isn't crowded today," she continued. "I believe we picked a very good day to shop."

Phil told Mother he wanted to run across to the Boy's Market.

"Joe may be due for a break just about now. I'll be back in a little while."

"You have plenty of time; the girls are going to be fitted for two pairs of shoes."

Phil raised his right leg, and kicked. He called what he was doing a karate kick.

"He is so crazy!" cried Mary Grace, as he darted across the street.

"He does act silly at times, but he is a good boy," said Mother. "Come, Priscilla and Mary Ann, you'll be fitted for shoes first."

Bessie and I headed for the costume jewelry counter. Every so often Mother would buy a pair of earrings for each of us girls. Mother believed we wanted them for when we played dress up. We did for a while; then one day we found Joe's car unlocked when he had gone rabbit hunting. We thought he wouldn't mind as long as we didn't hurt anything. We never dared to eat anything in his car, for that would really get us in trouble! We climbed into his car that day, and hung our play earrings on the sun visor. We suspected that he was either giving them to his date or they were helping themselves to them, because we never saw them again. I guess we didn't mind, because we continued to buy them and hang them on his sun visor. Hopefully Mother would buy some for us today. Bessie and I had plenty of time to look at all the different styles. We compared and agreed that the dangling earrings would hang very nicely in Joe's car.

When we joined the others in the shoe department, Mary Grace teased Bessie, "This may be your last pair of patent leather shoes. You're on your way to being a woman. Very soon now, you're gonna be too old for patent leather shoes."

Bessie rolled her eyes.

"Just leave me out of your woman talk! I'll get there when I get there, and not one minute sooner!"

I had a feeling there was more to this conversation, but I couldn't figure out the significance in the word "woman." Seeing the frown on Bessie's face told me not to ask her.

Mother winked at Bessie. I always felt reassured when Mother winked. I felt it was her way of saying, "Don't worry; everything is fine."

Mother said with a smile, "Come on, Bessie, don't look so serious. Mary Grace is just teasing."

"Leo does enough teasing!" cried Bessie. "We don't need another member of the family doing it too."

"Mary Grace is right though; you girls will get a pair of white patent leather shoes for church and a pair of oxfords for school."

It didn't take long to pick out our Easter outfits. I couldn't wait to get home to lay out my dress, slip, and socks.

Phil came in and announced to Mother, "Joe is working overtime. He wants me to drop you all off at home if you're done shopping, then return to pick him up."

Phil was like a third cousin to us. He was about 5'4" with a slender build. With his olive-colored complexion, brown eyes, and dark hair, he had average looks. He was a little showy and eager for praise.

Mother told Phil that was fine with her, but he was to go straight back to the Boy's Market to get Joe.

"Phil, you know how Joe feels about anyone driving his car."

"I know, but it was Joe's idea for me to drive back for him."

"All right then; you may come back with him and have dinner with us if you like."

"Thank you, Aunt Della! I love your homemade bread."

On the way home I searched my bag. Panic set in when I couldn't find my Easter bonnet.

"Mother!" I cried. "The lady didn't put my bonnet in the bag!"

"She didn't put them in any of your bags," Mother answered calmly. "I told her to put them separate from my other purchases. They're in the trunk of the car so they don't get smashed. All you girls check your bags to be sure you each have your dress, slip, white gloves, and the little white patent leather purses. Your socks are in the shoe boxes in the trunk."

We all eagerly checked, then nodded our heads.

"But there's nothing here for Mary Grace!" said Bessie.

Mary Grace answered that she would be wearing the same outfit that Mother had bought for her birthday on Easter Sunday.

That evening after dinner, as Bessie and I finished up the dishes, Mother came into the kitchen and handed each of us a whole quarter.

With widened eyes, I asked "What is this for?"

"Because you are good girls and this is extra money I did not expect to have. Mrs. Roth had me help her clean out all her closets today, and there were a couple of suits that her husband Dr. Roth never wears. She told me to take them and see if I had any use for them. Your father doesn't wear suits, but I told her I'd take them. The timing was right, because El Indio, an old friend of your father's, stopped by with your father's compadre. They reminisced about their old days when they worked for the city.

"I was going through the box of clothes that Mrs. Roth had given me, and El Indio asked, 'Mrs. Montoya, would you consider selling those suits to me?' I told him he could have them, but he insisted on giving me a few dollars and all the change he had on him. He said the quarters were for you girls."

"Is El Indio his name? It sounds like you're calling him Indian," said Bessie.

"That is what everyone at the yard called him when your father and his compadre Catalino started working for the city. He is an

Indian, but I don't know what tribe he belonged to. His hair is long, but it always looks clean and shiny."

"Hey, Pauline, do you think he might be an Apache like you?"

"That isn't funny, 'Bessie the cow'!"

"That's enough! Stop both of you before you start fighting," said Mother.

Priscilla and Mary Ann came running into the kitchen.

"Look what Mother gave me!" cried Mary Ann. "Bessie, will you save my quarter until I really need it?"

"Whatever you say. I'll save it for you."

"I plan to visit the candy room at school tomorrow at recess time," said Priscilla.

Aunt Vittoria's kitchen, 1954

Grandfather Pablo Montoya

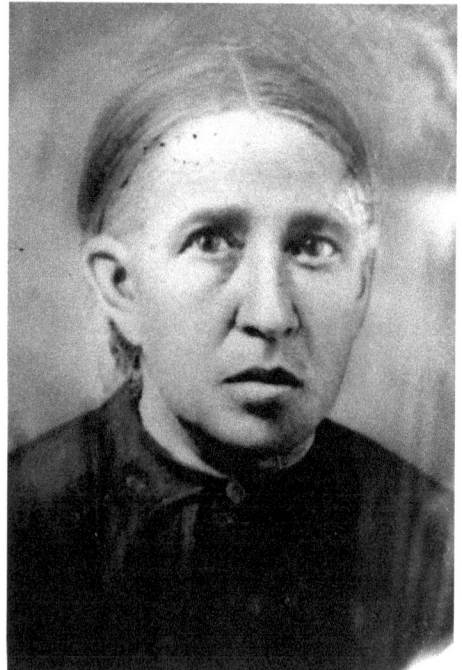

Grandmother Vicentia LeBlanc

Cousin Horacio
and his horse

Aunt Vittoria's home

Aunt Vittoria's spooky well

Alamosa River running alongside Aunt Vittoria's property

Cousin Haracio's horses grazing on their property

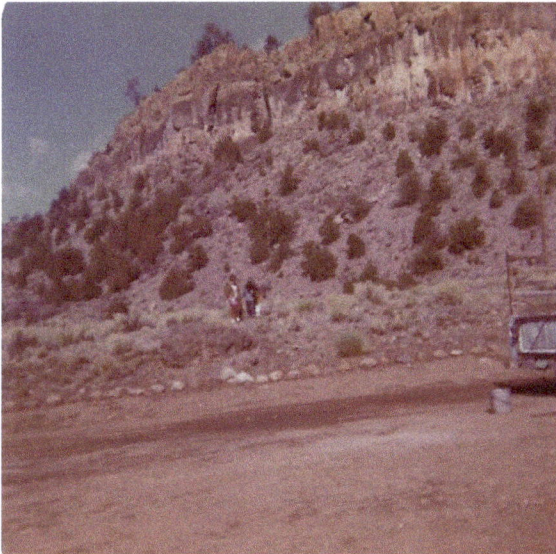

Mountains about 100 feet from Aunt Vittoria's front yard

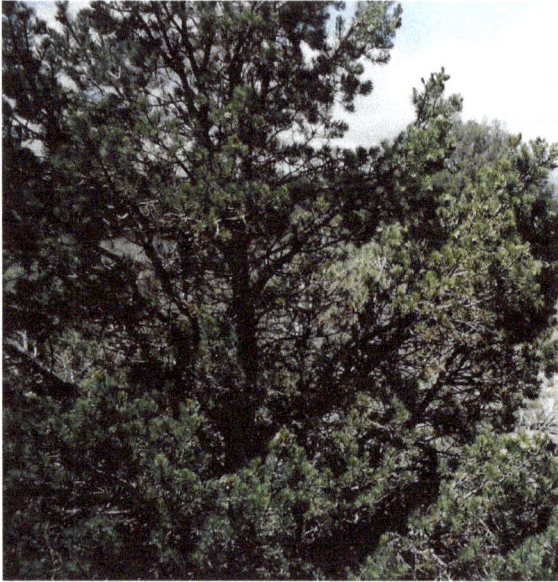

Pine tree we picked pine nuts from

Wolf Creek Pass heading toward Durango, Colorado

Chapter Three

On Tuesday morning I woke up to see Mary Grace sitting up in bed saying, "Just think, Bessie! Only four days to go and then my birthday party!"

Bessie was down on her knees reaching under the bed for her shoes. She didn't seem to be showing any interest in Mary Grace's excitement.

"Don't you have anything to say? It is my very first birthday party!"

Bessie shrugged her shoulders, and it was obvious to me that Bessie woke up "se passer de mot," as Father would say in French—without a word.

"Oh, I give up!" cried Mary Grace, as she got off the bed and left the room.

Bessie gave me a sidelong glance.

"Well, it's just too early," she said as she scratched her head. She always did that when she wanted to convey, "Don't bother me!"

Whenever she was very quiet, I left her alone until she got out of her bad mood. I knew she would talk when she was ready. She wouldn't be in that mood all day; and she was great to be around once that mood passed. It was always in the morning, and I wondered if she was thinking, "Will I be able to talk the girls into playing hooky today?" Then she'd get moody when she realized she shouldn't discourage the rest of us from going to school. That was Bessie Le Blanc for you: one had to give her the first hour of the morning to herself. I left the room to put my shoes on.

From the front room I could see into the kitchen. Mary Grace was combing each of Mary Ann's rag curls, trying to make them look freshly made after sleeping on them. Priscilla's had already been done and I was next. Bessie combed her own hair.

Mary Grace told me to sit at the table with Priscilla and have some oatmeal. It was nice when Mary Grace got up early enough to do this for us. Sometimes when she got up late in the morning, she'd part my hair crooked to make my braids.

Priscilla finished eating and went to look out the window. She announced that there was still snow on the ground.

"May I go out and fill my cup with snow, and add vanilla and milk to make ice milk?"

"I don't think it's a good idea," said our older sister. "It's not fresh fallen snow; it's dirty from the gas fumes."

"It looks clean from here!"

"No, Priscilla, it's getting late and the school bus will be here shortly. Bessie, go back into the bedroom and get the schoolbooks," ordered Mary Grace.

"Could you please grab my catechism book?" I asked. "It's on top of the radio in the front room."

"I've got it right here."

"Thank you, Bessie." Her mood seemed better already.

The school bus pulled up in front of our house just as Bessie finished her breakfast. We ran outside, the door opened and we climbed on. Our house was second to the last stop, followed by Billy McCoy's house.

In my class, we always started with the Lord's Prayer, our morning prayer, and the pledge of allegiance to the flag. The class sat down, and we got our reading books ready to start the lesson.

I checked my dress pocket to be sure my quarter hadn't fallen out. Yes! It was waiting to be carried to the candy room to be traded in for sweets. I checked my pocket two more times. My quarter sitting securely at the bottom of my pocket brought joy to my heart.

Sister Alquin opened the book in her hand.

"Now remember class, you are to study page eighty-one: 'Indian Children,' a poem by Annette Wynne. Two weeks from today, I will give a test on that poem, so you must memorize it. For today I will read it aloud.

> Where we walk to school each day
> Indian children used to play—
> All about our native land,
> Where the shops and houses stand.
>
> And the trees were very tall,
> And there were no streets at all,
> Not a church and not a steeple—
> Only woods and Indian people.
>
> Only wigwams on the ground.
> And at night bears prowling round—
> What a different place today
> Where we live and work and play!

"I like that poem. I know I can memorize it," I whispered to my best friend Julia who sat across from me in class.

"I think it is kind of long to memorize, and only two weeks to do it," whispered Julia.

"We can study together in our lunch hours," I offered.

It was time for math. I was glad I had memorized some of my times table. The time was going by so quickly.

"Okay, class, it's recess time. Sister Mary Julian will open the supply room in five minutes if anyone wants to purchase anything."

I called to Julia who was across the room reaching for her sweater.

"Come with me to the candy room!"

"It's the supply room. You keep calling it the candy room."

"That's because I never have enough money to buy anything else except small change for candy. And what does it hurt if I call it the candy room?"

"Do you have candy money today?"

"Yes, I have a whole quarter! What flavor sucker do you want? It's my treat today!"

"Cherry!"

"Me too!"

Sister Mary Julian took my quarter in exchange for two cherry suckers. She handed me my change: two dimes.

We walked down the hall that led to the door to the playground. Priscilla ran up to us.

"Pauline! I thought I wouldn't find you in time! I forgot my quarter at home." She stared at the sucker in my mouth.

"Here, you can borrow a dime from me and pay me back tomorrow."

"Thank you!"

"Don't lose the change you get back," I called after her.

Julia and I ran out to find free swings but they were all taken. We sat on some cement steps by the entrance of the classrooms and watched some girls play jacks. Sister Mary Joseph walked by, stopped, and said to all the girls sitting there, "Girls, be mindful that you sit like little ladies when you are wearing dresses."

We all said in unison, "Yes, Sister Mary Joseph."

Julia and I walked around the playground.

"Pauline, look at all the tumbleweeds!"

"How about tomorrow, if the wind doesn't blow them far, we line them up and use them as dividers? We can pretend they are walls if we lay them side by side to form big squares. We can design a front room and a bedroom and a kitchen. I'm sure someone will come along and do the same, and then we can call them neighbors!"

"That sounds like fun."

The recess bell rang: it was time to line up to return to class. Sister Alquin saw that we hadn't finished eating our suckers and said, "Girls, there is some wax paper on my desk. Each of you grab a piece and put them on the window sill with the suckers on top until lunch time. Be sure not to forget them because the janitor will toss them."

The school day came to an end. Sister Alquin was running late in dismissing the class. I was out the door the second we said the last word to the end of the day prayer.

Bessie, Priscilla and Mary Ann were waiting across the street in front of Saint Joseph's Church, our usual place to meet after school. As I walked toward them, I felt fear creeping up inside. Bessie was looking me in the eye as if she felt the same way.

"Let's take a different route to the public school to catch the bus today," she whispered. "Then we can avoid meeting up with the Ratenias!"

"Okay!" I whispered back. "Shall we take the next street down?"

Bessie gave me a look that meant I was whispering too loud. We didn't want to alert Priscilla and Mary Ann, and scare them.

Bessie tried to make light of it.

"Just for the heck of it, why don't we walk down three streets then turn left on Gunbarrel Road?"

"That sounds like fun!" said Priscilla.

Mary Ann nodded and reached for Bessie's hand. Bessie and I looked at each other, pleased. As we walked past homes on this unfamiliar street, we admired the green lawns and the flowers starting to bloom.

"Look at those pretty flowers of all different colors!"

Bessie smiled and nodded.

"I believe Mother calls those flowers pansies and some of those are sweet peas."

"I like the white boards," sighed Mary Ann.

"Baby, I do believe those boards are called a white picket fence," I volunteered.

"That's right," said Bessie.

"I like the black iron fence with the white flowers growing all over it!"

"Yeah, Pauline, I do too! I like the white shutters and boards that cover the windows of the house where we used to live."

"We've never lived in a house with shutters," I exclaimed.

"We haven't? Oh well, just the same I like the white shutters," sighed Priscilla.

We laughed.

"Priscilla, you are so funny!" said Mary Ann.

"I do believe we could fall in love with all the homes on this street," said Bessie.

"Oh, that's silly," said Mary Ann. "How could we fall in love with these houses? They are things, not people!"

"Just the same, these houses never looked so pretty from the car. We must walk down this street more often."

Soon we reached the public school, and to our delight, there were no Ratenias in sight! We reached our bus safely, and it began to fill. Mary Grace was among the students from the public school to climb onto the bus. She gave us a big smile as she made her way toward us.

"Did you girls have any trouble?"

We all shook our heads no.

The three sisters with the golden hair sat in front of us. I wondered where they came from. I thought they were so pretty that they must be part human and part angel. Their hair was so straight and shiny. We called them the three sisters, but we had never talked to them. We were too shy to let them catch us staring at them. We didn't know their names. They would always be the three sisters with the golden hair. The school bus dropped us off ahead of them. We liked to think that they lived in the next farmhouse, and that some-day we might visit and become good friends.

"The minute we get dropped off at home, I'm going to start cleaning house, so don't make plans to play baseball or whatever you girls do after school."

Before I could stop myself, I asked, "Are you saying that you are not going to fall asleep the second we walk in the door?"

Bessie, Priscilla and Mary Ann looked at our older sister for her response, knowing they wouldn't have dared to say that to Mary Grace. I guess the Apache in me had come out, and it was too late to take back my question.

Mary Grace looked at me and snapped, "Just for that, Pauline, you will be doing the breakfast dishes by yourself with no help from Bessie!"

Why can't I learn to think before I open my mouth? I thought. I needed to learn to keep my mouth shut. I hoped there weren't too many dishes. I liked washing dishes, but I liked company while I was doing them. I didn't like to be alone in the kitchen, especially when I had gotten myself into trouble. It made me feel left out of what the others were doing.

The bus pulled up in front of Bill McCoy's house. I turned to look up at him as he made his way to the front of the bus. He looked at me and gave me a quick half-smile. Better than no smile at all! Oh my! Once I had a secret love…

The bus pulled up in front of our house. We climbed off and ran toward the house. Leo opened the door.

"Did you beat the bus home on your bike or did you miss school again?" Mary Grace asked.

Leo didn't have the patience for riding on the bus. He always rode his bike to and from school.

Mary Grace looked at Bessie, who would know if he was in class or not.

"I'm not going to say anything to Mother, but sooner or later she will know how often you stay home from school."

When Joe was still in school, he had shown Leo the way to avoid getting Mother too upset. When the school called Mother to tell her that her boys were absent, she would come home to check and find them cleaning house.

Leo had learned well. The kitchen was swept and the dishes were washed, dried, and put away. He had also made a fire on the wood stove.

There were still some rolls left from the bread Mother had made. Priscilla, Mary Ann and I ate them with Mother's homemade chokecherry jam. I sat on the steps to the front door, with my roll and my schoolbooks to study. I decided to stay out of Mary Grace's way for a little while.

As it turned out, I'm the one that fell asleep. Mary Grace woke me up.

"That grass is damp! You may come down with a cold, get in the house!" she ordered.

Wednesday and Thursday came and went. Friday was another busy day, especially after school. Mary Grace mopped, washed windows, rearranged furniture and anything else she could think of to do in preparation for her party on Saturday.

Saturday finally arrived. The early morning hours were very busy. Everyone did their share to help prepare for Mary Grace's guests.

It turned out to be the best party ever, according to Mary Grace and her girlfriends. As Mary Grace predicted, Priscilla, Mary Ann and I did fall asleep before the party was over, but we'd had our fill of Dairy Queen ice cream! If they played "Spin the Bottle," we missed it. Mary Grace talked about her birthday party long afterward. Mary Grace and Phyllis had been upset with some girl that had been invited to the party. Word had it that she had been seen outside our house kissing Bobby Allen.

This girl Porfidia, according to Phyllis, knew full well that Mary Grace had invited Bobby Allen because she has the biggest crush on him. It was legal to kiss him in the game "Spin the Bottle," but not for her to go outside with him after Mother had made it clear that she wanted all the girls to stay indoors during the party. She would not be invited to return to our home; Mother had made that very clear.

Bessie, Priscilla, Mary Ann and I finally learned what "Spin the Bottle" was all about, but it was of no use to us, at our age. I assumed the nuns would recommend that Porfidia go make a good confession.

A whole week went by. We all attended school, with no absences. We made it to the bus each day and never met up with the Ratenias. My mouth didn't get me in any more hot water with my siblings. I was content.

After Easter Mass (from back row left
to right) Leo, Pauline, Bessie,
Joe, Mary, Mother, Father,
Mary Ann, and Priscilla

Uncle Charlie,
Mother's brother

Saint Joseph Church, Capulin, Colorado

Chapter Four

We were approaching the end of March. It had been a very festive month; we had joyously celebrated the Annunciation to Mary with songs. The girls and I memorized our favorite song to our Blessed Mother: "Immaculate Mary."

Immaculate Mary, your praises we sing.
You reign now in heaven with Jesus our King.
Ave, Ave, Ave, Maria! Ave, Ave, Mari—a!

We'd had a very snowy winter. The ice was taking longer to melt than usual, especially on the creeks and lakes that were shaded by pine trees.

On Saturday, the wind was cool and crisp. We had so much frost on the ground. We stayed indoors most of the day. We were beginning to get bored.

I suggested to my sisters that we go out by the creek and pick some of the long, narrow-pointed grass to weave.

Bessie agreed and said, "Remember to pick four blades to tie a knot at the top. Try to pull some that feel flexible to weave."

We made our way out the door.

When we stepped out, a very cool breeze had picked up. I felt chilled. We were not wearing our winter coats, because they were used only for school and church. We improvised a coat by using our dresses to keep warm. We placed the bottom hem of our dresses over our shoulders to keep our back and arms from the cold, while the back of our legs and our bloomers were exposed to the cold air.

Priscilla soon said, "I need to go to the bathroom."

"Ok, but make it fast; it's very cold out."

Priscilla asked me to accompany her to the bathroom. The farm house didn't come with indoor plumbing, so to the outhouse we went. Bessie followed behind us.

A short time later we were settled down in the front room, each with a comic book in hand. These weren't just any comic books; they were "love" comic books. Mary Grace and Phyllis would buy them to read in the evenings whenever Phyllis spent the night. Priscilla, Bessie and I would spot them, and it seemed like forever before we were able to get our hands on them. I'm sure it improved our reading skills, for we read them over and over again, and I'm almost sure there was a lesson or two to be learned. We certainly came to know that the good girl always got the guy to fall in love with her.

We heard the back door open, and Leo came running in.

"Mom! Mom! Where are you?"

"Here, in the front room," answered Mother from the sofa. She was wrapped up in a comforter quilt, where she liked to retire when she had one of her headaches.

Leo was tripping over his words in excitement.

"Now, Son, take a deep breath and tell me what's going on."

"I went to the lake by the Triangle Restaurant! The one on the way toward Alamosa!"

"Yes, Son, I know the one. You set some of your traps there, right? You went there this morning?"

"Yes, Mother, I went to check on the ones I set early this morning for muskrats! The police had the whole area blocked off! There was a lot of people there! A man asked me if I was a relative of the boys that drowned in the lake! I was shocked! This man said that one of the officers told him that four boys had been at the lake. Apparently they were crossing the frozen lake and at one point, the ice crashed and two of the boys went under! An older brother ten years old told the fourth boy who was a friend to go get help, and then he tried to help his brothers out. By the time the friend returned with help, all three brothers were gone! They were swept away from their parents' sight forever under the treacherous ice!"

Mother shook the tears from her cheeks. The girls and I were very still. We enjoyed finding ice on the lakes in winter months. How could this happen? How could the ice take the boys forever from their parents?

Mother asked Leo, "Do you know who they were?"

"I may have seen them at school, but they are much younger than I. The ten-year-old that tried to rescue his brothers was Ernest Pollock."

"Mother!" I cried out. "Ernest is in my class!" My eyes welled up with tears.

Priscilla got up and put her arm around me.

Mother signaled for me to come to her. Leo and Mary Ann just stared.

Bessie asked, "Is he the one that never wears socks?"

I nodded.

"Mother, poor Ernest! He must have been terror-stricken watching his little brothers go under the ice!"

"Come sit on the sofa with me. Let us bow our heads and say a prayer for the parents."

We were very quiet at the dinner table. Mother and Father talked about the drowning.

Father said to Leo, "Son, you recall that I told you a while back to stay near the shore when you go out to the rivers to set traps? The ice is smoother in the middle but it isn't safe! The man-made lakes are safe for ice skating; they are not deep and there is always a safety guard on duty. These boys must have been walking across the river where there was no one around."

"Yes, Father. I always stay on the edge of the shore."

"It is also very important to tell your mother when and where you are going to set traps."

Father turned to look at the rest of us.

"Girls, now do you understand why I forbid you crossing over to the neighbor's yard and have told you to stay away from the wooden plank that crosses over to the neighbor's house? In the winter months, one can never tell how deep the water is!"

We all listened intently, and I didn't believe any of us would disobey him.

Mary Grace came back into the kitchen.

"Mother, I was on the phone with Millie Espinosa, who called for Sister George. She needed to know if I could take the morning off from public school on Wednesday. The parents may want the funeral for their sons on Wednesday, and Sister George will need me and three other students from last year's choir to make up for any absent students. Sister George wants to prepare in advance; she doesn't want to be caught short-handed for the funeral. Millie would like me to let her know as soon as possible."

"That is fine. You may call Millie back after dinner. Tomorrow is Sunday Mass," said Mother.

After dinner, Mother helped Bessie and me wash the dishes. Father went into the front room to retire on his favorite chair to await the radio program "Boston Balky." Mary Ann joined him with crayons and coloring book in hand. Priscilla disappeared into one of the bedrooms. Leo went outdoors. Joe was most likely over at his girlfriend Dolly's house.

We finished the dishes and joined Father in the front room, but I wasn't in the mood to listen to the radio. Ernest's death weighed heavily on my mind. I went into the bedroom to join Priscilla, but there was no sign of her. I went into Mother's bedroom, but she wasn't there either.

"Pauline, where is Priscilla?" asked Bessie. "Mother wants to check her hair; she noticed at dinner that Priscilla had gum stuck to her hair."

"I don't know. I came looking for her, but as you can see she isn't here."

We heard Mother's voice in the kitchen. She had found Priscilla sitting inside one of the kitchen cabinets with the sugar bowl. She had done it again: she was on a sugar high.

"Priscilla, what am I to do with you? You can get very sick, eating all that sugar!"

The sugar bowl was empty. Priscilla's eyes were wide open.

I wanted to laugh, but Mother looked unhappy, so I restrained myself.

"Do I need to put the sugar and syrup under lock and key?"

Priscilla was now trying to hide behind one of the chairs.

"Come here now! Come to me!"

Priscilla twirled around the table when Mother reached for her.

"I'm sorry, Mother; I won't do it again! Please give me another chance to be good!"

Mother shook her head.

"Come here to me. You also have gum in your hair, young lady!"

Priscilla sat on a chair in front of Mother, and she began to work the gum out of her hair with an ice cube.

Bessie had returned to the front room. I sat next to her on the sofa. I couldn't get Ernest out of my mind. I had never felt this way, except when watching a sad movie. I didn't even remember feeling this sad when my great-grandmother died last year. We had only seen her once or twice per year, and I don't recall ever having talked with her. I remember standing in front of her, but only because Cousin Della was talking to her.

Mother would say to us, "Girls, say hello to your great-grandmother Mama-mina."

We'd do as we were told, but we never went up to her. Mama-mina was Mother's grandmother on her father's side. We had our own special Grandmother Genevieve. She had moved so far away, and we missed her so.

Our great-grandmother had never given us the love and affection that Grandmother Genevieve gave before she moved to California. I did feel sorry for Cousin Della when Mama-mina passed, because that was her grandmother. Della is Mother's first cousin, daughter of Great-aunt Louise. She was ten years old: my age, and she was named after Mother.

Aunt Louise's actions the day of Mama-mina's death had an effect on our attitude toward death. Mother had taken us with her to sit with Cousin Della and her brother, Cousin Frank Robert.

The girls and I walked into the front room to find Della. Mother was right behind us, but got held up in the kitchen greeting other family members. Della was kneeling on a stool in front of Mama-mina's coffin. Priscilla, Bessie, Mary Ann and I lined up against the wall. We didn't know what else to do. I was uncomfortable. Where was Mother?

Aunt Louise came into the room. She put her hand on Bessie's back and urged her to go forward. Bessie just smiled at her, but didn't move. Mary Ann, Priscilla and I just stared and waited for Bessie. Aunt Louise put her hand on Bessie's back again and whispered, "You and your sisters go on up to the coffin now. Kiss your great grandmother goodbye. You will need to help Priscilla and Mary Ann so they may reach up to kiss her."

Bessie stared at her and shook her head no. Aunt Louise was annoyed with Bessie. It was written all over her face.

"Go into the kitchen with your mother, you sassy little thing!" she ordered.

She then turned to look at the rest of us. Mary Ann was already making her way past me and Priscilla to join Bessie.

Before Aunt Louise had a chance to utter another word, Priscilla went into an act of sobbing and weeping. I couldn't believe what I was seeing. She even muttered, "Boohoo…"

Would Aunt Louise be able to see that she was faking? I didn't waste any time. I reached for Priscilla's hand and pulled her away from Aunt Louise's gaze.

I wanted to laugh. We found Mary Ann and Bessie in the kitchen, and I began to smile.

"What are you grinning about?" asked Priscilla.

"You! What do you think? I saw what you pulled in there. No one ever says, 'Boohoo' when they weep! It took everything I had to stop myself from laughing!"

Bessie and Mary Ann started to giggle.

"I did it for Aunt Louise, she so wanted us to feel sad."

I felt a little guilty for giggling. I supposed that this was not the time to have the giggles, but it felt so good to laugh with the girls.

Mother had said, "Mama-mina is in Heaven with Papa Kiko, her son Manuel, and her daughter and grandson who were shot dead that dreadful day, just nineteen days before Leo was born. Now that her time has come to join them, she would want everyone to be happy and to pray for their souls." But to giggle: I don't know if that's what Mother meant. Perhaps I was getting even with Aunt Louise for hurting Bessie's feelings by accusing her of being sassy.

We laughed about Priscilla all day, but also complained to each other about Aunt Louise's words. "How dare she call Bessie a sassy girl?"

Nonetheless that day affected our attitude toward death. Must we kiss the dead? I wondered.

On Monday, my class started the day with a prayer for the boys who had died under the ice.

Then Sister Alquin announced, "I want all those students who have received the sacrament of Penance to make a good confession on Tuesday after lunch, so that you may receive Holy Communion on Wednesday in memory of Ernest and his brothers. These boys died at such a young age."

Margaret, a new girl at our school, raised her hand.

"Yes, Margaret?"

"I haven't received the sacrament of Penance; what is it?"

"So you haven't yet made your First Holy Communion?"

"No I haven't. This is my first year attending Catholic school."

"I see. Well, Margaret, you receive the sacrament of Penance before you may receive the sacrament of Holy Eucharist. You've asked a very good question. I don't have time today to get into explaining all seven sacraments, but I will tell you a little about Penance.

"On Easter night, Jesus appeared to the apostles and said to them: 'Peace be to you! As the Father has sent Me, I also send you… Receive the Holy Spirit; Whose sins you shall forgive they are forgiven them.' We read this in St. John's Gospel, chapter 20, verses 21-23.

"Christ made confession part of the sacrament of Penance because of His understanding of the needs of the human heart. He knew that confession of sins helps the sinner. The urge to confess is natural to man. A sorrow or shame is lessened when shared with another. Confession makes us conscious of our sinfulness. It forces us to think of our sins."

Sister Alquin looked around at the class to see if we were listening. She had everyone's attention.

"When you children get older you will have a better understanding of the importance of the sacraments, and the graces we receive through them."

At lunch and recess, everyone at school was sharing their memories of the boys. After school we headed for the buses, once again hoping we wouldn't meet up with the Ratenias.

Mary Grace and Phyllis were standing close to the parked buses, talking to some girls. Mary Grace called us.

"We are going across the street to Strohmaier Mortuary to view the boys. Do you want to join us?"

"Do we just walk by and look at them?" asked Bessie.

"You may just walk by, or you can stop for a minute and say a prayer. You do whatever makes you comfortable." Mary Grace smiled at us.

Bessie started walking alongside Mary Grace and Phyllis. That was our cue. Priscilla, Mary Ann and I followed, knowing that we could visit the dead and no one would fuss at us. We didn't owe them a kiss.

On the day of the funeral services, the whole school streamed past their caskets. It was a gloomy and mournful day. I didn't like funerals but the hymns were beautiful.

I was fascinated by the Catholic Church and its rituals, and the devotion of the nuns. I thought I might like to study to become a nun one day.

The Easter season brought a very special time of the year for us: colored Easter eggs, Easter candy, and the hunting season. When I thought of Easter, patent leather shoes always came to mind, like Easter eggs and Easter baskets go together. We already had the shoes, now we needed the patience to wait for Easter Sunday. It was still a bit cold to play outside all day. We asked Mother if we could shine our patent leather shoes, the way we'd seen Joe shine his loafers: with a little petroleum jelly and a clean cloth. Mother gave each of us a small rag, and we shined to our hearts' content. We walked around the house in our shoes, and after a while we'd take them off and shine them again, though they didn't need it.

Easter Sunday arrived: April 18th. Mother removed the rags from our curly hair. I looked at myself in the mirror and thought I was the prettiest girl ever in my dressy Easter outfit. My sisters seemed to feel the same way about themselves. The morning was fine. Mother told us to wear our new sweaters; we didn't need jackets.

Mother borrowed Joe's car to make the drive to Capelin for Mass. I looked up at the altar. In front of the large crucifix was a banner with Jesus pictured on it. He was wearing a white gown and His Arms stretched up over His Head. After Mass, Mother and Father stood outside visiting with family and friends.

"Mother, remember when we went to the show and before our movie started a news reel came on? It showed a lady talking about her husband. Well, that lady was Eleanor Roosevelt and she reminds me of Aunt Rosa Bella. They comb their hair the same, and they are almost the same height. They look like they could pass for sisters. I couldn't see if Eleanor has green eyes like Aunt Rosa Bella."

Father laughed, and said, "You observed all that from a short news reel. I wonder what my sister would think if she heard that someone thinks she looks like President Roosevelt's wife."

While on our way home, Mother asked, "Should we go visit your sister Rosa Bella and her family?"

Aunt Rosa Bella's house stood in a prairie. It was a large area with no trees to shield the place from the wind, but today the weather was perfect. It was a glorious day—the Resurrection of our Lord Jesus Christ.

"You're right," said Father. "It's been a while since we've been over to see them. I ran into your brother Charlie at the lumber yard. He mentioned that they would be at Rosa Bella's house on Easter."

"Father, why is it that Mom's brother Charlie visits with your sister Rosa Bella more often than he visits with your other sister Vittoria?" I asked.

"When your mother and I got married, your mother's brother Charlie met my sister Rosa Bella's daughter Ida. Your uncle Charlie started courting my niece. When they married, your first cousin Ida became an aunt to you because of her marriage to your Uncle Charlie."

"Rosa Bella is now Charlie's mother-in-law, but Vittoria is just his wife's aunt. Hope I didn't confuse you!"

"Ask more questions, Pauline! It will make the ride to the ranch seem shorter."

"No, you ask questions, Bessie. I'm already called 'Parrot' because I ask too many questions!"

"Who calls you a parrot?" asked Mother.

"Mary Grace and Joe. It hurts my feelings."

We all looked at Mary Grace, who was grinning. When she opened her mouth, she didn't deny, but reinforced what I had just told Mother.

"Polly! Polly Parrot wants to have a carrot! Polly wants to ask a question!"

"See, Mother, I told you!"

"Don't worry, Pauline. It is alright to ask questions. One can't learn if one doesn't ask questions," said Mother.

Mary smiled and winked at me, but I knew that the next time I asked a question she didn't want to answer, she would say that the parrot was on its perch again.

"Then why don't you sing that new song I've heard you singing?" asked Priscilla.

"What song is that?"

"The one by Jim Reeves that's been playing on the radio; it says something about water in the desert."

"What am I, today's entertainment?"

"Come on, Pauline, I want to learn the words!"

Secretly I was pleased she asked again; nothing made me happier than to sing, especially when asked. I looked at Mom and Dad and the other girls. They seemed to be waiting to hear the new song, "Then I'll Stop Loving You." I started singing quietly, and when I saw that I had everyone's attention, I let the words flow.

"Very nice, Pauline," said Mother. "You're very good at memorizing all the words to a new song! Keep up the good work."

"Look, Girls!" said Father. "Farm horses crossing the road!"

"Father, look, there are six of them!" said Mary Ann.

"No, Mary Ann. There are only four!"

"You always count six," said Priscilla.

"I like the number six; I'm six years old!"

As Father turned into Aunt Rosa Bella's driveway, he honked the horn at the goat kids all around the car.

"They sure are cute little animals," said Mary Grace. "Look at their hollow horns."

Aunt Rosa Bella and her family came out to greet us. Since Father was their only younger brother, she, Aunt Victoria, and Aunt Raquel always made a fuss over him. They actually had other half-brothers, but they didn't share the same closeness.

Aunt Rosa Bella's house had a huge country kitchen where everyone congregated and could always find a place to sit. Even the floor was inviting because the conversation was always interesting. One could never forget the aroma: there was always something good cooking, and the wood stove was always burning.

Aunt Rosa Bella announced, "My daughter-in-law Isabella's parents, Mr. and Mrs. Macadio, want to visit with you and Della about the lost treasure."

Father shook his head and smiled.

"Everyone that knows Vicentia LeBlanc was my mother, approaches me to discuss their plan on how and where to find the lost treasure."

"Everyone has a dream," said Uncle Francisco, Rosa Bella's husband. "Gold can make a lot of dreams come true. But gold can't buy happiness," he added.

"You're right about that," said Father. "Look how many men lost their lives over the lost treasure of the Rockies."

"I once believed that the gold was buried up by Platoro Reservoir between Lookout Mountain and Elephant Mountain."

"I guess we will never know. Only the Indians know what happened to the Frenchman's gold, and the men that lost their lives running from them," said Father. "Thanks to my Grandmother Alvina."

I nudged Bessie, sitting next to me on the floor.

"Let's go outside. I don't want to hear Father talk that way. I want to hear that he is interested in searching for the treasure!"

"After all, we have our dreams to dream," she agreed. "And we need to find that treasure!"

We joined Priscilla and Mary Ann outdoors. Priscilla was chasing the farm animals as usual.

Uncle Charlie's boys, Philip and Orlando, were calling to her to stop chasing the kids.

"Please don't chase them! We want to watch the goats chew their cud."

"Chew their what?" asked Bessie.

"Cud," answered ten-year-old Cousin Carmelita, Uncle Charlie's only daughter. "Cud is a mouthful of swallowed food that cattle, sheep and goats bring back up from the first stomach to chew again slowly a second time."

"She is so smart," I whispered to Bessie. "You can tell she reads a lot."

"How many stomachs do we have, Pauline?" asked Priscilla.

"I don't know. Why, are you planning to chew your cud?"

Bessie, Mary Ann, and Carmelita's brothers laughed. Carmelita just shook her head and walked away.

"Carmelita has no sense of humor," said her brother Orlando.

"Carmelita, come join us," called Bessie. "We are going to the underground cellar to see what Aunt Rosa Bella has stored down there."

"Ok, but all Grandmother stores down there are sacks of potatoes and baskets of peas. In the winter months, Grandfather Francisco stores elk meat cut in long strips, then seasoned and hung to dry like beef jerky."

"Grandmother also hangs red chili peppers to dry them to crush and use for sauces," said her brother. "There are other foods down there."

"Entirely boring, if you ask me!" said Carmelita.

"Look who's talking. If you ask me, you act like an old lady," said Orlando. "Let's go down anyway."

"You are quite welcome to go down there. I'm going to watch my brother Herman and Cousin Leo shoot their BB guns."

"Why don't you just admit it, Sis? You're afraid that La Yorona is down there, waiting to take you with her!"

"I don't know what you are talking about! I'm gonna tell Daddy that you are being mean to me!"

"Who is La Yorona?" asked Bessie.

"Yeah! Who is La Yorona?" I wanted to know.

"No one! It's just a story my Uncle Miguel tells to scare me!"

"What is the story? Why would your uncle want to scare you?"

"Well, he says that my mom and dad could never go anywhere alone, because I never stopped crying for them. He says that no one wants to care for me when they are gone."

"Yeah, but who is La Yorona?" I asked again.

"La Yorona was a blind lady whose small children drowned in some river. They say that she died looking for her children."

"Now whenever she hears small children cry, she comes looking for her babies," explained Cousin Orlando. "Since my sister cries a lot, Miguel tells her that La Yorona is gonna get her."

"On second thought, why don't we all find Leo and Cousin Herman?" suggested Bessie.

"Yeah, I agree," I said. "We can go down to the cellar some other time when a grownup has to go down there."

"Only if that grownup is Father!" cried Priscilla.

Thankfully, Mary Ann didn't hear us talking about La Yorona, because she had run back to the house. Philip and Orlando ran off to find Leo and Herman, and Carmelita, Bessie, Priscilla and I decided to go inside and ask for homemade cookies.

My sisters and I reassured Carmelita, "Don't worry, we will say a rosary to St. Joseph so that he will watch over you as he watched over his little boy Jesus!"

Carmelita smiled as we all walked back into her grandmother's house.

Mary Ann was happily sitting on Father's lap, munching on a biscochito. Carmelita's other little brother Manuel was sitting on the floor playing with a sack full of marbles. Many thought Mary Ann and Manuel could pass for twins.

"They are first cousins after all," they said.

The kitchen smelled of food cooking. We knew we'd enjoy the meal prepared by Aunt Rosa Bella and her daughter Celina. Carmelita, the girls and I sat on the long bench at the table. We passed up the biscochitos, in favor of the pine nuts. They looked a lot bigger than the ones we had at Aunt Vittoria's.

"This half-gallon jar is the last of them," said Cousin Celina. "These are from last year's pick. Hopefully, this coming September we'll get another good fall of pine nuts." She winked at us. "Eating them can be addictive; once you start, you can't stop!"

The girls and I knew the end of the visit was nearing when we heard Mother and Aunt Rosa Bella making plans to get together to make homemade chokecherry jam.

We drove out onto Eleven Mile Road. Father drove about two miles on the dirt road and made the right turn onto the paved Gun Barrel Road. We girls fell asleep. If only one fell asleep, Father would carry us into the house, but this afternoon we were all asleep, so Mother woke us as we neared the house.

It was the best Sunday we'd enjoyed in a long time because it was still early in the evening. There was no need to go to bed early, because there would be no school tomorrow for Easter vacation.

Mother instructed us to remove our Easter outfits, hang them up, and get into our play clothes. Mary Ann sat on the couch with arms crossed and a pouting face.

"What is wrong, Baby?"

"Mother, why do we have to take off our new clothes?"

"Because it's still early and I thought you girls would like to go out and play. Your father and I plan to spend an hour or two in the vegetable garden. But if you wish to stay in your good clothes a while longer, you will need to stay indoors."

Mother headed for the kitchen door that led to the garden.

"Let's play Sisters," I suggested. "We haven't played 'Let's Pretend We're Sisters' in a long time."

We liked to play that we were grownups together.

"That is a good idea, especially since we all have purses! We can put homemade cigarettes in them."

"Can I be the one to carry them in my purse, and be the sister that offers them to the rest of you?" asked Priscilla.

"Do you remember the rule? The person that suggests that we play Sisters is the one that knocks at the door and gets to carry the cigarettes in her purse," Bessie said.

We picked up our purses and headed for the kitchen.

"I'll get writing paper from my binder so we can roll our cigarettes," said Bessie.

"I'll get the coffee can and some spoons," called Priscilla.

"Let me get the coffee can," I said. "I'm much taller and can reach for it without dropping and spilling half of it."

Mary Ann doubled over, laughing.

We looked in wonder at her.

"Mary Ann! What is so funny?" I asked.

"You are, Pauline! You told Priscilla that you're much taller than her!"

"What's so funny about that?"

"You and Priscilla are the same height! And I've heard people say, 'Pauline is going to be short. Pauline is a short stack.'"

"No, you are mistaken! I'm a little taller than Priscilla. Wouldn't you say I'm right, Bessie?"

"Yes, you are much taller and two whole years older."

Mary Ann shrugged her shoulders. "Well, maybe just a little."

Bessie filled a cup with coffee grounds from this morning's coffee pot.

"These are already wet! They'll stick to the paper much better."

I put the coffee can back in the cupboard, and we cut five pieces of paper for rolling. Then we each grabbed a spoon and scooped the grounds onto the papers.

I ran into Mother's bedroom for the little empty Coty face-powder box she had given to me. It was perfect to store the make-believe cigarettes, and the little box fit right into my Easter patent leather purse.

Bessie wiped off the table.

"Go outside, Pauline. But wait a minute or two before you knock at the front door."

I checked myself out. I looked quite grownup with my Easter bonnet and purse in hand. Leo was walking his bike out of the gate onto the road.

"Where are you going?" I called to him.

"I'm going over to Cousin Willie's. What are you doing standing there at the front door?"

"The girls and I are playing grownup sisters. We pretend we're sisters."

"Is that right?" As he peddled away, he hollered, "But you are sisters!"

I made a fist at him and proceeded to tap on the door. After a few more knocks, I still received no answer.

"Hello, is anyone at home?"

The door finally opened and Bessie appeared.

"What took so long for you to open the door?" I whispered.

"The last time you got to be the sister visiting, you complained that we didn't give you a chance to knock a few times on the door! Girls, we have a very important visitor! Come look! It's Pauline from California."

Priscilla greeted me. "Hello, Sis! How are you?"

"Come on in, Sis," said Mary Ann. "How are you?"

We spread out in the room and sat down. We all crossed our arms and legs. We were grown up after all, and would be for the next hour or two.

"Would you care for a cup of coffee?" asked Bessie.

"Not right now, but thank you."

I put my purse down on the floor. I paused a moment, then picked it up and set it on my lap. The girls' eyes were on the purse. They were ready for a cigarette, but it was my turn to be the "Cigarette Sis," and I was in no hurry to end my role. I stroked the front of the shiny smooth patent leather purse, and thought it felt more like hard plastic to me. It felt different than my patent leather shoes.

"The weather in California is so warm, I can sleep without blankets."

"Is that right? Tell me, Sis, how are Grandmother and Cousin Cecilia?"

"Grandmother Genevieve is great. She is still the sweetest grand lady. Cousin Cecilia is in a private Catholic school."

"My, that is just wonderful. Tell us more."

"People say around those parts, 'That girl is very book smart.' Yes, they are right about that. I recall when she lived here in Colorado so many years ago when we were children, back when we were in first grade, she could read Dick and Jane sentences faster than anyone in our class. I was so proud of her."

I tapped my fingers on my purse, then slowly moved my fingers across to open it. The girls waited eagerly. I very slowly opened it and proceeded to take out the little box with our cigarettes.

I looked at Bessie. "Would you like one of my cigarettes, Sis?"

"Why, don't mind if I do."

I handed her one, then turned to Priscilla.

"How about you, Sis?"

"I'd love one, I'm sure. Thank you, Sis."

I walked over to Mary Ann.

"Sis, do you still smoke?"

"Yes I do, a pack a day. I tried to quit, but I can't."

"Well, mine are very strong. One can only find these in California."

"My, you are right! They are very strong, just the way I like them."

It was fun pretending to light, puff, and flick ashes onto our make-believe ash trays: bottle caps. After about fifteen minutes of handling the cigarettes, we started to lose coffee grounds. We decided to clean up the little mess we'd made, change our clothes and go out to play baseball.

Mother and Father were out in the garden. They looked pleased, each with a tomato in their hand. They were taking turns with the salt shaker.

"Girls, would you like to try a tomato sprinkled with salt? They are excellent this year."

We each picked one off the bush. Soon we had juice and seeds running down our arms.

Every year, Mother and Father planted tomatoes, corn, zucchini, carrots, radishes, turnips and onions. Gardening in the evenings seemed to be their favorite pastime.

The sun was going down. We hated to see the day end. We helped Mother fill a basket with zucchini, a couple of tomatoes, an onion, and corn.

"Bessie, take these in the house and rinse them," she said. "I'd like to fry these up for supper tomorrow night. Mary Grace will need to clean the beans and cook them early."

"May we play jacks on the kitchen table?" asked Priscilla.

"Count me out," I said. "Mother, my head hurts."

Mother put her hand on my forehead.

"You don't have a fever. Have you drunk any water today? If not, drink a tall glass right now. Have you gone to the bathroom? After you do that, put your nightgown on and go to bed. I'll check on you later." She kissed me on the forehead.

I did as she instructed. I lay across the foot of the bed and closed my eyes. The sound of the jacks falling onto the table and the girls' voices in the distance put me to sleep.

I thought I had slept for at least an hour when I woke to the feel of Mother's warm hand on my forehead. But it hadn't been an hour: it was morning. Mother and Father were dressed and ready to leave for work.

"How do you feel? Does your head still hurt?"

"How do I feel this morning? Mother, I would have to describe it this way: 'Tra La La. Tweedle dee dee dee. It gives me a thrill to wake up in the morning to the mockingbirds' trill.'"

Mother and Father looked at each other and smiled. I blushed.

"I guess I can go to work without waking Mary Grace to have her check on you. If you're singing a Teresa Brewer song, you are feeling just fine. By all means, finish the song for Bessie."

Bessie was walking into the kitchen scratching her head, as she always did when she wasn't quite awake.

"There is no denying that Pauline has a love for singing," said Father to Mother as they left.

"Girls, don't let Mary Grace sleep too late," called Mother. "See you this afternoon."

I accepted Mother's invitation to finish my song; Bessie would be my audience.

"When the sun in the morning peeps over the hill and kisses the roses 'round my window sill—"

"Just what do you think you're doing? Knock it off! It's too early in the morning for singing."

"Cheer up, Bessie! We have all day to be at home and do whatever we want after we help Mary Grace clean house! We can play baseball, walk barefoot in the creek, pick flowers, play house with our play dishes, chase the sheep or the chickens—"

"Stop! I get the picture. We have no school all week. But do you mind? Let me wake up first. Mary Grace may have other plans for the day. You know how she gets if she is in the mood to clean house; we will be at it all day."

"But I just can't wait for our day to start. What do you think we should do today?"

"If Phyllis comes to spend the day with Mary Grace, we will be on our own. It's been a long time since we went up to the garret. I believe the Words catalog is still up there."

"But December is eight months away! It's too early to be flipping through the catalog for Christmas items."

"You're right. I just noticed yesterday that the wooden ladder is leaning against the house. It may also be too warm up there. We can decide later when Priscilla and Mary Ann get up."

"If Mary Grace gets up early, I'll ask her to fry some potatoes and eggs. I'm a bit hungry this morning. What did you girls do last night when I went to bed with a headache?"

"Father played his accordion, and Mother put pin curls in her hair. Mary Grace was on the phone, and Leo made a slingshot outside on the porch. The girls and I played grownup sisters again. We pretended that you had gone back to California."

"I wonder what it would be like to live in California for real."

"I would never want to move away from Colorado. I wonder if Cecilia likes it over there. We used to see her every day. Why, we even attended first grade together because we are only three months apart. And then one day she was gone, and Grandmother also!"

"I miss them both a lot," I said. "Mother must miss her mother plenty. Spending every day after school with Mother's sister Aunt Phyllis and Cousin Cecilia was almost like having two more sisters, and then along came Aunt Frances and she moved them all to California!"

"It's this way, Pauline. Mother's sister Aunt Frances and Uncle Tony are divorced. She has a daughter Cecilia to raise by herself. Grandmother is a widow with three unmarried children to finish raising: Uncle Frank, Uncle Paul and Aunt Phyllis. Since they're young adults, they wanted to move to make a better life for themselves."

"What do you mean, 'make a better life'? How will they do that?"

"Aunt Frances says there are more jobs with better pay in California. And Mother says that most of the work here is farming, and not everyone likes this kind of work."

Mary Grace came into the kitchen about an hour after Mother and Father had left for work.

"What have you two been up to?"

"We were peeling potatoes. We were hoping you would fry eggs and potatoes for us this morning. We also went ahead and peeled some for supper. Mother would like for you to clean and cook some beans. She said she'd fry zucchini and potatoes when she gets home from work. She made tortilla dough before she left; it's in the refrigerator."

"Will you make breakfast for us, please?" I pleaded. "Will you?"

"Yes, but let me wash up so I can wake up. Let Priscilla and Mary Ann sleep a little longer."

The phone rang. Mary Grace rushed into the front room to answer it.

"Hope that's Phyllis calling to let me know she'll be spending the day with us!"

"Oh goody! She is expecting Phyllis to come over today!"

"Pauline, please hand me the bowl with the lid so I can put the potatoes in water for tonight. Mary Grace or I can slice them just before Mother gets home."

Mary Grace came back into the kitchen with a big grin on her face.

"Guess what! Mother called to give us some good news. Mister Corlett called her at work to let her know that she and Father were approved for a loan to buy the house across the way: the one that caught on fire! The bank called to verify Father's employment and told him that Mother and Father would be notified by mail about the approved application. Mister Corlett wanted them to hear the good news right away."

"I had no idea they wanted that house."

"Mother said that she wasn't sure if it would go up for sale after the fire repairs were done. She didn't want to disappoint us if the owner decided not to sell. Do you girls know what this means? I'll probably get my own bedroom!"

"How many bedrooms are there?" asked Bessie.

"I don't know. Mother said she is getting off work early today so we could talk about the house. She has to clean Dr. Roth's medical office tonight and every Monday from now on. That means either you two or I will be going with her to help. It shouldn't take long; we just have to dust and empty wastebaskets."

"As long as I can remember, Mother has always had two jobs," I said.

"You know what Mother always says. 'My children will always sleep on clean mattresses and clean sheets, even if I have to work two jobs.'"

Mary Grace sent Bessie and me to make the beds and get the girls up to wash up for breakfast.

"I'll call you when the potatoes and eggs are done. Do you girls want coffee? Why Father allows you little ones to start drinking coffee at such a young age, I'll never understand. Maybe he doesn't realize you girls drink it every day. He may think you only drink it in the winter months and only when he serves you some."

Mary Grace removed one of the lids to the stove to add more wood. She would be doing that all day till the beans are cooked.

"Come on, 'Little One,'" I said with a grin, as we left the kitchen. "I've been called that by Phyllis, but never by Mary Grace."

"When one person spends a lot of time with another like Mary Grace and Phyllis do, they start picking up each other's ways and expressions."

"I see. Just like you do things the way I do."

"Don't you think it's the other way around? I am older than you! It looks like Mother made her bed this morning. Let's get the girls up so we can make the other bed. Priscilla! Mary Ann! It's time to get up; Mary Grace is making breakfast for us!"

"What time is it? Are we going to miss the bus and have to walk to school?"

"Not this morning! We are on Easter vacation! And Mary Grace has some exciting news to share with you two. Go on into the kitchen. Pauline, remove the blankets from the bed. I'll go get the dust mop, so we can use it before we make the bed."

After breakfast, Mary Grace told us to go out and play. Phyllis would be coming over for the day.

The creek water was still too cold to wade in. The lilac bushes that grew along the creek were loaded with flowers and the fragrance was wonderful. We were aware of every wildflower and green bush. We waved the flowers under our noses. We spent most of the morning hours placing them in each other's hair.

In the afternoon we played baseball. Priscilla hit the ball over the fence onto Mr. Buckhouse's property. We were not allowed to go over the fence. We would have to wait till Leo came home. He had gone to the dump with his friend Gilbert Gold. After that, we read "love" comic books. Priscilla and Mary Ann got Phyllis to polish their toenails.

In the evening, Mother and Father did most of the talking. They planned when to move into the new house. Since it was just across the way, they decided that Leo and Mary Grace could start moving the smaller items in Leo's wagon during the day while Mother, Father and Joe were at work.

"Bessie and Pauline can start putting the towels and sheets away and the kitchen items that aren't being used to prepare meals. Leo, you may start moving the ladders and other outside tools. Priscilla and Mary Ann can pick vegetables every day; what we can't eat, Leo can take over to Aunt Raquel or have Cousin Willie come on his bike to get some. Joe, Phil, Willie and Leo can help Father with the bigger furniture and appliances."

Mother and Mary Grace did all the packing. We spent the next few weeks moving and getting settled in our new home. Everything had a new home base.

Mother looked like she was having a great time.

"There is so much more room! I love this big kitchen, and the built-in kitchen cabinets, and the big linen closet! None of the homes we've rented ever had a linen closet; how I managed I'll never know."

Father also looked very pleased to hear Mother going on about the house.

"The middle bedroom will fit two double beds for all the girls; and they have their very own closet. The boys' room is so big that we can cut into it and add a bathroom. That room also has a large closet. I love the big pane windows—"

Joe interrupted, "I especially like that yours and Father's bedroom faces the street! You will be able to hear my car coming into the driveway at night!"

"Oh? And why is that?" asked Leo.

Before Joe had a chance to answer, Priscilla jumped off the kitchen counter. She had expected Joe to be ready to catch her, but he barely had enough time to step forward and catch her just before she hit the floor.

"Just what do you think you're doing, jumping off the counter like that? And what were you doing up there in the first place, young lady?"

"You are afraid of La Yorona, right? That is why you want Mother to hear the sound of your car, huh?"

"Don't you try to change the subject, Priscilla. Were you after the sugar bowl again?"

"No. Joe, don't you remember? You told me that I am Superman. And you are afraid of La Yorona, aren't you, Joe?"

"Mother, will you just listen to her? This little girl acts as though she did nothing wrong."

Priscilla shrugged her shoulders and ran out of the kitchen.

"Have you forgotten you're the one that told her to jump off the table into your arms the day you were so excited because Dolly said she would be your girl?" Leo reminded him.

"You're right, but that was such a long time ago. And I did not have my back to her."

"Well ever since then, she has been jumping off anything she can climb," said Mary Grace. "She is going to get hurt one day!"

"I didn't realize that. I'll have a talk with her."

Father came in from outside. He wanted Mother to come to the backyard so they could make a decision on how much lawn to plant and how much to section off for a vegetable garden.

They would also have to decide where to put the firewood that Father would bring down from the mountains. The outhouse was about one hundred feet from the house, and there was a small shed about thirty feet from there. Mother thought this would be a good place to store the sacks of potatoes and other bushels of fruit.

The people that had sold the property left a full size piano in the little wooden shed. Father played a few tunes for us, and promised to play again.

Our neighbors were now the Buckhouses, and the house we had been renting from Mr. Corlett was empty. I was happy too, because we were now one house closer to Billy McCoy. He lived on the other side of Mr. Buckhouse. Not that I'd be able to see him from our house; but I was thrilled that he was one house closer. I loved that he'd asked me to ride on his horse with him. It made me feel important, because I knew my sisters and I would never own a horse like the other farm children. Mister Corlett owned two horses, but Joe was the only one that attempted to ride them. Maybe one day Mother and Father would buy the house owned by the Buckhouses.

Father was happy that the yard had no potholes and no pigpen. We wouldn't have to deal with the smell every time we went out to play. We'd miss looking at the baby pigs with their curly tails, but that was the sacrifice we had to make for fresh air.

The girls and I were pleased that Leo had placed the wooden ladder against the house, right next to the door to the garret. The ladder was heavy and hard for us to handle. If it stayed where Leo had placed it, it would make our shopping days easier. We liked to do our Christmas shopping in the catalog in the garret. Climbing up the ladder into the garret was a small sacrifice. All we needed now was to place a new catalog up there. We were sure Mrs. Roth would provide. She always sent the fall catalog and each day's newspapers, a day late. I liked reading the funnies. I didn't always understand the story line in the Dick Tracy cartoons, but I liked looking at the many different characters' faces, and especially their hairdos.

When June arrived, we only had two weeks to wait for summer break. It was a very special time for all the family.

"Mother is so full of energy since we moved here, I can barely keep up with her," said Mary Grace one day. "She always has some project going on the weekends, like all those curtains she made! She is baking homemade bread and cinnamon rolls every week."

"Don't complain," said Bessie, "I like that Mother is so happy. She doesn't seem to get upset when she comes home from work and we've not done our chores. And don't those curtains in the bedrooms and the drapes in the front room look nice? This is the first house she painted and decorated and knows she won't have to move out if she chooses not to."

"I didn't mean to sound like I am complaining. I too like the mood Mother is in these days. I just wanted you to take notice of the change in her."

"I think there has been a change in all of us," announced Mother as she came back into the house. "And there is going to be a lot more." She smiled and winked at Mary Grace.

Bessie and I looked at each other. Mother's wink had to mean something. We would compare notes later. Mary Grace had planted the idea when she said, "There is a change in Mother."

I don't know why we held back from asking Mother if there was something she wanted to share with us. I just knew that if Bessie didn't ask, I sure wasn't going to. Somehow though, we sensed that we were in for a surprise.

Papa Cico and Mama Mina,
Manuel Ortega's parents

(from back right)
Mary Grace,
Bessie, Priscilla, Pauline,
and Mary Ann

Mary Ann, Pauline, and Priscilla

Bessie and Pauline's
Communion Day

(from back left to right)
Mother, Father, Mary Grace,
Bessie, Priscilla, Pauline, Mary Ann

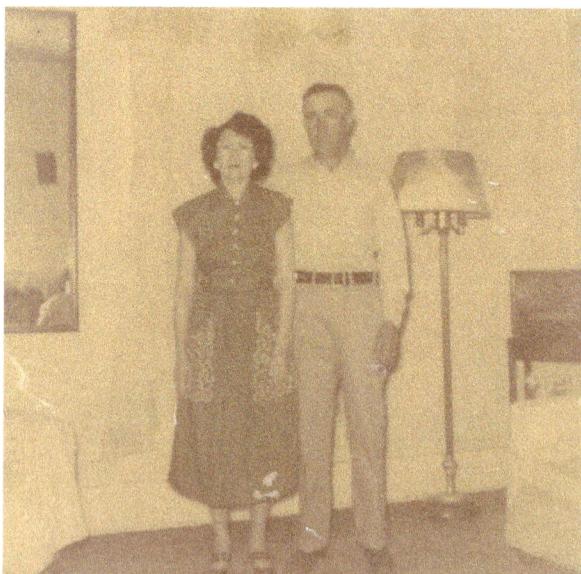

Mother and Father

Chapter Five

One beautiful Saturday afternoon, the girls and I were outside enjoying our time away from school. I wasn't feeling good. I hoped I wasn't getting a headache. I went back in the house and rested on the bed with my school reader in my hand. I flipped through the pages, and a prayer card fell out. I began to read it.

> To Our Lady
>
> Lovely Lady dressed in blue,
> Teach me how to pray!
> God was just your little Boy,
> Tell me what to say!
>
> Did you lift Him up, sometimes,
> Gently on your knee?
> Did you sing to Him the way
> Mother does to me?
>
> Did you hold His hand at night?
> Did you ever try
> Telling stories of the world?
> O! And did He cry?
>
> Do you really think He cares
> If I tell Him things,
> Little things that happen?
> Do the Angels' wings
> Make a noise? And can He hear

Me if I speak low?
Does He understand me now?
Tell me, for you know.

Lovely Lady, dressed in blue,
Teach me how to pray!
God was just your little Boy,
And you know the way.

I looked at the picture of our Blessed Mother standing on a cloud with a snake curled around from the back to the front of her feet. She wore a white gown with a blue robe and a gold veil covering her hair. She looked so beautiful with a halo over her head. Her arms extended outward with rays of light shining from her hands. I wanted to hold onto this card forever and ever; just looking at it made me feel safe. I placed the card on my chest with my hands over it.

"Pauline! Pauline, are you asleep?"

"Now I'm not. What do you want, Bessie?"

"Are you sick again, like you were at Easter time? Mother asked for you, and I told her you were lying down. I assumed you didn't feel good, so I told her."

"Is Mother in the kitchen now?"

"Nope. She, Father, Priscilla and Mary Ann left to go to the Boy's Market."

"And you stayed behind?"

"Mother said they would only be gone a few minutes."

I showed Bessie the card Sister Mary George had given me and Julia as a reward for pounding all the school erasers on the cement steps, on the last day before vacation.

"It's beautiful, except for the snake in the picture."

"Sister Alquin told the class that the snake at the Virgin Mary's feet means that God gave her power over the snake which represents the devil. She said that the devil can tempt everybody except Jesus' Mother Mary."

"She is blessed; she was picked by God to be the Mother of Jesus, and God wants us to love and pray to her above all other saints."

"And right before Jesus died on the cross, He looked down at one of the apostles and said, 'Behold thy mother.'"

"Yes He did! You know, you don't look sick to me."

"I never said I was sick. I just came in to lie down because my stomach felt queasy."

We heard Father's truck pulling into the back yard, and a moment later, Priscilla came in.

"Come on, Girls! Mother wants you in the kitchen," she said.

Mary Ann was sitting at the table. Mother was at the counter with a bowl of orange halves, a teaspoon and a bottle.

Mary Grace came into the kitchen.

"Oh no! Not that terrible stuff again, Mother!"

"Mother do we have to drink that awful castor oil?"

"I don't like the taste! Please, Mother, not me!"

"Baby, it's only a teaspoon, and if you suck on the orange right after, it will be easier. Doctor Roth told me it will help keep you girls from coming down with colds and flus. It helps to keep your system clean."

"Mother, I don't have a system! I never got one!" cried Mary Ann.

"Come on, Mary Ann, you can sit on my lap. I'll squeeze the orange juice into your mouth," suggested Mary Grace. "What Mother means is that it helps you go potty, therefore it cleans you out. So you see you do have a system. I don't like to take it either, but because Joe, Leo and I take it, we have very nice complexions. Look at how clear my face is! I never break out with pimples."

"Okay, Mother," Priscilla volunteered, "I'll be first!"

We formed a line. Priscilla was first, then Mary Ann in front of Mary Grace, then me, and last in line was Bessie. Mother handed Priscilla half an orange and a napkin. Priscilla opened her mouth and Mother put the teaspoon in her mouth.

Mother then took a step back to give Mary Ann her spoonful. Bessie nudged at me to look at Priscilla. I leaned over to look, but so did Mother. Her brave little soldier had lost the cause. Priscilla was pulling at the neck of her dress and spitting the castor oil down the front.

Mary Grace started to laugh.

"Volunteering to be first was pretty clever—so she could spit it out without being noticed."

We all laughed, but Mother told her to get in line again in front of Bessie.

"Priscilla! Have you been doing this all along? Now I know why some of your dresses have oil stains right in the front!"

Priscilla gave her usual sheepish grin.

"Not every time."

When she was finished administering the castor oil, Mother told us we could finish the oranges, rinse our hands, and go out to play.

"Pauline, you may stay in if you don't feel good. You'll feel better when the castor oil cleans you out, Sweetheart. I'll be outside if you need me."

"I think I will stay in and read a little."

Bessie stayed in too, which meant Mary Ann would be close by.

Priscilla headed for the back door, but came back quickly. She walked over to Mary Ann, who was stroking our cat in front of the stove. Priscilla bent down and whispered something in her ear. Mary Ann stood and walked out the door with Priscilla. Still feeling sick, I didn't bother to ask what she whispered to Mary Ann.

But a few moments later, Leo came into the kitchen, holding Priscilla and Mary Ann by an arm. Their faces were filled with guilt.

Mary Grace was at the counter washing dishes.

"What's going on?"

"Your little sisters were over by the woodpile spying on some boys swimming—actually skinny dipping! They had their faces so pressed against the fence, they didn't see me coming!"

Mary Grace stared at them, then shook her head and turned her back to them. Mary Ann and Priscilla looked at me and I turned away. I would be so embarrassed if Leo saw me grin.

He was firm.

"I don't ever want to catch you girls near that fence, ever again!"

He turned and walked out, leaving the girls waiting to see what Mary Grace had to say. Mary Grace instructed them to go the back door and check for mud on their shoes.

I went into the front room and lay on the couch. Bessie was sitting on the accent chair, flipping through the newspaper to look for paper doll cutouts.

When Priscilla and Mary Ann came in, Priscilla asked, "Do you want to go out and play baseball?"

"I heard what you two were up to," said Bessie. "Don't you think you should stay indoors for now, out of Leo's way?"

"Why? Mary Ann and I were just looking through the cracks in the fence to see if we could see the ball I hit over the fence yesterday. Is it my fault that those boys chose to swim in the nude just when we needed to look in that direction? Do we need to go to confession? I don't believe we do!"

"I suppose not," answered Bessie.

"But you did come in and invite me to go out and look at them," said Mary Ann. "Remember?"

"But that was only after I had been looking for the ball."

They thought quietly to themselves that confession was called for, since they disobeyed and went to the fence when they were told not to.

"Were you able to locate the ball?" I asked.

"No, but I found an old towel that we can wrap around a rock to hit with the bat till we get another ball."

"It's no fun to play unless we all play," said Bessie. "And Pauline doesn't feel good."

"What shall we do then?"

"You can read, or color, or play with the cat, or brush your hair. I'm sure you'll think of something."

Mary Ann sat on the floor where Bessie was cutting newspaper clippings.

Priscilla went into the kitchen. A few minutes later, we heard Mary Grace ask, "Priscilla, what are you doing behind that table radio?"

"Nothing!"

"Why aren't you in the front room with the other girls?"

"That's where I'm going right now."

It wasn't long before we were inviting each other to accompany us out to the toilet. The castor oil was starting to do its magic. Normally we used newspaper, but this time, Mother had bought real toilet paper. How exciting!

On one of our trips to the outdoor toilet, Bessie got a bright idea.

"Would you like me to dangle my legs into the round opening of the toilet after I lift up the lid like Mary Grace did that one time?"

"No! Please don't!" cried Mary Ann.

"You might fall in!" cried Priscilla.

"If you do that, Bessie, we are not coming with you the next time you have to come out here in the dark! So go ahead and do it if you want!"

"I'm not going to. I was just kidding. I won't."

For the longest time though, I feared that one day Bessie would try it. I prayed that the idea would never pop into her mind ever again.

Chapter Six

Monday morning arrived. No one seemed to mind getting ready for school, since there was only ten days left before we started summer vacation. Sister Alquin gave the class an oral spelling test. She started with the first row; I sat in the third row.

Albert Sanchez sat in front of me. I wondered if the class suspected that I thought he was cute, and that I never took my eyes off him. I wondered, with a nervous stomach, if he would turn around and talk to me. I prayed, "Please, Jesus, help me not to miss the spelling word she gives me on my turn!" I wouldn't want Albert to think that I wasn't smart.

Albert was given his spelling word, "healthy." He missed it, spelling it with an E at the end, instead of a Y. He didn't seem to mind; he just laughed.

I hoped I could take it the way he did, if I misspelled my word. Jesus answered my prayer. My spelling word was "attic." Easy!

At second recess time, right before Sister Alquin excused the class, Naomi Espinosa stopped by Albert's desk and whispered, "I'll see you outside after school."

I started to clear my desk. I was annoyed. What did Naomi want with him? I knew Albert Sanchez better than she did; his sister spent a lot of time at our house. Someday he might take a ride with his father to drop Phyllis off at our house and find out that Mary Grace and I are sisters.

Outside, I told Bessie about Naomi.

"I don't like that she is talking to him! She actually made a plan to see him after school!"

"Well, he is really cute; did you think you would be the only girl to notice?"

"You're right. Now I'm glad he doesn't know that I have a crush on him."

"Why? Wouldn't it be better if he did know?"

"No. The girls in the 'love' comic books don't let the boys know how much they like them because it's too hard to hide their jealousy when other girls spend time with the boys they like. And he does try to talk to me in class." I was too shy to answer him, though.

"Don't you think you are a bit young to be competing for the attention of this boy? What would the nuns think?"

"I hadn't given it much thought."

"You could have fooled me."

"Let's see how you react when you see another girl smitten with Raymond Sanchez."

"I'm sure I wouldn't like it much, but he doesn't belong to me. Besides, he is very shy; he probably won't even notice other girls."

"You wish!"

"Oh, what does it matter anyway? Have you forgotten Billy McCoy?"

"No, but I don't get to see Billy, except in the mornings on the bus, because he goes to public school!"

"Well, you'd better get used to girls paying attention to Albert. He's very cute, with that golden tan and those blond highlights in his hair."

"I know, and he always has that grin that says he is up to something."

"Here comes Sally; I'll see you after school."

Sally was Bessie's best friend. I ran off to find Julia.

Chapter Seven

On Tuesday morning, I got to see another side of Sister Alquin. Mary Grace had spent the night at Phyllis'. Bessie announced to Priscilla and Mary Ann that we would not be going to school.

"What reason do you have now for not getting ready for school? Last week it was that you didn't have clean socks!" I was frantic; I couldn't miss school again. "We have to go! I don't want to face Sister Alquin tomorrow with explanations as to why I wasn't in class today!"

"Pauline, we can't go; we don't have anything to make for lunch. I just can't go all day without eating. I can't face Priscilla and Mary Ann at recess knowing that they too are hungry!"

"I just can't miss! I'll eat that leftover oatmeal Dad made early this morning and hope it holds me over till I get home."

"You are really going to ride the bus by yourself?" asked Priscilla.

"Yes, I can't miss. I'll worry all day about tomorrow and facing Sister Alquin."

"But what about after school?" cried Mary Ann. "The Ratenias will get you by yourself!"

"I'll have to walk home."

The girls were very quiet while I was getting ready, until Priscilla announced that the bus had honked. I grabbed my books and headed for the door. I turned to look at the girls one more time. I hated the idea of being apart from them. At school I always knew they were nearby. I was scared. I would have to walk to my school from the bus alone.

I stepped onto the bus. I couldn't change my mind; the bus door had shut behind me. I wished that Mary Grace hadn't spent the night at Phyllis' house. I sat by myself. I looked out the window toward our house. I could see the girls clearly at the window. I don't think they believed I would actually get on the bus by myself; I couldn't believe it either.

The bus pulled up in front of Monte Vista's public school. I looked for those mean girls, the Ratenias, but I didn't see them. I walked as fast as I could. There were a couple of eighth-graders walking in front of me. They had come from the direction of Sunny Side. I breathed more easily as I neared Saint Joseph's School. I could see some students walking into the church. The steeple looked so wonderful and welcoming this morning. I missed my sisters, but I was safe at last.

At recess, I stayed in the classroom. I sat at my desk across from Margaret. She often stayed in because she hadn't made friends yet. I watched her color. I hoped she might ask me to color with her. I wished she would tear a page out and offer it to me. She didn't, so I just watched her color. I was always very shy around other students.

At lunch time I stayed in again. I put my head down on my desk. Other students came in and out. I finally fell asleep.

I woke up because Sister Alquin was pushing gently on my arm. Lunch hour was over. All my classmates were back. Sister Alquin asked me to step out into the hall and asked Margie Plane to follow us.

"Julia tells me that you stayed in class during lunch because you didn't have any lunch. She said that this occurs more than once a week."

I just looked at her. I was afraid that I was in trouble for falling asleep at my desk.

Sister Alquin turned to Margie.

"Take Pauline to the cafeteria, and ask your mother to please serve Pauline a plate. There is usually lunch food left over."

Mrs. Plane greeted her daughter.

"Margie, what are you doing here honey? Did you girls come to help me clean up?"

Mrs. Plane was the school's cafeteria cook and she also cooked for the nuns at their convent. Father McDevitt and Father Bargeman had their own cook at their home.

Margie whispered to her what Sister Alquin had said.

I watched as Mrs. Plane served me mashed potatoes, gravy, and chicken drumsticks, with a little bowl of applesauce. I was sure I was dreaming.

Mrs. Plane went back to cleaning tables. Margie walked alongside her mother. Each bite felt so good going down into my empty stomach, filling it up a little at a time. If the girls could see me now, they would say, "What the heck! How did you manage to get yourself into Mrs. Plane's kitchen?" No one was allowed back there.

I wished my sisters were here enjoying this meal too. I didn't know if I should be upset with Julia, or if I should thank her.

I thanked Mrs. Plane. I told her that she cooked chicken as well as my mother. She smiled and sent Margie and me on our way. We walked quietly back to our classroom.

We walked into the classroom. No one paid much attention. Sister Alquin thanked Margie, then turned to me and whispered, "Pauline, it isn't good to go without lunch; you need to bring lunch every day."

The rest of the afternoon, Sister read to the class. She explained that a long time ago, around 1884, the name for our town was Lariat. Three key ingredients led to the founding of Monte Vista: land, water (irrigation canals), and the railroad. Since the adoption of the new name in 1886, the question had arisen as to whether the name should be written as Monte Vista or Montevista. The Post Office had adopted Monte Vista as correct. They consulted the best scholars, who agreed that Monte Vista was the correct form.

The end of the school day neared; and I began to get a nervous stomach. I needed to make a decision. Should I take the chance of walking to the bus stop, hoping I'll miss seeing those mean girls? Or should I walk all the way to our farmhouse by myself?

A long time ago, Bessie had walked home alone from Grandmother's house to a brick house we had rented for a few short months, before Grandmother moved to California. Bessie told

Mother that every time she'd seen a car coming, she'd hide in the bushes.

"Weren't you embarrassed?" I had asked her. "I wouldn't have wanted the birds to know that I was scared! They probably thought you were a scaredy cat."

Sister Alquin excused the class. I decided I would walk home. I could run and hide if I needed. I walked with confidence. I walked about two blocks and reached some new track homes. I saw a man walking in my direction. I quickly walked to a pickup truck parked in a driveway and squatted down beside it. My heart was pounding. I could hear each footstep. I began to pray, *Saint Joseph, you who loved and protected Jesus as a little boy, please protect me now!*

Please hurry up and pass, I thought anxiously. Be on your way so I can stand up and continue on my way home. I waited, still hearing the sound of each step. I stood and looked to the front of the truck. He was right in front, and he looked at me. I must have looked as white as a sheet. He looked me straight in the eye; then turned and walked away. He surely must have seen my fright. He had a mean look. One leg was shorter than the other, so his body rocked from side to side as he walked. He wore a dark hat tilted to the side, so it blocked his right eye from view.

As he passed the front of the pickup, I leaped forward and started running as fast as my short legs would carry me. I ran without stopping as long as I could, in spite of the pain in my side. I finally reached the last of the track homes. I made a right turn onto Lariat Road, the country road leading to my house.

I finally caught sight of Mrs. McCoy's house. My house would be next. I slowed down, but kept looking back for that frightful man. I didn't see a soul; I was safe. I walked for about another ten minutes, expecting to see my sisters looking out for me, but no one was. If only they could hear my heart pounding! At last, I was safe at home! I opened the gate to the cyclone fence and dashed for the front door.

Priscilla was asleep on the couch. Bessie and Mary Ann were at the kitchen table eating sliced pears with cottage cheese. They both looked at me.

"What's wrong?" asked Bessie. "I didn't hear the bus. Have you been running?"

I started to cry. Priscilla came into the kitchen and looked at me, bewildered.

I told them how scared I had been, walking home alone, and how I had missed them all day.

"I never ever want to walk home alone again!"

"It's their fault!" cried Mary Ann. "Those mean girls made you walk home; what else could you do?"

"I think it was Sister Alquin's fault; you could have been at home with us if it wasn't for her!" cried Priscilla.

Bessie asked, "Didn't you see Leo at school? You could have told him you were the only one there, and he would have brought you home on his bike. Or if you made it to the public school, Mary Grace would have been on the bus with you to come home."

"But she would have had to walk by herself to the public school and the Ratenias would have gotten hold of her!" said Priscilla.

Bessie promised to bake biscuits for lunch the next day. We heard the school bus pull away. Mary Grace opened the front door, placed her books on the coffee table, and announced that she was going to lie down.

"Please wake me in half an hour, so I can start dinner."

I wanted to tell the girls about the good lunch I had had, but I was still upset about that frightful man.

"Pauline, do you want some pears or peaches with cottage cheese? Joe came home for lunch. As soon as he woke up from his nap to go back to work, we were able to have some of his left over lunch!" announced Mary Ann.

"Why didn't you ask him for it when he left the table, for Heaven's sake?"

"Oh, we could never do that! We would be too embarrassed," said Bessie.

"But if he left peaches, pears and cottage cheese out on the table, it was for you! But I guess if I'd been here I wouldn't have asked either. I wouldn't have wanted him to know that I was hungry. I will have some now though. I like peaches; thank you for saving some for me."

"Actually we did not save them; we were just too full to eat them all."

"Priscilla! What a thing to say! Why didn't you just let Pauline think we saved some for her? I could have had more, but chose not to," said Bessie. "Mary Ann and I had some more."

"I'm sorry, Pauline," cried Priscilla. "We really did save them for you! I was just kidding."

"Yes, we did," said Mary Ann. "When you are done eating, could you help me with my reading book 'Dick and Jane'?"

"Yes, I will; go find your reader. Priscilla, if you want I will sit in the middle between you and Mary Ann so you can listen to us read."

"I was going to go outside and play hopscotch. I've been thinking about it all day, but Bessie made us clean house all day."

Bessie glanced sideways at her, and shook her head.

"I'm a slave driver."

"I'm ready!" called Mary Ann.

Priscilla went out, and Bessie announced that she was going out to the little house to bring potatoes in to peel for dinner.

"Okay, Mary Ann, I will read a paragraph; and then we will take turns reading sentences."

"Jane said, 'We can go. Mother is here. Father is here. Dick is here. Sally is here. Away we go.' Dick said, 'Spot is not here. Puff is not here.' Jane said, 'Puff is here. Puff is here in the car.' Dick said, 'I see something. Look down, Jane. Look down and see something. It is funny. Can you see it?' 'Oh,' said Jane. 'Here is Spot.' Jane said, 'Come in Spot. Come in. You can go. You can go in the car.' Away we go in the car."

After about twenty minutes Mary Ann was ready to put her reader away. Mary Grace came in and turned on the radio. She tuned in to Rosemary Clooney, whose voice bellowed out "Half as Much" through the speakers.

Another song followed: "I Went to Your Wedding."

Mary Ann and I followed Mary Grace to the kitchen, where Bessie was already peeling potatoes. Outside the open kitchen door, Priscilla was holding a small hose to her mouth.

"Priscilla, take that dirty thing away from your mouth!" said Mary Grace.

"What is she doing?" asked Bessie.

"I have no idea. Pauline, will you please go out and play with her? I need to make tortilla dough. Once I put my hands into the wet flour; I won't be able to check on her. I'm afraid that little stinker might get into something she shouldn't."

As I walked out, I sang "Mr. Sandman" along with the voice on the radio.

"Why do you like to sing those sad songs?" asked Priscilla.

"I don't see them as sad; they're songs I can sing along with, and singing helps me take my mind off my worries. By the way, what were you doing with that hose to your mouth?"

"I was seeing how long I could hold my breath. Last Saturday, I put the hose in Joe's gas tank."

"Why?"

"To siphon gas out onto the dirt, light a match and throw it on the spill."

"What in the world for? That's terribly dangerous! Where do you get these ideas?"

"I saw Joe bring gasoline out of his car tank with that hose and put it in his friend's car tank. Lester was running low, and didn't think he could make it to the gas station."

"Mary Grace will probably get rid of that hose now. I wouldn't want to see Joe catch you putting that hose in his gas tank; and that hose is filthy."

"The matches wouldn't work anyway; they kept going out before I had a chance to throw them on the dirt."

The back door opened and Mary Ann popped her head out.

"Priscilla, will you please come play with me?"

"Okay, Baby, I'm coming."

Priscilla and Mary Ann sat on the floor in the front room cutting paper. I sat at the kitchen table. The girls had picked wild spinach earlier in the day, and Mary Grace was carefully rinsing the large dark-green leaves and patting them dry. Then she fried them with small pieces of bacon, onion, and chili seeds, so we could have them with fresh cooked beans and fried potatoes. Bessie was slicing potatoes so Mother could country-fry them.

My thoughts wandered back to the early hours of my day. I opened my mouth to relate Sister Alquin's reactions at finding out about our lunch situation, but Leo stormed into the house and threw his books on the table. He was crying.

Mother came in right behind him, looking grieved.

"What is going on with Leo?" asked Mary Grace. "Why are you home so early? Did Joe drop you off?"

"Father McDevitt called me at work to come to the school. Leo was very upset. I called Joe at work to bring us home."

Leo raised his head from the table where he had buried his face in his arms. He wiped away tears.

"I'll never set one foot at that church or school again!"

"Mother, please! What happened at school today?" Mary Grace begged.

Priscilla and Mary Ann came in quietly, as Mother explained, "I was called to school because some girl in Leo's class accused him of taking her change purse! Sister Devota told me that the young lady was sure that Leo had taken it because he had been standing next to her desk when the last bell rang for dismissal. She also accused another boy. As it turned out, no one took it; it was still in her desk. The school was having some work done to the floors, and all the desks were moved to one side of the room. When they were pushed back, a couple of the desks ended up in the wrong place. But by the time Sister Mary Joseph came in and asked Sister Devota to check every desk in the room, Leo just wasn't having it. He did not like being accused."

Leo burst out crying again.

"I hate going to school! Why can't you understand? I'm in the fifth grade, and still haven't learned to read! I'm not going back, I tell you! I'm not going to school anymore!"

Mother was at a loss. Leo left the room, and no one said a word. Mother walked over to the table, took off her jacket, and sat. She looked so very sad. Mary Ann walked over and sat next to her and put her arm around her waist, and Priscilla did the same.

Mary Grace suggested, "What if you just let Leo stay home the rest of the school year? There are only about nine days left, and he's so far behind, he won't catch up. I feel so bad for him."

"I know, dear. I do too, and I don't know how to help my little boy. School is so important, but it's so hard for him. You need to be able to read to succeed in other subjects."

"What do Sister Mary Joseph and Father McDevitt say?"

"They don't have any answers. I guess we will have to wait for September and hope that Leo feels differently. It's best for him to be around other children his age, even though he can't read."

"But he is so unhappy at school," said Bessie. "I see it every day."

"I know, honey, we will have to wait and see. I have to pray about it."

Leo came back into the kitchen. His cheeks were shiny from dried tears. I could see how helpless Mother felt.

"Honey," she said, "Your brother unloaded your bike from his car trunk. It's leaning against the house, but please don't go anywhere."

"I wasn't going to, Mother. I'll be out back chopping wood."

"Okay, Son. I see you girls have started dinner, thank you. I see you started cooking the beans I cleaned this morning; and we are also having spinach. Very good; thank you."

"The girls picked them and I just rinsed them. And the house is very nicely picked up; have you noticed? And furthermore, I didn't clean up. I woke up from my nap and found the rooms all tidy!"

Bessie was at the kitchen counter scooping up potato peelings to toss. She avoided Mother's eyes. Mother turned to me at the kitchen table.

"Pauline, I hear you had a very nice lunch today."

"Yes I did! How do you know that?"

"Leo and I met up with Sister Alquin on our way out. She told me you had not taken a lunch today and other days as well. She asked me to make sure you take a lunch every day."

Dinner was ready early. We sat down to dinner right after Father got home and washed up. Leo left the dinner table before anyone. Joe followed, and invited Leo to go with him to Cousin Phil's house.

Mother told Father what happened to Leo.

"He will not be returning to school tomorrow. He probably won't return at all."

"What can we do, Mi Vida?" asked Father.

It always made us feel so secure when Father addressed Mother as "Mi Vida"—Spanish for "My life." Mother's pet name for Father was "Mi Corazon"—"My Heart."

"We are blessed to have a son like Leo," she said. "He is such a good boy: honest, hard-working, and very loving."

"I don't believe we should push him to go to school; he just can't do it anymore. It gets harder and harder for him each day!"

"You are right, Ignacio. He can't deal with it any longer. I can't push him to go, when I see how unhappy he is. He learns by seeing and doing."

"I pray that he can get by with this. What else can we do?"

"For now, there are no easy answers."

Bessie and I started to clear the table, while Mother and Father enjoyed another cup of coffee. Priscilla sat at the table looking very busy putting something together with string and an empty thread spool. Mary Ann rested her head on her arms watching Priscilla. We could hear Mary Grace on the phone.

Mother went on, "Let me tell you about Pauline's day today!"

Bessie was washing dishes and I was drying. I looked at Bessie and raised my eyebrows in surprise.

"My day?" I whispered.

"It seems that she got to see the loving side of Sister Alquin today," Mother continued.

Bessie and I burst into laughter.

"Now girls, it's true," said Mother. "Sooner or later, one always shows a loving side, like Sister Alquin did. Her heart softened today when she saw Pauline had fallen asleep without lunch. You girls will go to school tomorrow and I will bring lunch to you. And for the rest of the week, you may walk to the Boy's Market and get lunch. Tell the grocery clerk to charge it to my account."

Bessie and I looked at each other and grinned. We listened as Mother went on to tell Father about the girl accusing Leo of taking her change purse. This was the straw that broke the camel's back.

"Did Sister Devota say who this girl was?" Bessie asked.

"I believe her name was Rose Mary."

"That girl is always counting her change in class. She always brings money with her to school. Leo was probably standing by her desk because his friend Gilbert Gold's desk is right behind her. But that did not give her the right to point the finger at Leo."

"She also accused another boy. In any case the coin purse was found with no money missing. Sister Mary Joseph told her not to bring money to school except what she needs for lunch."

"I walked home from school today," I said. "I was so scared! I saw this man walking, and he didn't talk to me or anything but he scared me! I was all by myself, so I ran as fast as I could all the way home!"

When I described him, Father said his name was Feles Co-ho.

"Co-ho is a nickname the townspeople gave him because he has a very bad limp. He is harmless. Everyone in town knows him; he was born and raised here."

"You girls always listen to your instincts," Mother said. "If something tells you to run, then you do just that. Remember to stay together. Wait for your sisters, and you will be fine."

We finished the dishes and tossed out the dishwater. Bessie and I went outside and told Priscilla and Mary Ann about our lunch plans.

"I suppose you want me to take the lunch bag to my classroom?" asked Priscilla.

"When will we go to the Boy's Market?" asked Mary Ann.

"Should we go before school or at lunch hour?" I asked Bessie.

"We could do it right after we get off the bus. The market is close to the public school."

"But what if we miss the bus in the morning?" asked Mary Ann.

"Let's make a plan not to!"

I was happy I wouldn't have to walk home alone anymore.

"I can't wait!"

"What should we buy to eat?" asked Priscilla excitedly. "We have to get those cupcakes that are folded in half with frosting in the middle. Or is it some kind of sweet cream?"

"Well, we could buy a loaf of white Rainbow bread, baloney and a little bottle of mayonnaise. We could also buy some Royal Crown soda pop," said Bessie.

"Can we also buy potato chips?"

"Yes, we can, Baby."

"I want an apple and a banana; we could get one apiece!" I added.

"Good idea!"

"But Priscilla, are you gonna get into the bag before lunchtime and eat your share and a little of ours?" Bessie asked.

"I promise I won't. But if you don't trust me, then one of you can take the bag with you."

Bessie and I looked at each other. We spoke together.

"No, Priscilla, that's okay! You can take the lunch bag with you to your classroom!"

"Okay then, but why are you embarrassed to take a lunch bag to class with you?"

"I'll tell you why! Because Bessie and Pauline don't want anyone to know that they get hungry and eat like everyone else."

We giggled at Mary Ann's explanation, which was very close to being true. But I didn't want to take it because Bessie didn't want to take it. She must be right.

"I just remembered! We can't go to the Boy's Market on Friday."

"That's right, Pauline! On Friday morning, we have to walk straight to school after we get off the bus."

"Why?" asked Mary Ann.

"Because on Thursday, we go to confession so that we may receive Holy Communion on Friday. Right after Mass on Friday, everyone who has made their First Holy Communion gets to eat breakfast for ten cents each."

"We need to go right now and ask Mother for our dime before we forget!"

"Sister Amelia told my class that Father McDevitt wants every student in school to make a good confession and receive Holy Communion on the last day of school," said Priscilla.

"He also wants us to make a conscientious effort to come and receive Communion over the summer," added Bessie.

"Bessie, please help me to prepare for confession; I don't have anything to confess," cried Mary Ann.

"Me too," said Priscilla.

"And me," I said. "I don't have any sins!"

"Ok, I'll get a piece of paper so we can make a list of sins."

Bessie came back quickly with her writing tablet and pencil in hand. I wondered why an old Indian was pictured on the covers of our writing tablets. I also wondered why there was a buffalo on the silver nickels.

"Let's sit on the front steps, the sun is hitting it just right."

I went into the house to ask Mother for our dimes for Friday morning, but Mary Grace told me that Mother and Father were on a long-distance call with Aunt Frances from California. I went back outside.

"What are you girls doing outside?"

"We're making a list of the Ten Commandments."

"Mary Grace, I have a question for you. Did Father McDevitt write the Ten Commandments?"

"No, silly! They came from the Hebrews, like Abraham, Moses, David, and his son Solomon, the four key Jewish leaders. They founded the religion of Judaism, the belief in one God and the Holy Scriptures. These are our beliefs also."

"Thanks, Mary Grace, I hope I can remember all that."

"Will you help me make up some sins?" asked Priscilla. "I don't have any. At least I don't think I do."

"We will need two pieces of paper," said Bessie. "On one page, we can list the Ten Commandments, and on the other, we can have four columns, with each of our names at the top. You may be surprised at how many sins you have committed.

"I will read each commandment and if anyone feels that we have sinned against it, we will say, 'put a check under my name.'"

"Here's another pencil, Pauline. You may be in charge of putting the check marks. Did Mother have a dime for each of us?"

"I didn't get a chance to ask her. Mary Grace said that they were talking to Aunt Frances."

"I hope everyone is okay in California. I would feel very, very sad if something happened to Grandmother! Can you imagine how we would feel never to see her again?"

"What a sad thing to be thinking of, Bessie!" cried Priscilla.

"Yes, don't even think it," I said. "I wish she would move back to Colorado. How could she move so far from us? She and Uncle Paul are my godparents."

"I'm sure it was very hard for her to leave us behind. Mother is her third child, but her very first daughter. She helped deliver each one of us. She loves all her grandbabies; it had to be very hard for her to make the move.

"Are you ready now to listen? I just want to read each commandment once. Let Pauline know if you need a check.

"First: I am the Lord thy God. Thou shalt not have strange gods before Me. Second: Thou shalt not take the name of the Lord thy God in vain. Third: Remember thou keep holy the Sabbath day. Fourth: Honor thy father and thy mother. Fifth: Thou shalt not kill. Sixth: Thou shalt not commit adultery. Seventh: Thou shalt not steal. Eighth: Thou shalt not bear false witness against thy neighbor. Ninth: Thou shalt not covet thy neighbor's wife. Tenth: Thou shalt not covet thy neighbor's goods. Girls, I didn't hear anyone call for a check!"

"You didn't either!"

"If you recall, Priscilla, I was busy reading!"

"You're right, I'm sorry. I just didn't want to be the first to ask for a check."

"I need a check on the fifth commandment. I stepped on a spider this morning and killed it purposely!" said Mary Ann.

"I need a check on the seventh; I took an extra cinnamon roll, after Mother said we could have only one," stated Priscilla.

"I need a check on the third," I said.

"I believe we all get a check on that one; we missed Mass a lot this past winter."

"What is adultery?"

"I don't know," said Bessie. "But I think that one is only for grownups."

"We don't have to worry about the eighth, ninth, and tenth, because we don't have neighbors. Mister Corlett's house is still empty and up for rent!" I said.

"I hope that the people that rent it have children our age to play with. But when it does get rented out, we will not be able to roller skate in that empty house."

"Let's see now, the eighth commandment means that we should always speak the truth about people," I said.

"You're right, and the ninth one is another one for adults," said Bessie. "The tenth one means that we should respect people's property, pay your bills, and always return things we have found."

"Sister Alquin told the class that there are a lot of different ways to sin against each commandment: a-lot-a-lot of different ways!"

"Okay, it looks like we each have a check."

"That is not enough; I want to tell Father McDevitt more! I want to make a real good confession!" cried Priscilla.

"Hey, what if we make some up?" suggested Mary Ann. "Then Father McDevitt will think that we are real good sinners! And then he can tell us, 'Go, my child, and sin no more.'"

Priscilla, Bessie, and I laughed at Mary Ann's idea.

"Baby, I don't think we would impress Father McDevitt by having sinned."

"Okay, but can you still help us make some up? How about saying that we told a lie two times? We could also say that we talked back to Mary Grace three times. We could say that we disobeyed Mother and Father two times."

"That reminds me, Mary Ann. I don't think you sinned against the fifth; killing a spider is not a sin. But it might be a venial sin if you did it in anger."

"I forgot—what is a venial sin?"

"Well, let me see...."

"A venial sin is a less serious offence against God, and does not ruin our relationship with God, but does weaken our love for God. I memorized that word for word."

"Very good, Pauline. It would be a mortal sin if you seriously hurt a person on purpose. A mortal sin is a serious offence against God; it makes man displeasing to God. I pretty sure none of us have committed a mortal sin."

"Now I don't have any checks under my name!" cried Mary Ann.

"Don't worry, Baby, you will when we are finished."

"Wouldn't it be a sin if we made up sins? It would be telling Father McDevitt a lie!"

"That's right!"

"Now you see, Mary Ann, you have two checks. You missed Mass on Sunday, and you wanted to tell Father McDevitt a lie. Priscilla, you disobeyed Mother when you took an extra cinnamon roll. Mary Ann, you could tell about the time that you were willing to go out and look at those boys skinny dipping.

"Pauline, I know what you could confess!"

"What? I don't remember doing anything recently?"

"Remember the mean description you gave of Feles Co-Jo? His only crime is that he has one leg shorter than the other."

"I guess you're right, but he did scare me so! It was the mean way he looked at me. I also fibbed to Sister Amalia when she caught me writing P+A all over my paper, meaning Pauline loves Albert. I told her it was just a reminder for my mother's P+A meeting."

"You're so smart, Bessie. Now let's talk about your sins: what have you done?" asked Priscilla.

"Well, let's see, I could confess the lie I told you girls last week when we stayed home from school. I said I couldn't find clean socks; that was not the truth. I had clean socks, but I didn't want to go to school because I hadn't studied for a test we were having that day."

"Why, you little fibber! We are going to have to watch you closely next time you want to stay home."

"Oh yeah, like I really twisted your arm to stay home with me."

"No, but you could have told us the real reason," said Priscilla.

"What would that change?"

"Mary Ann and I could have made our own decision to go or stay."

"My, my, look at Miss 'High and Mighty.' You are usually the first to run to the drapes in the front room and signal to the bus driver to be on his way."

Priscilla changed her haughty attitude and began to giggle.

"You're right, Bessie, I love to stay home from school just as much as the rest of you."

"So we are in agreement that we each have two checks, and Mary Ann has three. I stole an eraser, but I felt so guilty that I threw it away, never using it. I'll never take anything that doesn't belong to me! We can tell Father McDevitt that we can't recall any other sins."

Mary Grace must have finished her homework. She turned the radio up full blast. We could hear Earnest Tub. "I'm walking the floor over you. I can't sleep a wink, that is true...."

We heard Mother calling to us over the music.

"Girls, come here! I have some wonderful news!"

We ran inside to hear.

"What would you say if I told you that Aunt Frances, Grandmother, Phyllis, and Cecilia are driving from California to visit us?"

"Oh, goody, goody! We get to see Grandmother again!" shouted Priscilla.

"When will they be leaving? When will they get here?" I asked.

"Will they be here tomorrow?" asked Mary Ann.

"No, Baby, it takes at least three days. They will spend at least two nights in motels. They plan to leave California the day after school ends for Cecilia. I don't know if her summer break starts at the same time as our school's. Aunt Frances will call to let us know right before they leave their house in a week or so."

"Is that the reason you've been in such a good mood?" asked Bessie.

"I do feel very blessed these days. Now I need all of you to take extra care to put things away and help to keep the house tidy. I'll be baking a lot of bread and cinnamon rolls this coming weekend."

We all went to bed in a good mood; we had something great to anticipate.

Grandmother Genevieve
and Uncle Frank

Uncle Paul and Uncle Frank

Joe and Leo

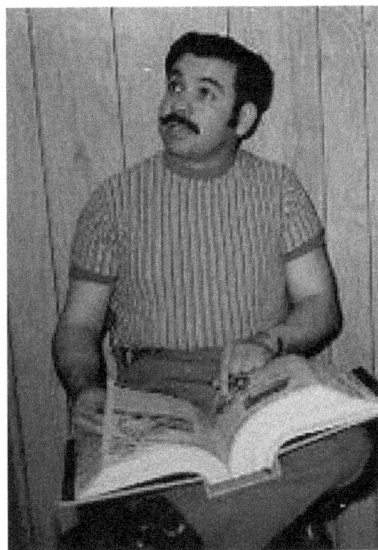

Uncle Jim

Uncle Paul

Chapter Eight

On Wednesday morning, I woke to the sound of Leo's voice.

"Mary Grace! Joe wants you to hurry; he said he will have time to pick up Phyllis at her house and drop you both off at school, but only if you leave in the next minute or two."

"I'm coming, I'm coming! Are you getting a ride with Joe too?"

"No, I'm headed for the woodpile to chop wood. Dad also wants me to dig post holes."

"Bessie, I'll see you and the girls on the bus after school; have Pauline and Priscilla brush their own hair. Please brush Mary Ann's. Thank you!" Mary Grace shouted as she closed the door behind her.

I rushed to get ready for school and joined the girls in the kitchen. I spotted the wide shallow bowl on the small cabinet filled with clean water and washed my face and hands.

"You don't have time to be playing with those suds," said Bessie. "Wash up quickly. The bus will be pulling up in another ten minutes."

"I need to go to the bathroom, please come with me!" cried Mary Ann.

"Baby, we don't have time. Can you hold it?"

"No, I can't!"

"Okay, then let's hurry! Pauline, Priscilla, watch for the bus."

Priscilla went into the front room, and I went into the bedroom to brush my hair. I heard the bus honk, and ran to the front room.

"Aren't the girls back yet?"

The bus was still honking.

"Pauline, what do we do now? The girls are still outside!"

"We can't miss school again!"

"I don't know, but we can't keep the bus waiting."

Priscilla went to the front window, pulled the flowered drapes open just enough to expose her arm and signaled the bus to go. The back door opened, and Priscilla told Bessie that we had missed the bus.

"What do we do now?"

"Well, it looks like we are just going to have to walk. So we need to leave right now."

We started down the road, and in the distance we could hear Leo chopping wood. Suddenly, to my surprise, I saw Bessie drop to her knees. When I saw her make the Sign of the Cross, I dropped to my knees, and so did Priscilla and Mary Ann.

I whispered, "What the heck are we doing kneeling in the middle of the road?"

Bessie whispered back, "Look up to the sky! Jesus' eyes are upon us!"

"Where?"

"I don't see Him!"

"No, but He can see us."

Priscilla and Mary Ann were very still as they gazed up to the sky in wonder.

Bessie whispered, "See the narrow beams of light? All the lines are pointing at us! Jesus' Arms are spread out; They are spread out and the rays are coming from His Heart!"

"Oh yes, the lines are pointing to us!"

"I wish Leo was right here with us," said Mary Ann.

"Oh, I'm sure this has happened to him when he is on his bike. He has never mentioned it to us, but Jesus watches over him all the time because he always gets home safe."

"How long do we need to stay on our knees?" asked Priscilla. "I have a little rock embedded in my right knee."

Bessie stood up and signaled to us to rise.

"Jesus will still watch over us as we walk. I don't think He would want us to be late for school. We don't need to whisper anymore, but let's just make the Sign of the Cross all together. In the Name of the Father, and of the Son, and of the Holy Ghost. Amen."

The school and the church were soon in our sights, as we reached Batterson Street. We weren't late; there were still students on the playground. The eighth graders were lining up outside to march across to the church.

Father McDevitt would be hearing confessions, but my third grade class would not be going to confession until after lunch.

Bessie started to walk away toward her classroom.

"See you girls at lunch! Have a good confession; we did prepare!"

Priscilla, Mary Ann, and I walked to the left side of the school building where the younger grades were. I went to the right of the hall; my class room was in the center of the building.

"Bye, Girls! See you at lunch."

I spotted my friend Julia standing with the new girl Margaret. I smiled at her, but I felt the smile leave my face when I got closer and saw Albert talking with Naomi. Albert looked up at me and gave me a huge smile, which surprised both me and Naomi.

Julia walked up to me.

"Did you see the dirty look Naomi Espinosa gave you? What was that about?"

"I don't know."

Julia had no idea that I had a crush on Albert, and I was not about to tell her. I couldn't imagine what would happen if it got back to the nuns that I liked a boy. I was too young to be thinking about them. It could get around and people might think that I was boy crazy. Nope, I thought, the only ones I can share my feelings with are my sisters. But what was that smile all about? Did he know that my sister is his sister Phyllis' best friend? I wondered what Bessie would think.

"Come on, Julia, let's go to our desks," I said aloud. "I want to tell you about my walk to school today."

"Class, please come to order now," said Sister Alquin a few minutes later. "We will skip morning recess time today. Father McDevitt announced that he will hear confessions today instead of tomorrow, because on Thursday, the Catholic students from public school will be released so they can go to confession."

Sister Alquin instructed the class to stand and face the flag. We all put our hands to our chests and pledged allegiance to our red, white and blue flag hanging in the corner of the room.

Next we faced the statue of Jesus, our little King, as a Boy. We said the Lord's Prayer.

Our Father, Who art in Heaven,
hallowed be Thy name.
Thy kingdom come; Thy Will be done,
on earth as it is in Heaven.
Give us this day our daily bread;
and forgive us our trespasses
as we forgive those who trespass against us;
and lead us not into temptation,
but deliver us from evil. Amen.

The morning hours flew by. There was a knock at the door. Sister Alquin got up from her desk to answer it. I was surprised to see my mother greet Sister and hand her a bag. Then I remembered that Mother had said she would bring lunch to school for us. She left quickly to return to work. I was thrilled to have seen her; we didn't always get to see her before she left for work in the mornings.

Sister Alquin walked over to the wall with the coat hooks and placed the bag under my sweater. I was embarrassed of course, but relieved, when she said, "Pauline, this grocery bag is lunch for you and your sisters."

I was thankful that she mentioned my sisters; now the class knew it was not just for me!

From where I was sitting, I could see that there was a quart of milk in the bag: a whole quart! I wondered what else it contained.

There was another knock at the door; this time it was Sister Mary Georgia.

"Class, it's our turn to go over to the church for confession."

We came back just in time for lunch, so Sister dismissed us as we reached our classroom door. I picked up the paper bag, and went to find my sisters.

Priscilla and Mary Ann ran up to me.

"Let's go find Bessie; Mother brought lunch for us!"

We soon found her, coming down the cement steps. I handed her the big grocery bag.

"It's lunch from Mother; it's heavy."

"Mother brought it to your classroom?"

"Yes! Now let's go find a table in the cafeteria; I want to see what she brought."

"Do we need to take turns putting our heads close to the opening of the bag to take a bite?"

"No, Baby. She didn't bring scrambled egg tortilla sandwiches like we do. Here…"

She handed each of us a ham sandwich wrapped in wax paper. We started to bite into them as she pulled out four paper cups.

"What else is in the bag?" asked Priscilla.

"There is an apple for each of us and some Fig Newtons: Mother's favorite cookies."

We enjoyed every bite we took; we ate with our heads held high.

"How did you girls do in confession this morning?"

We shook our heads yes; we were too busy eating to speak.

"I take your nods to mean you did well."

We shook our heads again. Bessie smiled and took a bite of her apple. She knew that she had coached us well.

That afternoon, Sister Alquin told each student to partner with another student to quiz each other on the times tables. The end of the school day finally came. I was busily gathering my work papers to take home when I felt someone walk up and stop at the side of my desk. I looked up. It was Naomi Espinosa.

I gave a half smile. She bent down and whispered, "Pauline, I'll be outside waiting for you. I'm going to beat you up."

"Why? What did I do?"

Naomi walked away without another word.

I was scared. What should I do? What did she mean, she's going to beat me up? My sisters are waiting for me outside, but I can't go out there! I'm scared. Do my sisters and I have a sign on us reading, "Here we are…beat us up?" First the Ratenias, and now a girl in my own classroom! What do I do? I prayed, "Mother of Jesus, please help me."

To my surprise, another girl walked up to me.

"Are you Pauline?" she asked.

"Yes, I am."

I was glad to buy some more time, talking to this girl.

"I'm Sally, Naomi's sister. Don't be afraid to go out; your sisters are waiting for you. My sister told me what she was up to. I told her, 'Naomi, you have another think coming if you think I will just stand here and let you behave like a bully!' She didn't make a fuss. She has already started to walk home."

"Really? Thank you! Where do you live?"

"We live on the other side of Gun Barrel Road, on Sunny Side. Now go home, and don't worry; she will not bother you again. I plan to tell my parents."

She was right: my sisters were waiting for me, and Naomi was not. Sally told Bessie what had detained me.

"Pauline, hurry! We have to walk fast to catch the bus!"

I looked in the direction of Sunny Side Road, and I couldn't believe my eyes. I saw Naomi, and she was walking with Albert Sanchez!

"Do you see what I see? What is he doing with her? Was he going to watch while she beat me up?"

"Maybe he doesn't know what she had in mind."

Bessie's reasoning gave me a little peace of mind, but not for long. On the bus ride home, I was very quiet. My heart was broken for I knew that I had to stop liking Albert just like the girls in our "love" comic books. The thought bubble would read: Once a cheater, always a cheater. The comic book girls knew that one has to forget a boy that likes too many girls at one time.

I knew that Albert liked me, but he also liked Naomi, and I couldn't have that. It had to be only me!

We climbed off the bus and ran into the house. The one that reached the kitchen table first might just be the one to get the last tortilla. Leo was feeding wood to the stove, looking content. We changed our shoes and went out to play softball.

We decided to make our own ball, with a rock wrapped in a thick rag and masking tape. We used the stick from an old broken broom as a bat. We played most of the afternoon, until Mary Grace called us in to help wash dishes while she made the beds and swept the floors.

For dinner, Mother steamed vegetables and potatoes, and baked lamb chops. Mary Grace sliced a loaf of homemade bread. The subject of Leo staying home from school was not discussed. The girls and I thanked Mother for the wonderful lunch. She told us that Mrs. Roth helped put it together from her kitchen.

"Mrs. Roth has a good heart. She told me that you girls never have to go without lunch. She said that I can fix lunch for you from her kitchen whenever the need arises. Do you have room for a cinnamon roll?"

We looked at Bessie.

"I'll have one a little later," she said. "I don't have homework tonight, but I want to play outdoors after we do dishes."

Priscilla, Mary Ann, and I agreed that we would also wait.

"Aunt Frances called me at work today to say that they will come the second week of July, for the Sky-High Stampede," said Mother. "Your grandmother would like Cecilia to see her Uncle Louie on his Appaloosa in the parade. He has ridden in the parade every year since the War. Cecilia has never been to a rodeo."

We knew that this event brought thousands of visitors to the San Luis Valley.

"Frances wants me to buy Cecilia the same cowgirl outfit that I buy for you girls. She thinks she's the same size as you, Pauline."

After dishes and sweeping, we went outside to discuss Cousin Cecilia's visit.

"We'll spend three days of their visit at the fair, so that leaves eleven days."

"That's right, Pauline. I also heard Leo ask about pea-picking. Mother told him that Aunt Frances might take us kids to pick our own to bring home, but that if we want to pick for pay, Aunt Frances probably won't want to stay."

"Hey, we could ask Aunt Frances to let us pick for pay to spend at the Sky-High Stampede," suggested Priscilla.

"Let's plan for the days we stay at home."

"We could show her how we place flowers in our hair; every day, we could walk barefoot in the creek."

"We could roller skate in the empty house," said Mary Ann.

"We could roll cigarettes another day and play grownup sisters," I suggested.

"Absolutely not!" said Bessie. "Playing grownup sisters and going up to the garret are two activities we share with no one! But if she likes to sing country songs, we can take her out to the hay wagon."

"That's a good idea, but she has to join in the singing, even if we have to teach her the words to our favorite songs. I would like to teach her 'Jambalaya'!"

"Everyone knows the words to Jambalaya!"

I started to sing and the girls joined in.

"Pauline, what does 'veer-o' mean in the second line of this song?"

"I asked Joe the same question, Priscilla. He said, 'Veer means to change direction, to shift or turn in a different direction.' I think the song invites us to be happy; wouldn't you girls agree?"

"Yes! And Joe would agree; he sings it every time he picks up his guitar."

"What else can we do when Cecilia is here?"

"She may have something to share."

"Yes, and they might not spend every day at home with us; I'm sure they will be out visiting family."

"Uncle Jim, Uncle Manuel, and Uncle Louie are Grandmother's sons; she will want to spend time with them and her other grandchildren."

"I've heard Mother say that Uncle Tony lives in Denver."

"But he comes every year for the Sky-High Stampede," said Bessie. "He is so handsome; I wonder if Cecilia still looks like him."

"I think Mary Ann is right: we should let Cecilia play grownup sisters with us! She's almost like a sister to us. It's not her fault that she moved away."

"That's right," said Priscilla. "I bet she would love pretending to smoke."

"Okay," said Bessie, "but if she makes fun of us, that is the last time we offer our game to anyone! Are we in agreement?"

We all agreed.

Mother called, "Girls, please collect the wood kindling. Leo chopped wood all day so there is plenty to pick up."

We picked and fooled around, chasing each other around the yard until Father's compadre drove onto our property.

Primo Catalano was Father's very best friend. Primo and his wife Star had no children. The girls and I wondered why he never brought his wife with him. We only saw her at Christmastime. She wore a lot of rouge on her cheeks, but Primo was very affectionate toward her. Father came out to greet him and they went into the house, Primo carrying his guitar as usual.

There was no more kindling to be picked, so we carried the basket into the kitchen. We walked straight over to Primo to shake his hand. Father winked at us. He had taught us always to greet company with a hello, a hand shake, or a hug depending on who was visiting; it made him proud of us. It wasn't always easy, because we were painfully shy.

Father had his accordion on his lap. We all enjoyed listening to Father play, so we made ourselves comfortable.

Mother busily cleaned yellow peas, so that Mary Grace could cook them after school tomorrow. When Mother came home, she would season them with salt and pepper, and add sautéed onions.

Primo sang a little and the two of them tapped their feet. Primo sang the lyrics to a Spanish song, "Solamente Una Vez"—Only Once. It told of falling in love only once in a lifetime. Then Father played the tune to Bill Monroe's "Blue Moon of Kentucky." I sang the words in my head.

I couldn't sing in front of Primo; I'd be too embarrassed!

Father also played some tunes he had learned as a very young man from his mother, Mama Vicentia. I had never heard them before; they were not Spanish nor Country. We watched in amazement as Father made music come out of his instrument by pulling out and pressing together the bellows to force air through the metal reeds, which were then opened by his fingering the keys.

Mother offered Primo and Father coffee and cinnamon rolls; they stopped playing and moved closer to the table. After Primo left, Mother told us to get ready for bed.

Jesus' Eyes Are Upon Us

Uncle Tony

Uncle Manuel,
Aunt Francis, and
Uncle Tony

Chapter Nine

On Thursday morning, we left ten minutes before the bus was due to arrive and walked quickly and eagerly to the Boy's Market for our lunch. It was empty of other customers. The salesperson, busy with a calculator, looked up and smiled. That gave us the confidence to shop to our hearts' content.

We placed on the counter four Hostess cream-filled puff pastries, four bright yellow bananas, four bottles of Royal Crown soda pop, a loaf of white Rambo bread, and a small bottle of mayonnaise.

"Is there anything else I can help you with, Young Ladies?"

Bessie asked for half a pound of sliced bologna and added four red delicious apples to our wonderful pile.

The lady gave us the total.

"We are Della Montoya's daughters," said Bessie. "Could you please put this purchase on her grocery account?"

"Of course! I know your mother very well. Your brother Joe is on a delivery run right now. I'd better double-bag; the pop bottles and apples make the bag heavy."

She handed Bessie the bag.

"We will take turns carrying the bag; we don't have far to walk."

"You're headed to Saint Joseph's School?"

"Yes, ma'am."

All the buses at the public school had come and gone; there were no students around. We crossed the street, and headed for Saint Joseph's. As we neared 4th and Batterson, we realized that we had taken longer than we had anticipated. There weren't any students in our schoolyard either.

Bessie and I looked at each other. We knew we couldn't show up late, especially with this heavy grocer's bag. Everyone would ask: "What's in the huge bag?"

Not only were my sisters and I connected in our heads, we always agreed with each other. Well, on important matters, anyway.

I told Bessie what she wanted to hear.

"I think we should just go home. We can't go to school late."

"Will I be questioned in front of the class?" asked Priscilla.

"Yes, you girls would also need to explain why you were late."

Priscilla and Mary Ann didn't seem to mind going home. We walked past the school and the nuns' convent right next door, terrified that one of the nuns would see us. We finally reached Lariat Road, which ran in front of our house.

We crossed an irrigation ditch, and Bessie handed the bag to me.

"My arm is beginning to ache."

"Can we eat something?" asked Mary Ann. "Can we?"

"I'll make a deal with you girls: if we start cleaning house the minute we get home, then we can play grownup sisters, meeting for lunch. We will enjoy the food more if we are surrounded by tidiness."

"What if Leo is home? Oh, I know! We can share our food with him!" said Priscilla.

"He won't be home. I heard Father ask Leo to go with him to check on the sheep. He said he has a few sheep ready to drop their lambs and some of them have two."

"Oh good! No one will know that we didn't go to school!" said Priscilla.

"Don't kid yourself," I said. "Mother always knows. She just knows. Don't even try to deny it if she asks."

"That's right," said Bessie. "Mother always knows what we are up to. And don't forget—we went to confession yesterday."

It was a beautiful spring morning. The flowers in our yard were blooming; the birds were singing; the chickens were prancing around the yard. The horses and cows with their calves were grazing on Mr. Corlett's property. I began to sing:

On top of old Smokey,
all covered with grass,
I lost my true love for courting and such…

"Come on, Girls! I can't wait to have our lunch! Let's hurry and make the beds, and wash the dishes," said Bessie.

We ran to the house and worked quickly. Afterward, we placed a blanket on the front lawn to have our lunch. We ate slowly.

We heard the familiar sound of sheep bleating. Mister Crawford, who had roto-tilled the front yard when we planted the lawn, was herding fifty to seventy sheep past our house.

"Where the heck is he taking all those sheep?" asked Priscilla.

"He'll probably turn right when he reaches Gun Barrel Road," said Bessie. "There are many ranches at that end of town."

"Look at that one! It has five legs!" cried Mary Ann, pointing.

Bessie whispered in my ear, "It is a baby lamb's leg. The sheep is giving birth!"

I was shocked. I didn't know what the heck she meant. But I couldn't ask, because it would alert Priscilla and Mary Ann, and Bessie obviously didn't want them to hear.

We watched and listened, as the sheep passed: small ones and big ones, fat ones and skinny ones. After the sound of their bleats faded, we went back to enjoying our wonderful lunch.

We took our apples down by the creek, which was shallow enough for us to wade. We took off our shoes and stepped into the cool spring water.

"Look at all those baby fish!" said Priscilla.

"Those are tadpoles developing into frogs," I said.

"How did you know that?" asked Bessie. "Leo told me that too. He said that when those are gone, more will come through the summer months."

Bessie pulled out a milkweed. Priscilla had a wart on her index finger, and Grandmother had told us that this plant with the milky juice in its stems and leaves would make the growth on the skin harden and fall off. Grandmother had a remedy for every ailment, and Mother believed in her cures. Her home remedies and Father's prayers had saved Leo from death when he was an infant.

Mary Ann wanted to lie down, so we all went into our parents' bedroom and fell asleep in their bed with our full tummies. After about an hour or two, the sound of Father's truck woke me up, and I roused the other girls.

We forgot that we were not supposed to be at home and ran out to greet and hug Father. Father let each have her turn, patted each on the head, and then went to unload some lambs he had brought home.

Leo asked, "Did school let out early today?"

We didn't answer, and he did not pursue it.

"Guess what?" said Mary Ann. "We saw a man and a lot of sheep go by the house earlier today!"

"He was probably taking them to higher, cooler ground to graze," said Leo.

We saw the bus go by. Father must have thought it had just dropped us off. He didn't ask, and we didn't tell.

"Why did you bring this sheep home with you, Daddy?" asked Priscilla.

"They are in need of some care."

"Can we help you care for them?" asked Mary Ann.

"Yes, Daddy, we can give them some tender, loving care!" I said.

"Why do these lambs need special care, Daddy?" asked Bessie.

"Let's see now. This little one lost his mother and needs to be bottle fed. Would you like to care for this one, Bessie? The rest of you girls can help your sister if she is busy doing other house chores. Pauline, you may keep an eye on this chunky one. He has an infection on his right leg. He got it hung up on some barbed wire. Priscilla, you may keep an eye on this one. He has very weak legs and he falls a lot. He feeds well but can't gain weight."

"What about me?" Mary Ann asked.

"Well, because you are so little, we all need to care for you. Don't forget: you are the baby right now."

"Oh yes. I forgot."

Mary Ann was satisfied with Father's answer; she had a very pleased look on her face.

Father winked at the rest of us. He asked Leo to unload a bag of wheat and barley, then he handed Bessie two old soda-pop bottles with huge black nipples for feeding milk to the lambs.

Phyllis' father drove in and delivered her and Mary Grace. They greeted Father and went into the house.

Father told us we could go play, so we went in to check on the older girls. Mary Grace was feeding the wood stove with newspaper and kindling. I didn't think my sisters and I would have much of an appetite after our big lunch, but it's hard to walk away from country fried potatoes.

On Friday morning, we stayed out of the kitchen, so we could fast the three hours before Holy Communion. Mrs. Plane and her help would already be preparing breakfast for the students who received the Holy Eucharist.

After Mass, all our classes headed across the street back to the school. Three lines of students who had received Communion headed for the cafeteria. I stood behind Bessie.

We waited with anticipation; hoping Mrs. Plane would serve wheat cereal with milk and a blend of honey and butter spread on toast. Betty Montacelli was standing in front of Bessie, looking in the direction of the first line. Gilbert Samara was cutting across the lines. He cut in between Bessie and me, and to our surprise, he pinched Bessie right where she stood!

Bessie looked at me in shock.

"Do you think anyone else noticed? I'm so embarrassed! How could he do that to me? He risked getting caught! What kind of boy would do that? That was Joe's friend Earnest's brother!"

"I know! He is in my class! Why would he do that to you and not me?"

"You would want him to goose you!?"

"No! That is not what I meant. It's just that he—"

"It's just that he—what!?"

"I don't know what I'm saying. Don't turn it on me. Gilbert is the one that behaved badly, not me!"

"We can't tell the girls. They wouldn't understand. And he did this right after Mass—shame on him!"

The line had shortened. We would be getting served soon. Bessie's friend Betty had left the line without saying anything, and that nasty boy Gilbert was nowhere to be seen.

Mrs. Plane gave us a big smile as she handed us our food trays. We loved the toast with honey and butter. The tiny bowls of cream of wheat probably held only one fourth of a cup, but with the bread and milk, it was satisfying.

"We must try making this at home, Pauline. It's just real butter mixed with honey. We must remember to ask Mother to get us a jar of honey."

All the classes returned to their rooms. Thank the good Lord Gilbert was not at his desk. Maybe he cut school. Maybe he got caught. Maybe his conscience got the better of him.

We spent the day reviewing for tests we'd take the following week. After we came in from last recess, Sister Alquin asked the class to quiet down and take our seats right away.

"Sister Mary Joseph has informed us that our Sister Mary Julian is very ill. We don't know yet what's wrong, but she is in the hospital. All the classes will be praying the rosary for her. We need to pray with all our hearts. The Blessed Virgin Mary wants us to pray; she cannot help those who do not pray."

I asked sister Amelia, "Why do we say the rosary?"

"Because it pleases Mary when we ask her to intercede for us."

"What does that mean?" I wanted to know.

"Well, Pauline, when Jesus started His ministry, a wedding took place in Cana in Galilee and Jesus' mother Mary was there. When the wine was gone, Jesus' mother said to Him, 'They have no more wine.' Jesus then turned the water into wine which was the first of His miracles.

"So, you see, Pauline, if we are in need of something and we pray to Jesus' mother, that pleases Him and He will answer our prayers, if what we ask is good and if it is His will."

We were allowed to sit at our desks to say the rosary. There would be fewer interruptions if we didn't have aching knees.

After school we walked quickly, hoping to avoid the Ratenias. We thought we could climb on to the bus before they got out of their classes. But luck was not on our side today. We saw about five of them walking toward us. When we were face to face with them, one of them said, "That's them!"

They stared at us. As we passed, they placed their hands on our backs and pushed hard, but none of us girls tripped. We walked faster. Bessie held Mary Ann's hand and I held Priscilla's hand. They didn't follow us, but we could hear them laughing. I felt humiliated. We couldn't stand up to them. We didn't know how to fight back, and we were scared!

Safely on the bus, we saw the "Three Sisters" with the golden hair, quiet manner, and the nice lunch pails. Mary Grace was not riding the bus home today. We would have to share our scare with her later. I was sure there would be more from those mean girls. We just needed to pray harder and longer for them to be converted along with the Russians and their Iron Curtain. I wanted to know why the Ratenias hated us. We didn't even know each other.

The house was empty when we got home. We sat in the kitchen eating homemade bread and butter. The phone rang; it was Mother calling to check on us. Leo and Cousin Willie walked in, so Bessie told her, "Leo is home with us."

Mother told Bessie that she and I needed to take all the white kitchen chairs outside and wash and dry them. Mother also said that Cousin Phil was giving Mary Grace a ride home, that she knew to wash the kitchen floor when she got home, and that Uncle Manuel and family were coming over tomorrow.

Priscilla and Mary Ann followed Leo and Cousin Willie outside. Willy was our first cousin on Father's side. Willy was a short and husky youth with olive-colored skin and green eyes. He was always very quiet. He never spoke much, except when spoken to.

"Bessie, do you think Willy purchased his bike in green to match his eyes? Green might be his favorite color or maybe that model only came in green. It is a nice looking bike, with its foot and hand-operated brake lever mounted on the handlebars, but on the other hand I don't care for the cable attached."

Bessie and I washed the chairs, swept the floors, made the beds, and emptied the bed pot. When Mary Grace came home, I went out to play with the girls.

Leo and Willie had gone rabbit hunting, and Priscilla and Mary Ann were jumping rope. They asked me to join them. We sang as we took turns jumping.

My mother, your mother
Lived across the street
And every time they had a fight,
This is what they said,
'E...ca baca, E...ca baca,
E...ca baca, boo—
Soda crackers, Soda crackers,
and out goes you."

Bessie came out to join us and sang along as we jumped some more.

"Blue bell, crack a shell E...V...I...V... over."

I asked Bessie, "Do you think Willie would mind if we rode his bike?"

"We don't know how to ride a bike."

"Well, that's what I mean; we could teach ourselves how to ride."

Bessie and I took turns with the bike, falling off on our bottoms. The impact knocked the wind out of us, but we got right up and tried again.

Mary Grace came out.

"I don't think Willie would appreciate it if you girls crash and dent his new bike. Put it back."

We all went into the house to play.

When Father got home, he stayed outside working on the pump at the irrigation ditch, which pumped water for the front lawn and the vegetable garden. When Mother got home, she made salmon patties, since we abstained from meat on Fridays. Salmon was our favorite sea food because we didn't have to be as careful of bones as when we ate trout. When Mother fried trout, Father very carefully checked that it was free of bones for "his little girls."

The girls and I sat at the kitchen table, taking turns coloring. Most of the time we had only one coloring book for all of us. Mother was cutting cores out of apples, so she could place them on a cookie sheet, sprinkled with cinnamon and brown sugar, and bake them in the oven until they were golden brown.

I watched as Mother next combined the salmon, some crushed saltine crackers, finely chopped green onions, lemon juice, salt and pepper. She shaped the mixture into patties and began to fry them in a skillet. Soon we sat down to eat salmon patties, steamed green beans, homemade bread, and baked apples.

After dinner, Mother surprised us by announcing that we were going to Monte Vista's Town Theater after the dinner dishes were done. Mother, Father and Mary Ann went outside to check on the vegetable garden; they picked almost every evening. Priscilla swept the kitchen as quickly as she could so she could join them.

Bessie and I were excited about going to the movies, but we knew that we had to heat the water first to wash the dishes. Then one of us had a bright idea—I don't remember which of us it was. We decided that we'd clean the dishes of excess food, and then hide them and wash them in the morning. We hurriedly hid them in the big drawer at the bottom of the refrigerator and put the dirty silverware in the freezer part. We rinsed the coffee cups, wiped them, and put them away. The kitchen looked very nice and tidy. No one would know.

We went into the bedroom to brush our hair, then went out and announced that we were ready to go. Mother looked up and smiled at us. Priscilla and Mary Ann were helping her fill her apron with zucchini, tomatoes, and cucumbers.

"That was fast!" said Father. "You girls work pretty quick, don't you?"

I felt guilty, and Bessie glanced over at me. We didn't want to hear any more compliments. I whispered to her, "We went to confession on Wednesday!"

"I know," she whispered back, "But we never said that we washed the dishes; we just said we were ready to go!"

We went into the house. Mother told us to grab sweaters.

"It might be a little chilly when we leave the theater. It's Friday so there will be a double feature. Who will be the first to fall asleep?"

"Not me! I took a short nap after school today," said Priscilla.

"Me too!" said Mary Ann.

"What about you two?" asked Father as he opened the door to the refrigerator.

Bessie and I didn't answer. We just stood there pop-eyed. But if Father saw the dirty dishes, he never said a word.

During the ride downtown, Bessie and I were very quiet. But thanks to Rex Allen and his horse on the big screen, we quickly forgot what we had done.

Priscilla fell asleep on Father's lap, and Mary Ann on Mother's lap. It was just as well, because the second feature was a Science Fiction, and it spooked me good. "The Day the Earth Stood Still" was about a spaceship that landed in Washington D.C.

The lady in the movie almost forgot what she was supposed to say to the iron man with the burning eyes. But I knew that I would never forget the words, if ever I met up with him! "Klaatu barada nikto."

"That iron man scares me way, way more than Feles CoJo," I whispered to Bessie.

"I'm sure glad Mary Ann and Priscilla fell asleep," she whispered back.

I must have fallen asleep on the way home because when I woke up, it was Saturday morning. Priscilla and Mary Ann were having coffee with Father. Mother was grilling pancakes. The radio was playing the song it played at that time every Saturday morning: "Las Mananitas."

Mother sang along:

> Estas son las mananitas
> Que cantaba el Rey David
> A las muchachas Bonitas
> Te las contomos Asi.

> Despierta mi bien despierta
> Mira que ya amanecio
> Ya los pajaritos cantan
> La Luna ya se oculto.

> Que Linda esta` la manana
> En que vengo a saludarte
> Venimos todos con gusto
> Y placer a felicitarte.

El dia enque tu naciste
Nacioren todas las Flores
Y en la pila Del bautismo
Cantaron los ruisenores.

Ya viene amaneciendo
Ya la Luz del dia nos dio
Levantate de manana
Mira que ya amanecio.

Bessie came into the kitchen, rubbing her eyes.

"Where is Mary Grace?"

"Joe dropped her off at Phyllis' early this morning on his way to work. Phyllis' mother has given birth to a little girl. Why? Did you need her for any special reason, Sweetheart?"

"No, Mother. No special reason. I was just wondering."

Mother served up some much buttered pancakes.

"Thank you, Mother! I thought my coffee might get cold before I got my hot-cakes," said Priscilla.

"Oh, you did; did you?" Mother looked at Father. "Now look at what you've made of your little girls: coffee drinkers! And they even take it black, like you do!"

Father smiled at us and asked if Bessie and I were ready for our cups. We washed our hands and faces and quickly sat down at the table.

Leo came in with an armful of firewood. Mother put her hand on his back.

"You are a good son, thank you. That will do for today; now wash up and sit down to breakfast."

Father and Leo talked, and Bessie and I ate quietly. The buttered pancakes were so good and the coffee went well with them. Mother was singing "Amorsito Corazon."

Mother's singing was interrupted by the ringing of the phone. She went into the front room. Father walked outside with his coffee cup, and Leo followed. Bessie and I served ourselves another pancake each.

Mother came back into the kitchen and poured another cup of coffee. Father popped his head back in.

"I'm going to tighten the wire on the clothesline. Mary Grace complained the sheets were dragging on the ground when she went to bring the clothes in from the line."

"Okay, Mi Corazon," said Mother.

The girls and I spent the morning in the house with Mother; it was a treat to have her home with us. She made rice pudding and put a meatloaf together to go with mashed potatoes, brown gravy and corn. This was a favorite of Uncle Manuel's. He, Aunt Elsie and their children were coming over for dinner this evening. He always said, "Della, you are the best cook ever! Next to Elsie of course."

And Aunt Elsie always responded, "Oh sure! We all know that Della's meatloaf is the best; that is why I don't make it for you. Mine would never measure up to your sister's."

By mid-afternoon, Mother suggested we go out and play so she could bathe. We decided to go across to Mr. Corlett's still empty house. Mrs. Corlett had given Mother some roller skates for us. They weren't new, but they were barely used. We skated from kitchen to front room and back again.

Mary Ann kept saying, "Stop passing me up! That is cheating!"

We loved that we had the house to ourselves, and we knew it well, for it had once been our home.

Leo popped his head in the door.

"Just checking on you girls. Father wants you to check in with him whenever you are over here; one of you can run across every so often. Hear me?"

"We will!" answered Bessie.

"Next time we come across to play, let's remember to bring the formal wedding dresses! We can play dress-up with the black high-tie boots," said Bessie.

"Good idea!" said Mary Ann. "I get to put the boots on first since we only have two pairs. Since I'm so little, you may forget to give me my turn!"

"We have to take turns. We only have two wedding dresses," said Priscilla.

"Why do you suppose Aunt Dolores and Aunt Mary left their wedding dresses behind when they moved to California?" I asked Bessie.

"I think Mary Grace told me a while back that Aunt Dolores and Aunt Mary were not happily married women like Mother. Mother's sisters were both in a divorce. Aunt Frances also was in a divorce."

"How do you get in a divorce? What does that mean?" Priscilla wanted to know.

"I think it means that their husbands were not ready to be settled like father is. What do you think Bessie?"

"I'm not sure, but it could be that they did not take enough time to pick the right mate for life."

"They must have been happy on their wedding day, because they look so beautiful in their wedding picture."

"They couldn't have been good men like our father, or our aunties would not have left their dresses behind. I do believe that the ones we play with were not their actual wedding dresses. I think they were formal dresses they wore on Aunt Frances' wedding day. Aunt Dolores sewed them."

Mother called us, and we all ran back to the house. She told us to take baths and put on clean underclothes and socks, for we'd be going to Sunday Mass the next morning.

We decided to shine our patent leather shoes after bathing. We placed newspaper on the kitchen table for the shoes, so we could spend more time with Mother. She had made a banana cream pie—Joe's favorite—and was now beating egg whites for the lemon pie she had baked.

"Mother, could you buy some bobby pins for us so that we could pin curl our hair?" asked Bessie. "We are getting too old for rag curls."

I hadn't given that much thought, but Bessie was right as usual.

"I don't know about that," replied Mother. "I love to see you girls in 'Reesos.'"

"I'll make a deal with you, Mother," said Bessie. "If we take our school pictures in September with our hair curled in 'Reesos,' then after that can we stop wearing rag curls?"

"That sounds fair. We'll see. I hate to give up our family tradition of seeing you girls in rag curls and flannel nightgowns sitting in front of the tree on Christmas Eve. If only time could stand still so that

I could enjoy seeing you girls little. If only I could stay home from work, I would love to be here when you girls get home from school.

"Enough of this kind of thinking," she continued. "I have to thank our Lord Jesus that I am able to go to work and help your father to pay for our new home, and that He watches over you girls when I can't be with you! I believe Manuel's truck just pulled in. Be on your best behavior!"

Mother didn't need to worry: we would never misbehave around Uncle Manuel! We looked up to him. He was always good to us and gave us attention, unlike Mother's other brothers: Uncle Jim and Uncle Louie. We also thought he was very handsome, like a movie star. He looked like Fess Parker, who played Davy Crockett. But most importantly, Mother loved him very much. They were very close, since Mother had helped Grandmother care for Uncle Manuel and Aunt Frances when they were toddlers.

The girls and I ran out to meet them. We enjoyed playing with our cousins Robert, Ruth, Virginia, and Andy. After dinner, Mother and Aunt Elsie washed the dishes, giving Bessie and me the night off.

I whispered to Bessie, "Whatever happened to the dirty dishes we left in the refrigerator last night?"

"Mary Grace left a note on the bed before she left with Joe this morning. It read, 'Bessie: Guess what Father was doing this morning while Mother and you girls were still sleeping? Washing dishes! I wonder why?' I believe Father kept our secret, because Mother never said a word about it."

Uncle Manuel, Father, Leo and Cousin Robert left right after dinner to go see a Hop-along Cassidy cowboy movie. Father loved cowboy movies. He never missed a Gene Autry or Gary Cooper movie.

Aunt Elsie helped Mother empty our wool-filled mattress. They placed the wool in a box. The soft, curly hair resembled our little lambs outside.

"Remember the days when we would pick wool off the fences along the country roads?" Mother asked her sister-in-law.

"Yes, those were real hard times, but we did sleep on comfortable wool-filled pillows. Della, the Lord's Day is a day for rest."

Mother explained that she wouldn't wash the wool on Sunday, but on Monday.

"Mary Grace will heat water and fill the wringer washer so that when I get home from work, I can do it."

We knew that Mother would then spread the washed wool on a clean sheet in the back of the truck to dry in the sun. Next she would re-stuff the pin-striped mattress sheet and sew up the corner she had taken apart to get the wool out. The next day she would start on another mattress. Mother did this every year when the weather warmer.

Priscilla loved to help Mother with her wool washing. Bessie and I shied away from this job; it didn't look like much fun pulling apart the knotted up wool. Mary Ann sometimes helped, depending on her mood that day.

I didn't like when Mother had to wash clothes. The little house in the back was tiny, half the size of the little room at our old house. There was barely room for the piano and baskets of fruit and vegetables, so Mother now had to keep the washer in a corner of the kitchen. Although it was a big kitchen, it became terribly untidy when Mother was washing. There were clothes and baskets all over the kitchen. I preferred the kitchen to be filled with the aroma of cooking and baking: that was what kitchens were all about.

On wash days, Bessie and I preferred to be outside hanging clothes on the clothesline, although it seemed unreasonable to do it in the winter months. All we could do was pray that the sun would come out, so the clothes on the line could dry.

Mother and Aunt Elsie sat at the kitchen table chatting. Mother peeled green chili peppers which she had roasted on the stove. She'd serve them with fresh cooked pinto beans and fried potatoes. Andy was sound asleep in his mother's arms, and Ruth and Virginia were falling asleep on the couch. We soon went to bed and fell asleep too.

Chapter Ten

Right after Mass the next day, we changed into play clothes and hurried out to feed the little lambs. We held the milk bottles as high as we could with our arms stretched out in front of us, but the lambs still bent their legs at the knees as if they were feeding from their mothers.

Father had built an open fire to heat water in a round galvanized tin tub. He placed big rocks in a circle, about two feet high. Mother plugged in the wringer washer and filled it with wool. Father carried buckets of water into the house for washing and rinsing and continued filling the tin tub. Mary Grace helped Mother spread wool on the sheet laid on Father's truck bed.

Leo was helping Joe build wood and screen cages, because Joe wanted to breed rabbits. He had brought home lattice discarded by his store.

"Bessie, Pauline!" called Father. "Go to the shed and fill a pan with potatoes, then bring them here, please."

We brought the potatoes and watched as Father threw them into the open fire. Leo asked him why.

"As soon as these potatoes bake, we will have them for lunch. Your mother is too busy to cook right now and it's getting close to lunch time."

We loved potatoes, but we had never had open-fire potatoes. Bessie and I waited and watched as Father tended the fire. He cooked and heated water at the same time. He filled buckets of hot water and carried them into the house. When he came back, he grabbed a small shovel and began to sort the charred potatoes from the hot coals.

When the shovel was filled with baked potatoes, he set it on the ground.

"Wait a few minutes for them to cool, and then you may eat them."

"But Dad! They look like black balls."

"That's all right. When you break them open and add salt and pepper, you will find out how tasty they can be!"

Father was right! We quickly ate two each.

Joe laughed.

"You girls look like the guy in the movie 'My Dear Old Swanee'!"

We looked at each other and started to laugh; our faces were black from eating the charred skin on the potatoes. Joe laughed again.

"You look like the people in a fifth-grade play I was in! We sang 'The Battle of Jericho.'"

He walked away, laughing and singing, "Joshua fought the battle of Jericho, Jericho, Jericho, and the walls came a-tumbling down!"

Joe picked up his hammer and went on nailing his rabbit cages and singing.

Mother came outside.

"Ignacio, Mi Corazon, you may stop heating water. We've done three mattresses. We need to rest the rest of the day; we can do our mattress during the week."

"Mother, I thought we were not supposed to work on Sundays," said Bessie.

"Well, sweetheart, Father McDevitt says, 'Some work is necessary and permitted for the common good.' For example, it is necessary for policemen, railroad men, drug store and hospital workers, and working mothers and fathers to do work that is necessary. Washing wool is permitted because one has to do this on a sunny day. It needs a whole day to dry."

Father poured water on the hot coals. Mother took the tin tub and hung it on a nail on the side of the little wood shed.

Priscilla and Mary Ann played school on the porch. Bessie and I went into the kitchen and found that Mary Grace had the kitchen back to normal: very nice and tidy. She was blending garlic and salt into the green chili peppers Mother had roasted and peeled last night, but there were no beans cooking on the stove.

"Are we having that chili with fried potatoes and beans for dinner?" I asked.

"Not today; we didn't get a chance to cook beans today, so Mother said we are having homemade hamburgers and French fries."

"Oh, I love the way Mother cooks hamburger patties! Even well-done, they are still juicy."

"I like mine with a lot of pickles," said Bessie.

Mary Grace turned up the volume on the radio and sang along to "Dear John."

"Mary Grace!" I exclaimed. "That song is scandalous! How can you sing that? Don't you have any feelings for poor John? That girl is leaving John for his brother—shameful!"

She laughed.

"Pauline! It is just a song! This poor John will fall in love again, with someone way better for him, and where did you pick up such a big word 'scandalous'!?"

"On the radio program that Mother listens to sometimes. You must admit that that song is very sad—poor John! Don't you think what she did was shameful?"

"I think you girls need to not spend so much time reading my comic books!"

Mother came in from outside to rest for a little while before she started dinner. We followed her into the front room.

"Hopefully this week will go by quickly," she said. "I'm looking forward to spending time with my mother. I have missed her so! Aunt Frances called this morning and said that they will definitely be here the second week in July. The Sky-High Stampede will take place the following week."

Joe and Leo returned from Meloff's Foods with Royal Crown soda pop, and we all sat down to supper. Father said grace, and we dug into those wonderful homemade hamburgers, a rare treat. Mother and Father went into the front room afterward; they looked worn out. Priscilla and Mary Ann joined them, while Mary Grace cleared the table. The boys went out again, and Bessie and I worked on the dishes.

"What shall we do the first week of summer vacation?" I asked. Mary Grace said, "I've got plans to teach myself how to drive!" "How are you going to manage that?" asked Bessie.

"I heard Father tell Mother that Mr. Corlett hired Cousin Faustino to work for him, so they'll take turns driving to work. On the weeks that Cousin Faustino picks Father up for work, Father's truck will be sitting out front calling to me to get behind the wheel!"

"What if you wreck Father's truck?"

"How could I? I'll have the entire open field on Mr. Corlett's for my driver's training, and I'll just honk at the animals. You girls can come with me for moral support."

"That sounds like a lot of fun!" I exclaimed. "Thank you for inviting us to go with you!"

"You're very welcome! Now don't say anything to Priscilla and Mary Ann—we will surprise them."

Bessie put her hands into the soapy dish water, looking thoughtful. My thoughts drifted back to the time when Grandmother Genevieve took care of us, before Mary Grace was old enough to watch over us. Grandmother would make us gingerbread cookies. The cookies were very hard in texture, but because they came from her special stash, we loved to eat them.

I also loved when Grandmother would go outdoors to stop the trucks selling fruit. The trucks drove up and down every street in her neighborhood. They had no tail gates and had boxes stacked with all kinds of fruit. Sometimes Grandmother would give us a whole apple and sometimes just a quarter of it, depending on how many grandkids she was watching that day.

I have only two unhappy memories of our days at Grandmother's house. Cousin Cecilia, Bessie, Priscilla, and I had to hide in Grandmother's bedroom whenever "La Visitant"—the social worker—was due to arrive.

"You girls have to be very, very still, or this lady will cut off your ears!"

I can't remember which of Grandmother's older children told us that, but we waited in dread until the woman left.

The other unhappy memory was when Cousin Louie and Priscilla would fight. Then Mary Grace would defend Priscilla, and Aunt Phyllis would defend her nephew Louie.

But now that they had all moved to California, we missed them. It seemed that most of Mother's family had moved away.

"Pauline..."

Bessie blew bubbles toward my face from the palm of her hand. I caught them with my hands, and blew them back. She continued to wash.

"I'm excited about going to school tomorrow and the rest of the week!"

"Why is that?"

"Well, I memorized my poem 'Indian Children,' and I'm pretty confident that I know my times table, and I've studied all the lessons at the end of my catechism book!"

"Then you should have a very good last week at school."

"There is just one more thing that would really make it perfect for me."

"What is that, Pauline?"

"I...I was wondering if you would consider letting me wear your very nice outfit to school tomorrow. Please?"

"You mean my white top with the three little buttons in front and my full skirt with the pink flowers?"

"Yes, please?"

"Yes you may, but..."

"I know. I promise to do the dinner dishes two nights by myself. And there is just one more thing."

I squinted my eyes before I dared to spill the words.

"May I please also wear your black shoes with the three little white buttons?"

"I kind of thought you would get around to that, and yes you may. We don't have any other shoes that could go with that skirt."

"Thank you, thank you, Bessie! I promise to be kind and take them off the minute we get home from school!"

We finished the dishes and went into the front room where Mother and Priscilla were sewing up the ends of our clean mattresses. Bessie curled up on the couch with Mary Ann. Father nodded in the accent chair. The radio played very softly, so that we could barely make out the words to a country song.

I went into the bedroom to check for the bed pot. I had drunk all the soda pop left in everyone's glasses when Mary Grace cleared the table after supper. I knew I would need the pot in the middle of the night. After doing the pot check, I joined the girls in the front room.

Mary Ann unbraided her hair. Priscilla flipped the pages of her reader. Bessie and Mother tried to carry the mattress into the bedroom, until finally Father stood up from his chair and did it for them.

"Mommy, do I have a fever?" asked Priscilla. "I don't feel good. My tummy hurts."

Mother put her hand on Priscilla's forehead.

"No, you don't have a fever. Did you go potty today?"

When she nodded, Mother went on, "Mary Grace and Bessie are making the beds; go put your nightgown on and get into bed. If you still don't feel good in the morning, I'll let you stay home with Mary Grace."

"Is Mary Grace sick?"

"No, but she doesn't have classes tomorrow. There is a field trip, and she prefers not to go."

"May I stay home too?" cried Mary Ann. "I may not feel good either tomorrow!"

Mother smiled at her.

"We will see how it goes in the morning. Now get to bed."

When Mary Grace and Bessie came back in, Mother said, "Dr. Roth mentioned to me that there is a bug going around. He said I should have my girls drink plenty of water. Mary Grace, would you please make some atole? And have them drink plenty of water all day."

"What is atole?" I wanted to know.

"Atole is made from roasted blue cornmeal; I like to make a hot cereal out of it. I've been feeding it to you girls since you were toddlers. I like it with salt and pepper and hot milk. It is wholesome nutrition."

Chapter Eleven

Monday morning I jumped out of bed and brushed my hair plenty. I washed my face in a rush. I couldn't wait to get dressed in the full skirt and white top along with the little black shoes.

I climbed on to the bus feeling very smart in my outfit for the day.

Bessie and I walked quickly toward our school, never saying a word about the Ratenias. Maybe if we didn't mention them, they wouldn't appear. It worked; we did not meet up with them. We made our way to our classes.

It was a very good day for me, except when I didn't hear Sister Devota talking to me. Sister Alquin had sent Margie Plane and me into the candy room to return a stack of books. I was busy admiring myself in the outfit I was wearing and was embarrassed when Sister Devota finally got my attention. I felt her eyes tell me, "Pauline, one should not put so much importance on clothes."

I did not have lunch with Bessie. I saw her and Betty Montacelli still in their classroom helping Sister Devota sort books. They would probably have their lunch in the classroom. Bessie had made Spam sandwiches for us to take for lunch. My friend Julia also shared her orange with me. I wondered how Priscilla and Mary Ann were doing at home.

After school, Bessie and I walked down Gun Barrel Road, the next street, so we could avoid meeting up with those mean girls. We were admiring the amazing flowers when we came upon a prone bulldog. Bessie yelped, then moved very slowly behind me. She put her hands on my shoulders and used me as her shield as she talked to the dog. He did not attempt to stand.

Bessie whispered, "Make me me, go to sleep. Make me me, don't wake up."

I tiptoed around him, wondering why he had chosen the middle of the sidewalk to take his nap. We had safely distanced ourselves from the bulldog before Bessie took her hands off my shoulders.

"I'm so sorry, Pauline," she said. "I just reacted. I would not have let him bite you!"

"Oh really? And how would you have stopped him with your hands on my shoulders?"

"I'm really sorry. But look, we are safe now. I'll make a deal with you. You can wear my shoes again tomorrow, okay?"

"Promise? Because for the longest seconds, I was sure he'd wake up, and that I would feel the stubborn grip of his teeth on my leg! And all the time hoping that you could talk this short-haired, stocky, square-jawed dog into going back to sleep if he did wake up!"

"Yes, Yes, Yes. I promise my shoes are yours for another day."

We didn't get to stop and smell the flowers. We hurried to catch our bus. When we got home, Mary Grace was making macaroni con leche. Priscilla and Mary Ann were sitting in the front room curled up on the couch, looking at books.

"Were the girls really sick today?" Bessie asked.

"Well, Priscilla slept off and on all day; she was not active at all. Mary Ann did not complain, but wasn't interested in eating any food. I washed all the windows and window sills. I made enough macaroni for you girls and Leo. I'm going to take a nap."

Leo came in with some news.

"You know that truck we saw drive in to Mr. Corlett's yard? They are looking to rent the house; they asked if the owner was around."

"I just hope Mr. Corlett gets some good people in there. By the way, your friend Gilbert Gold wants you to go by his house whenever you are going out to find scrap metal. He wants to know when you will be returning to school."

"And did you remind him that there are only four days left of this school year?"

"Yes," said Bessie. "I suspect he knows you will not be returning to school."

Mary Grace pushed her macaroni con leche bowl to the side and ripped open a new bag of lentils. She began to remove all foreign material, so that Mother had only to rinse before cooking.

"I wish pinto beans came as clean as these lentils," she said. "Both foods are a very good source of protein. They both taste so good with fried potatoes. I need to go out to the wood shed for potatoes to peel."

"There are some potatoes on the counter," said Bessie. "Leo must have brought them in earlier."

"Oh, good. I think I will go and lie down for a bit. Bessie, please keep an eye on Priscilla and Mary Ann. It looks like they've fallen asleep again. When I get up from my nap we need to make tortilla dough."

Leo came in to tell us that Joe and Cousin Phil were at Mr. Corlett's place.

"Joe is taking the horses out of the corral."

Mary Grace gave Bessie and me permission to go with Leo. We liked watching Joe ride Gypsy. Gypsy, whom Joe had named, was very handsome, with solid hoofs and black flowing mane and tail.

We watched as Joe tried to get Cousin Phil to ride Gypsy.

"I'm not getting on that wild horse! I'll just ride Chopo, thank you!"

"You're crazy. He is not wild; he is just fast!"

"In comparison to Chopo, I say he is wild!"

"Come on, Leo. Ride with me," Joe called as he mounted Gypsy.

Joe reached down and gave Leo his hand and helped him up. Joe was skilled at riding Gypsy. He flicked him with the crop and off they went. Leo held on tightly.

Phil asked Bessie and me, "Do you girls want to climb on Chopo, and I'll walk him around a little?"

We agreed, but wanted to ride together. We were afraid to be up there alone. After about fifteen minutes, we spotted Joe and Leo coming back. Phil helped us down, and I ran back to the house. I felt uneasy seeing Gypsy galloping toward us. He was fast and somehow looked even bigger when he was breathing heavily.

I went into the kitchen singing:

Jimmy Crack corn and I don't care
Jimmy Crack corn and I don't care
Jimmy crack corn and I don't care
My master's gone away
See the pony run, he jump he kick,
He threw my master in the ditch!
All the people wondered why
He was trying to brush away the blue-tail fly.

Mary Grace was at the window watching the boys with the horses.

"Pauline, you have a song for every situation, even for horses."

"I know. I just like to sing a lot."

Bessie came in and asked Mary Grace if she had gotten her nap.

"No. I guess I'm not tired; one would think I'd be bushed after all the housework I did today."

"Maybe it's the excitement about Grandmother's visit, and the school year coming to an end!" said Bessie.

I went outside. Leo was raking the ground where he chops wood. I still had the bulldog on my mind.

"Leo, why would a dog take a nap on the sidewalk instead of the soft lawn?"

"Most likely he had been running and wanted to cool off. Cement is a lot cooler than grass."

"Oh yeah. That would explain it."

Joe and Cousin Phil were gone, leaving only hoof prints on the muddy ground.

I went back into the front room. Priscilla sang "How Much Is That Doggie in the Window?" at the top of her lungs. Mary Ann stroked Goldie our cat, asleep next to her.

I sat next to Mary Ann on the couch. Priscilla stopped singing and asked, "Wouldn't it be wonderful if Grandmother took us back to California with her for a visit?"

"Priscilla and Mary Ann, you two are world travelers! You both have been to California! Father has been there to look for work. Joe and Leo attended school there one year, and you two went with Mother when she went to visit Grandmother."

"Bessie and I are the only ones that have dared set a foot out of Colorado."

Priscilla stood up.

"Come on, Mary Ann, get up off that couch. Let's go travel around the yard! I'm tired of being in the house all day. I feel much better; don't you?"

Mary Grace, Priscilla and Mary Ann returned to school on Tuesday, and soon school was over for the summer.

Archie, Aunt Dolores,
Horacio, and Aunt Mary

Lariat Road running in front of our home

Stone house that Father helped build on Eleven Mile Road

My family pictures from the 1950s

We are sisters, my sisters and I

Father, Mother, and brother Joe

Father and brother Leo

Chapter Twelve

The last week of June and the first week of July were the best. We slept in, woke up to see Mother, Father and Joe leave for work, then we could crawl back into bed if we wanted. Most mornings we'd sleep in till about eight, have breakfast, and play Ball and Jacks until Mary Grace decided it was time to clean house. Leo always did his chores, then went off on some adventure.

Right before noon, Mary Grace would turn on the radio and Roy Rogers' Sons of the Pioneers would entertain us with "Tumbling Tumbleweeds" and "Cool Water." I think Priscilla and I learned to tell time with the Sons of the Pioneers. The clock struck twelve, Father walked in for lunch at 12:15, and they sang these two songs every day at the same time.

After Father was done with the lunch Mary Grace had prepared for us, he would take a short nap. We would take turns combing his hair, and he always fell asleep. We made sure to take out the small braids before he woke up. At 12:45, Father would leave to go back to work, and Joe would arrive with lunch in hand. He too took a fifteen-minute nap, but we never went anywhere near his hair. He would not allow it. Every hair on his head was in place and not to be disturbed.

We finally ran out of days to count, and Grandmother and Aunt Frances would arrive the next day. Then they would rest the whole weekend and visit other family members on Monday and Tuesday. Mother had bought cowboy hats, boots, jeans, and pearlized button pocket shirts for us girls and Cousin Cecilia. The jeans also had pearlized buttons on the back and front pockets.

On Friday morning, we woke early. Mother had taken the day off work. She had us bathe early, so the house could look nice and tidy.

I couldn't believe my eyes when the back door of their car opened and Cecilia stepped out. I saw the most beautiful shoes on her feet. We all ran up to the car to hug and kiss, then hug and kiss again. I never wanted to let go of Grandmother. We all hung on to her; she and Mother hugged and cried. Aunt Phyllis wanted to bring her suitcase in right away.

Cecilia bent down and took her shoes off. They were white flats with ornamental detail. The beads were so small, but they looked like jewels. I had never seen shoes like this. She took them in her hand and prepared to throw them back into the car through the open window.

"Cecilia, you may put your shoes in our closet if you like."

"Will you do that for me, please?"

"Sure I will; they are the prettiest shoes I've ever seen."

"You may wear them if they fit you. They hurt my feet."

"Oh thank you, I will! I mean they do fit!"

Cecilia smiled at me, and I thought how she was still as nice as she was when we were in first grade together. We picked up where we left off; it was as though she had never moved away. She remembered all our names, even though it had been three years. I really believed she had missed us as much as we had missed her.

We all stayed indoors for a couple of hours, getting reacquainted with Grandmother, Mother's youngest sister Aunt Phyllis, and Mother's other sister Aunt Frances.

Mother had arranged with Father's sister Aunt Raquel for Leo and Joe to sleep at her house for the days that we had our California family with us. That evening, Cecilia suggested that after Leo and Joe left for the night, she and I could entertain the adults. She told me we could have a powwow and dance around like Indians. I was glad when Mother said, "Okay, Girls, go put on your nightgowns now."

We spent Monday and Tuesday showing Cecilia around the farm. She seemed to have fun being a country girl, except when she stepped on broken glass in the creek. The California gal had a big gash on her foot.

The Sky-High Stampede finally arrived with its daily parades. Mother braided our hair, and we dressed in our boots and cowgirl outfits. Cecilia could only be half a cowgirl, because she couldn't wear her boots over her bandaged foot.

The girls and I felt bad for her, but she didn't seem to mind. She was a good sport. She was happy with the moccasins her mother bought for her. She told us she was so happy to spend time with her very favorite cousins. In a day or so, she was walking in the creek again.

In the days that followed, we enjoyed looking at the handsome floats. Monte Vista Flour Mill, Monte Vista Creamery, L. L. Fassett Lumber Company, Dairy Queen, and a dozen other businesses were represented. The cowgirls looked so smart on their well-groomed horses.

The highlight of the parade for us was seeing Uncle Louie on his Appaloosa horse. Mother's brother Louie was a real cowboy. As a young man he was known for breaking in wild horses. Grandmother was very pleased to see her eldest boy in the parade, but happy that he had stopped breaking in wild horses. Grandmother had feared that one day he would fall and break his neck.

After a few days of playing the part of cowgirls, the Sky-High Stampede was finished for another year. We went back to enjoying our summer break, thrilled that we still had our wonderful company for another week.

Cecilia made a fuss whenever Aunt Frances announced that they were going to visit other families. Grandmother pacified her by suggesting that one of us girls could go along to keep her company. On the day Cecilia picked me to go visiting with them, we went to visit her Uncle Eloy, her father Antonio's brother. She had a lot of cousins. It was a fun visit, but I missed being with my sisters.

Sometimes we just did things around the farm. The last two days of their visit, Grandmother just stayed home with us. On their last day, we took Cecilia over to Mr. Corlett's property to play on the hay wagon. We asked Cecilia questions about her life in California. We also introduced her to Leo's favorite song.

"Would you like us to sing this Acuff song for you?"

"Sure, Mary Ann, but what is an Acuff?"

"Acuff is a country singer and songwriter. Roy Acuff," said Priscilla.

"Where have you been that you don't know this?" asked Bessie.

"I guess I haven't been listening to all this country music like you cowgirls! But do go right ahead and sing for me. I'll enjoy listening." She didn't need to ask us twice. We sang:

From the great Atlantic Ocean to the wide Pacific shore,
From the queen of flowy mountains to the south bell by the shore,
She is mighty tall and handsome, and known quite well by all
She's the combination called the Wabash Cannonball.
Listen to the jingle, the rumble and the roar
As she glides along the woodlands,
Through the hills and by the shore.
Hear the mighty rush of that engine
Hear the lonesome hoboes call
He's a riding through the jungle on the Wabash Cannonball.

"That was very nice! What exactly is a Wabash Cannonball?" My sisters and I looked at each other.

"You must know, Pauline. You were singing the loudest."

"Leo told me that Wabash is the name of a railroad company, and they called a train that carried both people and freight the combination of the Wabash Cannonball."

"Very interesting. I like that song! You girls sing it very nicely."

The hour arrived when we had to hug and kiss Grandmother goodbye. Cecilia was so lucky to have Grandmother in her life every day. I handed Cecilia her white beaded shoes and waved goodbye.

Mother kept us busy over the weekend. I knew she was feeling blue after her mother and sisters had driven away. All her sisters had moved to California. The girls and I promised each other that when we grew up, we would never move so far away that years had to go by before we could see each other.

On Monday morning, Mary Grace got us up for breakfast after Mother and Father had left for work.

"I think it's time we stopped moping around," she said. "It's not as though we'll never see Grandmother again. Being gloomy is not going to bring her and Cecilia back to us. Cheer up! I have something to share with you!

"Cousin Faustino came by this morning to pick Father up for work! So, after we clean house, we are going for a very slow ride in Father's truck."

Priscilla and Mary Ann looked at each other with widened eyes. "But you don't drive!"

"That is the whole point, Priscilla. I'm going to do some driver's training, and you girls will give me moral support."

"I can give a lot of that!" said Mary Ann.

"I can too," said Priscilla, "if you'll just tell me what it is."

"Moral support means that if I make a mistake or get scared behind the wheel, you can encourage me to take it slow and try again."

"Okay, we know how to do that," said Priscilla.

"It also means that Father is not to know until I get really good behind the wheel!"

We were done with breakfast in no time at all. Bessie and I started in the kitchen. Mary Grace asked Priscilla to sweep all along the baseboards in the kitchen and the front room.

"Priscilla, you may have Mary Ann hold the dust pan for you. Okay, sweetie? I'll be doing the bedrooms. It won't take me long to make the beds and dust mop."

Leo came in to let us know he'd be going to Cousin Jimmy's house.

"Bessie, will you please tell Mary Grace that I'll be home sometime after lunch."

Mary Grace came into the kitchen to see if we were done with the dishes.

"We need to get going now, Girls. Father is coming home for lunch, and it is already after nine. I heard Leo say he was leaving for a couple of hours. It's best if he is not here. He would shake his head 'no' and then I would lose my nerve!"

We piled into the truck, and Mary Grace got behind the wheel. My sisters and I knew to be very quiet, and let her do whatever she

needed to do to get the truck moving. She put the key in the ignition
and turned on the motor. She began to talk to herself.

"Let's see now. I shall put my foot on the gas pedal. It will feed
gas to the engine and this will make the truck go."

The truck started to move forward slowly.

"Now, Girls, I want you all to be very still, because I need to
concentrate. I need to get on the public road for a little bit, so we can
get across to Mr. Corlett's property. There is more open range to drive
without hitting anything."

We did as she instructed and were very quiet. We slowly crept to
the end of our driveway. Mary Grace brought the truck to a stop as
we approached Lariat Road. She looked to the left, to the right, then
to the left again, and then to the right again.

"No cars coming in either direction."

She again looked to the left, and then to the right. My sisters
and I just looked and listened.

"Okay, here we go!"

"No cars coming, Mary! Let's go!" said Bessie finally.

We all laughed as we drove over to Mr. Corlett's place.

"So far, so good. I've been watching Father and Joe when they
drive, and I think I've got the hang of it!"

"Come on, Mary Grace! Let's drive far! Over by where the cows
crowd," Mary Ann suggested.

"I don't want to run over the cow pies; we won't have time to
wash the tires before Father comes home for lunch."

"I know!" cried Priscilla, "We can wash the truck while you fix
lunch for us!"

"Okay, but let me know if I'm coming too close to a cow, or
we'll be eating beef every day for six months!"

We all laughed. We drove back and forth and around in circles.

"This is so much fun!" said Priscilla.

"Will you please watch out for the potholes?" Bessie begged. "I
don't want to get one of Mother's headaches!"

"Well...excuse me! It's not like I've been driving forever."

"I know, but the truck is bouncing up and down."

"I think I just need to go slower and head back. I don't want to
use up all the gasoline."

As we approached the little house at the back of the property, Mary Grace accidentally accelerated. We rammed into the one-room shed and jerked to a stop.

We looked at Mary Grace, and she began to laugh.

"That reminded me of a ride at the Sky-High Stampede last week! I'd better check to see if there's any damage done to Father's truck! Are you girls okay?"

We all jumped out to look. There was a small dent in the wall of the shed, and the truck looked fine.

"Fortunately, there is no damage to the truck and you girls are not injured! Thank Jesus my foot must have been light on the gas pedal!"

Mary Grace parked the truck where Father had left it.

"Do you want us to wash it?" I asked.

"No. After lunch we can all go out to wash it, after Father and Cousin Faustino return to work. Remember, Girls, not a word!"

Father came in for lunch at the usual time. He and Cousin Faustino were out the door by twelve-thirty. Father didn't take a nap, and Joe did not come home for lunch today.

We walked out to say goodbye to Father, and Mary Grace followed with a bucket and rags. We tagged along after her.

"Bessie, will you please pull the water hose this way?"

Mary Ann and Priscilla both wanted to hold the hose to rinse the soap off the truck.

"How about you both get in the cab of the truck and wash the windows?" suggested Mary Grace. "When I rinse the outside of the truck, you can pretend that it's raining."

They each grabbed a wet rag and climbed inside.

Bessie and I did the outside of the windows. Soon we were done, and Mary Grace told us to play outside, so she could nap. We removed our shoes and cleaned off the mud.

Bessie started to laugh.

"Look at your shoes, and then look at your feet."

We all giggled. We had mud between our toes; our shoes now looked cleaner than our feet. We followed Bessie to the creek and waded until the skin on our feet wrinkled. We loved walking in the creek when the warm sun glared on the water.

Sometime after that, Mary Grace got her driver's license, and we'd often see her drive, with Father on the passenger side. It pleased us, because they usually exited the truck with white bags in their hands. Sometimes Mary Grace drove to the bakery and treated him to those wonderful cream puffs. Then she got to drive home while Father enjoyed the pastry. It was a dead giveaway when we saw white powdered sugar on his mustache.

By the second week of August, the weather was perfect. We spent our days outside. Leo was staying close to home these days; Mary Grace had taken a job at the Dairy Queen. On the days that she was scheduled to close, she was allowed to bring home the ice cream left in the ice cream maker. Life was great!

One Friday around midday, Leo and Cousin Jimmy knocked at the kitchen window. Bessie and I were at the counter cleaning pinto beans. Leo signaled, and Bessie opened the back door for them. Jimmy and Leo dropped two gunny sacks on the floor. Priscilla and Mary Ann came running into the kitchen.

"What are you carrying in those gunny sacks?"

"Candy and more candy!" announced Jimmy.

We all looked at Leo. He smiled and nodded as he knelt on the floor and began to untie the knot on one of the sacks.

"That's right! A whole sack just for you girls! The second one is for Jimmy, his brother Danny and his sisters."

"But, Leo," said Bessie. "How did you get all this candy?"

Leo continued to pull and tug on the tight knot.

"Well, one could call this candy 'half and half,'" he said with a chuckle.

"Half and Half is Mother's favorite drink!" said Priscilla.

"You'd better explain what you are talking about," said Jimmy.

Leo stopped tugging on the sack.

"You know how there are two little grocery stores not far from each other? One is on Gun Barrel Road, and the other is on Lariat where you see most of the adobe houses."

"Yes, of course," said Bessie.

"Well, the one by the adobe homes caught on fire early this morning. On my way to Jimmy's house, I saw the firemen working to put it out. Later, we rode by on our bicycles, and one of the firemen called to us and asked if we would like to take the half-burnt candy. Jimmy and I filled our scrap metal gunny sacks. We picked the boxes that were not burned too badly. I found one box that had not been touched by the flames, and I believe it's the candy you girls always buy!"

"Lipstick candy! Lipstick candy!" called Priscilla.

By this time Jimmy had worked the knot out and handed the opened sack to Leo.

Leo dumped it out on the kitchen floor. We were so pleased to see all that candy; we didn't care that some of the corners were burnt. We ate some and saved the lipstick candy for when we played grownup sisters.

After dinner, Joe, Leo, and Mary Grace left right away. They were going with friends to the drive-in. Tonight was the first showing of some pirate movie that would be running weekly episodes starring Richard Egan. We had seen the previews. I thought Richard Egan was very handsome, but I did not like to see him in that black and white striped tight-fitting t-shirt.

Mother had made fried trout and had told us to be very careful because of the small bones. The girls and I each had our turn with Father standing behind our chair and reaching over to our dinner plate to check our fish for bones.

"I don't think I want to eat this fish," I said. "I only like Mother's breaded salmon patties."

"Let me ask you something, Pauline," said Father. "Do you know what Jesus fed the multitude of people that had come to the hillside where He preached the word of the Lord?"

"Yes, Daddy. He fed them loaves of bread and some fish."

"Well, it would please your mother and me if you would learn to eat trout. Look, I've cleaned it for you. No bone left to worry about. Trout is a small fish of the salmon family. So you see, if you like salmon, you will like trout."

Bessie was quietly working on her piece of fish, double checking for any bones. Father smiled at Mother and they continued with their conversation.

"Oh Daddy," said Priscilla. "Look at Mary Ann and me eating! We love this fish, especially since you cleaned it for us! May we have a cup of black coffee just the way you like you it, to enjoy with a cinnamon roll when we are done with our supper?"

"You are allowed to have a little black coffee, but only on Saturdays when your mother fixes hot cakes."

Bessie whispered to Priscilla, "Nice try, but your sweet talk of 'good fish' didn't work with Father. It didn't get you a cup of coffee."

Priscilla rolled her eyes at Bessie and stuck out her tongue.

"Well, like Joe always says, 'There is no harm in trying.'"

Bessie smiled and shook her head.

Priscilla was finished.

"Come on, Mary Ann! Let's go color in your Jimmy Duarte coloring book."

I didn't want to leave the table, although I too was done with my supper. I wanted to listen to Mother and Father's conversation. Joe also said one can't learn if one doesn't listen. But then, he would turn around and call me a listening parrot. It hurt my feelings when he and Mary Grace called me a parrot, but I liked listening to grownups talk. Mother didn't scold me for it, so I wasn't doing anything wrong.

Bessie got up and started to clear the table of dishes. I didn't make a move to help, and she didn't invite my help. After a while, I joined Priscilla and Mary Ann in the front room. Mother and Father would not be gardening this evening, because it was windy outside.

"Guess what?" I said. "We are going to attend a wedding tomorrow! I heard Mother tell Father that she'd like him to help her in the morning by heating water for us to bathe. She is preparing to bake a couple of cakes to take tomorrow."

We returned to the kitchen. Mother always made a little cake that we got to taste before she made the big ones. She'd say, "I make this little one to see if my batter came out right, and to see if it is going to rise, and not go flat. This little one is a tester."

Mary Ann yelled, "Pi-do-me; el cake-e-toe!"

"Mary Ann! Bessie and I called it already, but you know Mother always makes us share."

"I know," Mary Ann replied, "but I always have to call for it."

Bessie had stacked the few dinner dishes to be washed with the baking dishes afterward. Mother sent us to bed early, so we could get an early start.

On Saturday, we drove to the church in Alamosa. I had never been in this church before, but it did have a big cross with Jesus on it, just like ours at Saint Joseph's. After the ceremony, we drove to the bride's home for the reception. I liked listening to the music; the musicians played guitars, harmonicas and banjos. There was a lot of food, including cakes and sweet breads. Mother's cakes were the best, with her special homemade caramelized frosting made from brown sugar, butter, and cream.

Mother told us to go to the food tables and serve ourselves. She said the dancing would begin soon. Mother knew we would want to get good seats to watch the grownups dance.

Bessie, standing behind me in line, nudged me and whispered, "Look!"

To my surprise, I saw my best girlfriend standing with her brother.

"How funny!"

"Her parents might be related to the bride."

"Are we?"

"No, but Mother and Father are good friends with the groom's parents, Mr. and Mrs. Mercado. The groom is brother to Cousin Faustino's wife."

Julia finally looked up and saw me looking at her. She smiled and looked away shyly.

We hadn't seen each other since school let out for the summer. It hadn't been that long, and we were acting like distant friends. I hoped we would continue to be best friends when we got back to school.

After we ate, the musicians took their places in one corner of the room. A man sang a dedication to the married couple. We didn't know the bride, but she looked so beautiful we couldn't help but stare. After a while, she left the room, and we stepped outside where other children were playing. Leo and another boy were tying different knots on a rope.

Suddenly there was a commotion, and everyone began talking at the same time in excited voices.

Julia ran up to me and said, "Pauline, isn't it exciting?"

"What is going on?"

"The bride has been stolen from the groom!"

"What do you mean?"

"It happens all the time at home weddings! The teens and young adults steal the bride, and they will only return her if the groom makes arrangements to rent a hall for a dance. If he has to, he will pass the hat for money to pay for it."

"But why?" I asked. "The musicians in the house play very good music."

"Yes, but the young people want to dance and this house is too small! Only two or three couples can dance at a time."

We went to find Mother and Father. We watched them dance a little. They danced to "La Valse Li Ana." One of the musicians sang, "Put your little foot; put your little foot; put your little foot right out! Put a step to the right; put a step to the left," and so on. We loved to see Mother in Father's arms as they danced, especially to the "Tennessee Waltz."

The reception was over and it was time to head home, but there was still no sign of the bride.

I said goodbye to Julia.

"I hope we run into each other again before school starts!"

"Yeah, me too!"

On the way home, I fell asleep worrying about the groom who had lost his bride. I woke up when I heard Mother's voice telling Leo not to be gone too long.

"Come on, Girls, wake up. We are home."

"Mother, when will the groom get his bride back? This is terrible! How will we ever find out?"

"It's okay, Pauline," she assured me. "He will get her back as soon as the owner of the hall opens the doors for the young folks to dance. The hall is only a mile from the bride's home. The owner is happy for the business, so I'm sure he won't mind such short notice. Now go in and change before you play. As soon as your father changes from his gabardine slacks into jeans, we will join you outside."

Soon Father headed for the woodpile and grabbed an axe. Mother began taking towels off the clothesline. Priscilla and Mary Ann made little mounds of dirt and ran magnets over them to see how much iron their magnet could draw to it. Bessie sat on a log and watched as Father sharpened the axe.

"Mother, do you think the bride and groom stayed to dance with the young folks or was the groom upset with them?"

I was still worried.

"I hope he isn't too upset, Sweetheart. This happens all the time. Usually, even when a bride and groom don't want a big dance, they are still prepared in case the bride gets taken away."

"Did the young folks take you away at your wedding?"

"No, Sweetie. Your father didn't leave my side for a second. Not for a second. His sisters escorted me to the ladies' room, but other than that I stayed just where I wanted to be—close to your father through the reception.

"Pauline, it will probably make you feel better to know that the groom's parents, Mr. and Mrs. Mercado, are coming for a visit tomorrow afternoon. I'm sure we will hear all about the dance."

Father walked over to Mother and added, "I'm sure, though, that 'El Tesoro' talks will dominate the conversation."

Bessie and I took notice. We would definitely be hanging around the adults tomorrow, to hear what they had to say about finding "the treasure."

Leo and Jimmy raced up on their bikes, put on their brakes, and skidded to a stop right in front of Father.

"Just another few inches and you'd have run me down!"

"Sorry, Dad."

"Sorry, Uncle Ignacio."

"Father! We just came from the dumps, and they have a new caretaker!"

"Oh yeah!" put in Jimmy. "I have never seen a man like him! His skin is very, very dark, and his hair is black and curly! Uncle, why is he so dark?"

"He is from a large group of people who come from Africa. He is a black man. Only four percent of our state population has African roots as he does. I don't believe he has any family here; he is the only one that I have seen here. When I was in California, I saw many ethnic groups of people from all over the world."

"May we go to the dumps to see this man?"

"If and when I have the need to go to the dumps, you girls may come along," said Father. "But I will not make a special trip to stare at this man. He is just a man like me; the only thing different is the color of his skin. We are all God's children."

Right after Mass on Sunday morning, a couple of Joe's friends drove up to go rabbit hunting. Leo and Jimmy went, with Joe, Phil, and some other young men. Mary Grace spent time with Phyllis. Mister and Mrs. Mercado's visit was welcomed, but we didn't learn much more about "El Tesoro." The discussion only led to more speculation as to where the treasure could have been buried when the French ran from the Indians.

"If you think about it," said Father, "there was no going back for the treasure. Colorado settlers and the Army fought the Indians until around 1885, so the French had no chance to return for what the Indians felt belonged to them. My great-grandfather probably lost the desire to return after watching the men of the French Expedition being killed by the Indians. He was one of only two to survive. He went back to France, and I don't know what happened to the other man. My grandfather Guillermo said that the two men parted ways and did not keep in touch. My great-grandfather kept the map and gave it to Grandfather Guillermo LeBlanc."

Mr. Mercado listened and asked Father questions, but Father knew only what his mother had told him.

"We had better never lose our silver rings where the Ratenias live," I said to Bessie. "The ones Father made for us at Lariat. We would never be able to go back to look for them because they would chase us, just like the Indians chased the French men."

It was still early in the evening when the Mercados said their goodbyes, assuring us that their son the groom had gotten his bride back.

Joe came in and took a short nap, then cleaned up to go see his girlfriend Dolly. I watched as Joe brushed his teeth, brushed his tongue, and gargled.

Leo came in.

"Father, Mr. Corlett asked if I could take my BB gun and shoot at the magpies. He said, 'Those darn black and white birds with the long tails and dark bills perch on my cattle and sheep to pick off the ticks and maggots, but they're overdoing it and causing infections on these poor animals.' He gave me a one-dollar bill!"

"All right, Son. You'll earn money doing what you like to do—hunting!"

"I'll be back in about an hour."

"Okay, Son."

Mother fried chicken breasts and drumsticks at the kitchen stove. She seemed deep in thought. A pot of potatoes and a pot of corn boiled.

Cousin Jimmy had left behind a comic book, and my sisters and I examined it. It was awful! One page showed a man sitting at a table with a bottle of liquor. In the bottle, he could see an ear, a nose, and a finger floating. If that's what alcohol does to you, when I grow up I'd never have any! This was the most horrible comic book I'd ever seen! But I couldn't put it down.

Bessie glanced through the newspaper, and Priscilla showed Mary Ann how to outline with a color crayon in the coloring book.

Mary Grace and Phyllis came in.

"Mother, I'll put my stuff away and then help you mash potatoes."

Mother didn't reply; she seemed very quiet.

Father came in to wash his hands with cold running water.

"What's wrong, Mi Vida? You look worried."

"I've been thinking about that awful day."

"Yes, I know. I've also had that day on my mind, ever since Don Mercado brought it up. He told me that he had come across an old newspaper that covered it."

Father kissed Mother on the cheek as he finished drying his hands.

"A sheep man, Pat Maes, killed three men with a heavy C rifle after the Deputy Sheriff shot his wife and son. The three men were Raymond Martinez, Edward Dominguez, and Manuel Ortega."

I lost interest in the comic book. I thought I'd probably stick to "love" comic books in the future anyway. Bessie looked up from her reading and watched Mother and Father too. Priscilla and Mary Ann had followed Mary Grace and Phyllis into the bedroom.

The conversation saddened Mother, as any remembrance of that awful day always did.

Mother said, "The question that haunts me is, if it was true that the Deputy Sheriff did shoot Maes's wife and son as the newspaper stated, what possible reason would Maes have for turning his rifle on his brother-in-law Manuel, who was just sitting in his truck while the sheriff questioned Maes on stolen sheep."

A witness had claimed that there was another side to the story, but that didn't change the fact that Mother lost her father that day. He left behind a very large family.

Thank goodness for Mary Grace. At that moment, she and Phyllis came into the kitchen laughing, and Mother seemed to snap out of her sadness.

"Mrs. Montoya, what is that liquid you added to your gravy mixture?"

"Oh, Phyllis dear, I mustn't reveal my family secret to you. Some recipes are meant to stay in the family."

We all saw the surprised look on Phyllis' face. Mother put her arm around her quickly.

"I'm just teasing, Sweetheart. Of course you may see what I add to my gravy!"

Phyllis smiled as Mother showed her secret ingredient. Then Mother took a teaspoon and spooned some gravy for Phyllis to taste.

"Yummy! This is the best brown gravy I've ever tasted! It is so good!"

"Just wait till you pour some over mashed potatoes; it's to die for!" said Mary Grace.

We agreed; Mother was the best cook in the world. After dinner, a car pulled into our yard. Uncle Jim, Mother's brother and Jimmy's dad had come to visit Mother and Father. It was a beautiful warm summer evening, so they visited outside. Uncle Jim had come by himself, leaving Aunt Louisa, Danny, Jimmy, Grace, Norma, Eileen, and Brenda at home.

Mother called to Bessie and me to come out and greet Uncle Jim.

"Your Uncle Jim came over to invite the four of you girls and Leo to join him and his family on an outing tomorrow. Would you like him to pick you up in the morning?"

We looked at Uncle Jim, who smiled and added, "I want to take your cousins on what I believe will be our last summer picnic. You need to be ready early if you wish to join us. Your Aunt Louisa is packing lunch for us all as we speak."

We thanked him for the invitation and promised to be ready.

"Where are you taking them?" Mother wanted to know.

"Louisa and I took the children out to picnic off of Conejos River a couple of weeks ago. The mountainous area is breathtakingly beautiful, and we were surrounded by acres of National Forest. One feels hugged by the aspen and pine trees."

Father added, "No matter where you end up in the San Luis Valley, you will be surrounded by spectacular views."

"Jim, if you happen to drive by Our Lady of Guadalupe Catholic Church, please point it out to my children," requested Mother. "It was the first church to be built in the San Luis Valley and the oldest parish in Colorado."

"The original adobe church was destroyed and rebuilt. Actually, it has been rebuilt twice," added Uncle Jim.

Mother laid out our blue jeans and shirts, and sent us to bed early. The next morning, bright and early, we all piled into Uncle Jim's car.

He parked the car near a small river where we settled for our wonderful picnic. The cold mountain water moved swiftly and produced small rapids. The water splashed hard against the rocks and the Nehi soda-pop bottles that Uncle Jim had placed in the river.

We had our choice of strawberry, orange, grape, and chocolate, along with Royal Crown and Coke. A watermelon sat alone between some rocks. Seeing all the different colors in the water gave me a warm joyous feeling, like when Mother and Father put up our Christmas tree. I will never forget that special outing with our cousins, Uncle Jim and Aunt Louisa.

By the end of the month, Mr. Corlett had rented our old home, so our roller-skating rink was ours no longer. Soon we had only a few weeks left of summer break. We spent hours playing baseball. Cousin

Jimmy had taken pity on us when he saw us improvising with a stick and homemade ball made from rags, and given us a real ball and bat.

We spent a lot of time in the creek too, from which we could spy on the new tenants next door. This family consisted of a mother and father, three daughters and two sons. After a couple of days, the older of the two boys came over and introduced himself to Leo as Felix Maes. He was no relation to Pat Maes, who shot Grandfather Manuel. He told Leo that his father, Don Maes, would be working for Mr. Corlett's brother at another farm. He also mentioned that his older sister Beatrice was three years older than Joe; his other sister Perfidia was sixteen; and the youngest girl Juana was eight. His baby brother Eugene was two years old. Felix himself was fourteen and would be attending public school. His mother was a homemaker.

Mother told us that she expected us to keep to ourselves whenever she and Mary Grace were at work.

"You may play with the little girl, but only if Mary Grace or I are at home."

She told Leo, "Please don't encourage Felix to come over to our house. I would like to get to know these people a little better before we get too friendly. I need you to watch over your sisters more now that your older sister is working, please."

Bessie began to talk to Mother about school clothes and supplies. She suggested that it might be good to buy a few things on Saturday if we went grocery shopping. The moment Bessie mentioned school supplies, I could smell the aroma of clear paste and the rubber of an eraser. The thought of a chalkboard gave me a nervous stomach. On the other hand, summer ends and autumn follows. Autumn was my favorite season, with the welcome heat from the coal-burning furnace, the smell from the wood stove of baked apples, cinnamon rolls, roasted pine nuts, and apple butter—Mother's favorite jam.

Cecilia, Aunt Phyllis, Priscilla, Bessie, and Pauline

Mother Della and
Grandmother Genevieve

Brother Joe

Jr. and Uncle Louie

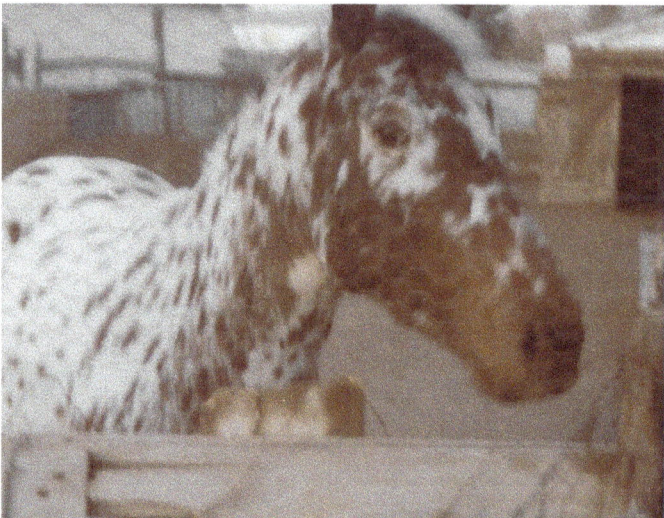

Uncle Louie's show horse for yearly parades
in Monte Vista, Colorado

Chapter Thirteen

On Saturday morning, I woke to the sound of country music. I jumped out of bed to join my family in the kitchen. Mother had scrambled eggs and fried bacon. She also had the washing machine out.

"After breakfast, I want you to get cleaned up, but no baths this morning. I only have two more loads to wash, and then we will be going to shop for groceries."

Father parked the truck in front of the Boy's Market, but he didn't come into the store with us. A friend or relative always happened to see Father sitting in the truck and Father enjoyed these visits, for they made his waiting time go by quickly.

Bessie and I checked out the comic books. We didn't notice one of Father's long lost cousins come up on us. She swung a loaf of bread and hit Bessie gently on the head with it. Mother winked at the bewildered Bessie.

"That lady Amanda is kind of crazy," she whispered to me. "What kind of way is that to greet a person?"

I giggled and said, "And what kind of way is that to treat white Rainbo bread?"

Bessie gave me a sideways look and continued to complain of the injustice done to her.

"I don't get it," she grumbled. "First Aunt Louise tells me that I am a sassy young lady, then our good Bishop tapped me hard on the cheek on my Confirmation day, and now I'm greeted in this manner? What have I done to be treated this way?"

"Bessie, I think you are having one of those moments. You know, an 'I'm feeling sorry for myself' moment."

"Oh, really? Is that what you think I'm doing? Feeling sorry for myself?"

"Look, I don't mean to sound insensitive."

"Oh, really? Do tell!"

"Well, just think about it. You were not the only one that got a light slap on the cheek; your whole Confirmation class did too. And Aunt Louise wasn't too happy with the rest of us girls, either!"

"Oh, come on, Pauline; let's go find Mother and the girls."

By this time, Mother's groceries had been checked, boxed, and placed in front of a window to be carried out when one of the baggers was free to help. Bessie and I placed our large bag of Spanish salted peanuts and "love" comic books into one of the boxes. We didn't realize that this meant we were not charged for them.

"God works in mysterious ways," I said later, when Mary Grace brought this to our attention.

"You may justify getting these items free today, Pauline, but now that you know, it will be stealing if you put them in a box after Mother's groceries have been rung up."

"I know. We would never do it intentionally, Missy!"

"See that you don't, or you will have to confess that to Father McDevitt."

"Mary Grace, may we just enjoy here what we got free?" asked Bessie.

"You may indeed, because it wasn't intentional. But put extra money in the collection basket this Sunday!"

I felt much better when I heard that. Priscilla and Mary Ann stayed outdoors with Father and our dog Blacky. I helped put groceries away. Bessie peeled and sliced potatoes for frying. Mary Grace rolled and cooked tortillas. Mother fried ground beef to add to a thickened mixture of flour, water, salt and powdered New Mexico chili. After cooking, we knew Mother would serve it over country-fried potatoes with freshly-cooked pinto beans—yummy!

Priscilla and Mary Ann came in to announce that the neighbor was outside.

"Joe and Cousin Phil called out to that girl Perfidia."

"What do you mean they called out to her?" asked Mary Grace. "What did they say to her?"

"'It's not the beauty, it's the butte!' What does that mean?"

"Never mind," said Mother. "You girls go into the front room until supper is ready."

She stepped out and called to the boys; she did not look happy.

"I've never heard that one before," said Mary Grace. "It sounds like something Phil would say. I don't care much for that girl, but that is not a nice thing to say to a girl."

"Why don't you like her?" asked Bessie. "You don't even know her."

"She is not very friendly. I waved to her the other day and she turned and looked the other way."

"Maybe she is very shy."

"I don't know. It's not like I was trying to carry on a conversation with her. I only waved. She's just strange."

After dinner, Mother and Father pulled the weeds that had invaded our beautiful green lawn. Priscilla and Mary Ann turned somersaults on the grass. Blacky and Goldie were also relaxing on the lawn.

Mary Grace and Phyllis gave Bessie and me a break from the dinner dishes. We grabbed our comic books and peanuts and went out to lie in the grass to read.

"Bessie, I turned ten this past July, so that means that I will make my Confirmation this year, right?"

"Yes. I made mine when I was ten years old. You will need to know all your prayers, the Ten Commandments, the seven sacraments, how to pray the rosary, and the Stations of the Cross. If I were you, I would start today to memorize the Apostles' Creed. For me it was the longest and hardest. Sister Devota told our class that it's our Blessed Mother Mary's favorite prayer. It came down to us from the time of the Apostles, and she wants us to say it frequently as a profession of faith. You will find it in your catechism book on the page where it shows how to pray the rosary. It is the first prayer you say after you look at the crucifix for a moment, and make the Sign of the Cross: 'In the name of the Father, and of the Son, and of the Holy Spirit, Amen.'"

"And after you memorize the Apostles' Creed, Pauline, you can pray it out loud so that I can learn it from you!" said Priscilla.

"It wouldn't hurt for you to get a head start for when you make your Confirmation," agreed Bessie.

On Sunday morning, Father fixed oatmeal for breakfast. Mother stayed in bed with one of her migraine headaches.

After we cleaned up the kitchen, Father said we would go to the dumps. Bessie, Priscilla, Mary Ann, and I climbed into the truck. We drove about five miles, and as we approached, the burnt odor hit our nostrils. We walked around the perimeter looking at the trash people had tossed. We spotted a small box full of comic books, but Bessie reminded us that they would be full of germs and would be smelly. Mother wouldn't want us picking up anything from the dumps. As we neared the truck, Father was talking with the caretaker, and we realized that this was the man Cousin Jimmy and Leo had mentioned. He was indeed very dark, but as Father had said, he was just a man.

Mother was up and dressed when we returned home. She was at the stove making Panocha, a sweet dessert made from blue cornmeal and sugar. After a couple of hours, she asked us if we wanted to take a ride with her and Father to visit her brother, Uncle Louie. Visits to Uncle Louie were very rare. Bessie wanted to stay home with Mary Grace, and Mary Ann wanted to stay with Bessie, so Priscilla and I went. We watched Cousin Gilbert and Cousin Joseph feed the Appaloosa horses.

On our way home, Mother told Father that Uncle Louie had mentioned that Cousin Estella, Phil's mother, had had a baby boy. She named him Johnny Ray after his father.

Priscilla asked if Cousin Phil had any sisters.

"He has one sister named Sophie, who's the same age as Bessie. We will have to invite her over one day."

When we returned home in the afternoon, we saw that Cousin Faustino and his family had arrived. Priscilla ran into the house and beat me to the baby. We called little Bobby, "Bobbito."

Mary Grace and Bessie were getting ready to go see a movie.

"May I go too, please?" I begged.

"What about Priscilla and Mary Ann? They will want to go too."

Priscilla and Mary Ann were taking turns holding the baby. Mary Grace told Mother that she, Bessie, and I would be back in a couple of hours. Priscilla and Mary Ann didn't take any interest in going.

"I can't wait to see this movie! Joe and Dolly saw it last evening and Dolly told me, 'Mary Grace, you just have to see this film! It's entitled "Three Coins in the Fountain"; it is so romantic.'"

When we returned home, Joe, Phil, and Leo jumped into the truck.

"Bessie, Pauline, will you girls heat water for me to bathe when I return from rabbit hunting, and place the tub in the bedroom for me, please?" Joe smiled at us, and as usual, we aimed to please him.

Mother was baking a leg of lamb in the oven. We could use the whole top of the wood burning stove. We placed four pots of water on the burners, and a bucket of cold water in the bedroom next to the tin tub. We watched and waited for Joe's return, standing guard over the hot water on the stove so no one could take a drop. We finally heard the truck pull into the yard. We could now go out to play.

Joe was impressed that we had done what he asked.

"I didn't think you even heard me ask you to heat water! You may go sit in my car, listen to the radio, chew some gum, and you can help yourselves to my pack of cigarettes."

Bessie and I looked at each other. Did we hear the word "cigarettes"?

Joe laughed at the expressions on our faces.

"Yes, you heard me right. You may play pretend smoking—just don't light them up."

We ran off to find Priscilla and Mary Ann. We sat in Joe's car for the longest time puffing, flicking make-believe ashes, chewing gum, and singing along to the songs on the radio.

"Girls, don't wet the filter, or put your teeth on it; we can play with this pack for a long time!"

"You're right, Bessie! Tomorrow after we clean house, we can play grownup sisters. I want to sing 'Three Coins in the Fountain.'"

"But we can't because there are four of us!" cried Mary Ann.

"Well, we can sing 'Four Coins in the Fountain,' each thinking happily, 'which one will the fountain bless?'"

"That's a good idea! We can sing the word 'four' instead of 'three.' Who is to know, but us?"

Soon, Mother called us in for supper. Bessie placed the pack of cigarettes in her pocket for safekeeping. Joe left to see Dolly. We nicknamed her Esther Williams. Dolly did look like she should be in a movie, and Joe was very much in love with his first love.

Soon, Mary Grace will have her first love. Leo is not interested in girls yet, as far as we know. As for us girls, we will be playing grownup sisters for many more years, I hope. There is no need for Bessie to think of a first love. We need her to be just as she is.

As summer wound down, plans were made to prepare for the first school days. Mother took a very important step in her life: she applied for a driver's license and was issued this very important document.

"I will now be able to take lunch to you or pick you girls up at lunch time, whenever the need arises. It is going to make a world of difference for us all now that I can drive."

She also took us shopping for school clothes.

Leo did not return to school. This decision weighed heavily on Mother and Father, but it was made. Leo was on top of the world: laughing, joking and teasing, a totally different person.

We cherished the last of our summer days and evenings. Very soon it would be early to bed and early to rise.

In the second week of September, Uncle Jim moved his family into the house where Lariat Road begins: only a mile from our ranch house. Leo and Jimmy were pleased. They didn't have far to ride their bikes. Mother said that Jimmy's sisters "made a path to our house" to spend time with us girls. It was no secret that Mother didn't want the girls over every day. As much as she loved her nieces, she did not welcome the extra worry of having so many children in her home with no adult supervision. She sent them home and told them they could come over on Saturdays, when she and Father were home. They seemed to understand, and they were pleased that they were allowed to come to the house when she was home. Nothing kept Jimmy away though; he came almost every day.

Cousin Phil also brought his sister Sophie and little brother Johnny Ray Aragon when he came looking for Joe. Priscilla, Mary Ann, and I had to share Bessie with Sophie a lot. She came over every day to spend time with us.

At this time, we also became acquainted with the new neighbors. Priscilla and I started to spend time there. Priscilla and the little girl became playmates. Beatrice, the eldest, was very nice too. She'd come outside and talk to us. The other sister, Perfidia, was always washing diapers on a washboard. She didn't talk much.

"Pauline, will you come with me to get Jenny?" asked Priscilla one day.

"Who the heck is Jenny?" I asked.

"Our new neighbor: the little girl named Juana. I nicknamed her Jenny."

"Oh, really? What does she think about her new name?"

"She thinks I am funny. She doesn't mind her new name."

"Yes, I will go over with you, because it sure looks like Sophie is getting all Bessie's attention today! I never thought I'd say this, but I just can't wait until school starts. Then all this young company will need to stay home, and we can go back to being just us girls again!"

"You're right, Pauline. We haven't been alone, just the four of us, for what seems like weeks!"

As we walked over to get Juana, I giggled to myself. Juana thinks that Priscilla is funny for naming her Jenny. Well, she is right, because she sure doesn't look like a little girl named Jenny. She looks like the comic character "Little Red Rider," an Indian boy. She doesn't carry herself like a girl, but Priscilla loves her new playmate. Maybe, by spending time with Priscilla, Juana will be transformed into a girly girl, but I just don't see Juana giving up her boy cowboy boots. Time will tell. In any case, Priscilla is thrilled to have someone her own age nearby.

I was happy for Priscilla, and I did like Sophie and our other cousins, but I felt that my sisters and I needed to get back to the business of being together with no outside distractions. Mother always said, "You girls have each other; what better friends could you have than your sisters?" My mind was set on that belief. That was how it was and should be. We made each other shine: my sisters and I.

We woke up to a very nice Friday morning, the last weekend before the start of school. Mother took the day off from work and let us sleep in. At about nine, we all staggered into the kitchen, one by one. Mary Grace dusted in the front room; Leo chopped wood outside. Felix, the new neighbor, stood talking to him with one hand on his hip and the other holding a BB gun.

Mother set the table for breakfast. Leo came in with an arm full of firewood. Felix followed. He stopped at the table and tried to make conversation with us, but we ignored him.

"Boy, Leo! Your sisters don't talk much, do they?"

Leo shrugged his shoulders and headed out the door. Felix tagged along behind him.

"Leo hasn't taken a shine to that young man, I believe," said Mother. "He seems to brag a lot, but he is a neighbor, so we must be polite. It doesn't hurt to show good manners. We always need to treat people in the way that we would like to be treated. Leo tired quickly of his boasting; he doesn't have much patience for Felix's self-centered ways."

"I wonder how he picked up this characteristic. He is only fourteen years old," said Mary Grace.

"Your father says that Mr. Maes is a very pleasant man, but that his wife likes her Coors beer. In any case, I don't want you to be rude to any of them. Okay, Girls, when you are done with breakfast, Mary Grace and I will braid your hair. I am having a Stanley party this afternoon, so please stay tidy for my guests. You may also help me fill the candy dishes with peanuts and creamy butter mints."

Mother began to grind a roll of bologna in the hand grinder, then added mayonnaise to spread it on sandwich bread. She cut it into small squares to offer her guests as an appetizer. She had made caramel-pecan cinnamon rolls too. This made them very sweet, which is why she didn't always add caramel and pecan to her cinnamon rolls. She also made a big pot of coffee for her guests.

We felt blessed to have Mother home from work on a Friday. It made our weekend even more special. The Stanley party was an added bonus. I admired the way Mother carried herself with confidence as she entertained her lady friends. I wished my sisters and I could be more like her in that respect. Maybe one day we'd outgrow our shyness, and be more like her and Mary Grace.

After Mother's guests left, she asked Mary Grace to accompany her to visit with Father McDevitt.

"Your sister and I will not be gone long; Leo is out back."

"Mother, may we have the peanuts and mints left over in the candy dishes?"

"Yes, Priscilla. You girls may share, but don't eat too many. I will fix dinner as soon as we get back."

"We have time to play grownup sisters!" said Bessie. "You girls go into the front room; I'll go into the bedroom and get the pack of cigarettes Joe gave us."

We took our places in the front room, crossed our arms and legs, and waited eagerly for our "grownup time" together. Bessie handed us each a cigarette.

"I know!" said Priscilla. "We can pretend that I'm the Stanley lady taking some orders from you girls for cleaning products!"

"We can do that for a little while. Then we can sit and visit like Mother's friends did this afternoon," said Bessie.

Mary Ann and I agreed. We didn't get to play for very long; Mother and Mary Grace came back, in no time at all.

Mother washed her hands and started on dinner. She poured elbow macaroni into a skillet with a little oil and began to brown it. We sat at the table eating peanuts.

"Father McDevitt and I discussed tuition fees," she told us. "He had a list of the students and their teachers for this year."

"Who did I get this year?" I asked excitedly.

"You will be in Sister Amelia's class. Priscilla, you will be in Sister Alquin's class."

"Oh no! Not Sister Alquin!"

"It will be okay, Priscilla. I know what she expects and I will help you," I said. "I had her and I'm still here, right?"

"Bessie, you will be in Sister Mary Joseph's class."

"Oh, you will love her, Bessie," said Mary Grace. "She is the oldest nun at Saint Joseph's, but the nicest. She is like a sweet old grandmother and she always smells so good. She must use a special soap, not Lava, that's for sure. Joe and I both had her in eighth grade."

"Who did I get, Mother?"

"Mary Ann, you hit the jackpot. You have Sister Devota. I know all you girls like her."

"Last year, Sister Alquin put my name up on the blackboard under the word 'Tuition'!"

"If that happens again, just let Sister know that your mother will be calling Father McDevitt. You are not to worry about tuition fees."

Priscilla seemed troubled, so I tried to reassure her.

"Don't worry about Sister Alquin, Priscilla. We just need to make sure that we attend Mass on Sundays. Once she sees you there for the first few weeks after school starts, she will not bother you."

"Mother, did you hear what Pauline said?"

"Yes, I did, Sweetie. She would know; she had her for a full year."

"You also must learn your times tables, and 'Indian Children.' Your experience in her class will be much better than mine was in the beginning. I have to admit that, although she is hard on her students, I learned good study habits by being in her class. We mustn't miss school unless we are sick or the buses are snowed in. Okay?"

"Okay, Pauline, if you say so."

Mother added fried, ground round beef, sautéed onion, diced tomatoes and a small can of tomato sauce into the browned pasta.

The phone rang.

"Mother, it's for you," called Mary Grace. "It's your Uncle Eloy."

"Bessie, please keep an eye on my pasta and don't let it dry out; it needs to simmer for half an hour. Uncle Eloy likes to chat."

Mother soon came back into the kitchen. She smiled and said, "Uncle Eloy didn't say much this time, except that he is on his way over. What a surprise! It's too bad he didn't make the trip from Trinidad in July, when my mother was here, so he could see his sister. He said he wants to spend the weekend with us and leave for home on Monday.

"He wants your father to take him for a drive up Wolf Creek Pass. When he came some years ago, we went up there and picked pine nuts. I think it would be nice to spend the day up in the mountains tomorrow. We can take fixings for a picnic. What do you girls think about that?"

"Yes, yes! Can we pick pine nuts?" asked Priscilla excitedly.

"I don't see why not," answered Mother.

Father came in from work, and we sat down to eat pasta, salad and Mother's French bread. Mother gave Father the good news about Uncle Eloy. She fixed a food plate and set it aside for him, since she expected him to arrive before dusk.

Phyllis' parents dropped her off to spend the night, so she came with us on the picnic.

Uncle Eloy was the youngest of Grandfather Manuel's three brothers. Mother claimed that he looked more like her father than the rest. He was about five-foot-five, not as tall as her dad who was five-foot-eleven, but just as handsome. Uncle Eloy had a kind disposition. Mother always looked forward to his visits. He was the only brother who moved to Utah after his brother's death. He looked happy to spend time with Mother and Father on our picnic, even though he went home empty handed: no *piñón* this year.

Pauline, Bessie, Mary Ann, mother Della, and Priscilla

Lilacs starting to bloom

Father Ignacio

Grandmother Genevieve

Chapter Fourteen

On Monday morning, we woke up with butterflies in our tummies. Mine quickly faded when I thought of walking into my classroom and seeing Sister Amelia at her desk.

"Pauline, which dress are you wearing to school this morning?"

"I think I want to wear the red and white plaid dress. What about you, Priscilla?"

"I want to wear the pale-yellow dress. Mary Ann is wearing her lime green, and Bessie laid out her baby blue."

Mary Grace called to us.

"Girls, come into the kitchen so I can take the rags out of your hair. It might be picture day today."

Bessie joined us, but she wasn't ready to talk yet. We knew that it was just too early for Bessie to be communicating.

Leo came into the kitchen.

"Mother will be bringing a bagged lunch for you girls."

The bus honked; we climbed on. The bus driver greeted us, probably the only time he would do it for the rest of the year. A couple of times during the school year, he turned and asked some of the high school boys to keep it down, but that was it. Mary Grace was comparing programs with another girl.

Everyone seemed to have something to say to another. We four just sat quietly, looked and listened. The bus pulled up in front of the public school. Mary Grace waved goodbye as we walked to Saint Joseph's, with lots of other laughing and talking students.

The bell had not yet rung when we arrived. I looked for Julia. At the playground, Priscilla and Mary Ann grabbed swings, and Bessie and I watched. The school building had a new paint job.

I got butterflies in my tummy again when I saw six of the nuns walking toward the school from the convent. I felt proud of them too. These were our teachers, with their black and white habits and black rosaries hanging from their waists. Their hands were neatly tucked into the sleeves of their habits: never exposed when walking. Seeing their hands tucked away gave me the feeling that, if I went up to them, they would give me their full attention, and that nothing was more important than the person standing in front of them.

When I grow up, I think I might become a Benedictine nun, I thought. I'd like to teach children about Jesus and help them prepare to receive the sacraments. This would be a very good thing, I think. Only time will tell what Jesus wants for me. It could be that Jesus and I have already decided what I am to do in this lifetime: be a nun!

The nuns waved and walked up the cement steps of the school building. Moments later, the bell rang. Bessie and I walked to our classrooms, which were right next to each other. Priscilla walked Mary Ann to her class.

"Priscilla, go straight to your class afterward; remember, you don't want to be late to Sister Alquin's class."

"I know, Pauline."

Sister Amelia led us in the Lord's Prayer, and then we pledged allegiance to our American flag. She told the class to pull out writing tablets and write down the names of all the prayers we would learn in preparation for Confirmation.

"Most of you are ten years of age: the usual age for the reception of Confirmation."

"Sister Amelia, what is Confirmation and why do we need to receive this sacrament?" asked a boy named Tony.

"That is a good question, Tony; I was coming to that. Confirmation is the sacrament through which we receive the Holy Spirit. We receive His gifts: wisdom, understanding, knowledge, counsel, fortitude, piety, and fear of the Lord. In Baptism, we received these gifts in the early stages of development, and through Confirmation, these gifts are more fully developed.

"The bishop will come from Denver to Saint Joseph's to administer the sacrament, and you girls will wear beanies on your heads. You will need to pick a sponsor and a saint's name. But you still have plenty of time for that; as we get closer to Confirmation day I will remind you. And now, Class, Pauline and Tony will pass out math books and readers."

I knew right then that I was going to be very happy in her class. I felt special as I walked from desk to desk and handed each student their math book. I thought that Tony was probably feeling the same way. Did Sister know that she had picked the shyest students in class to help her?

After all the students had math books and readers, Tony and I went to the candy room to return the extra ones. She told us to knock on the door because Sister Mary Julian would be there.

Sister Mary Julian looked wonderful; one could never tell that she had been so ill. She was not ready to teach an eight-hour class though. She did substitute for the first and second graders a couple of hours a week. Tony and I stacked the books neatly. I noticed how very cute Tony was, but I also noticed that his nose beaded up with sweat, which was very unattractive.

Sister Amelia thanked us and told us to return to our desks, which were right across from each other. Albert Sanchez sat at the front of the room across from Sister's desk. Naomi, the girl who had liked him last year, sat a few desks behind me. Every once in a while, Albert would turn, look at me and smile. I still had a crush on him, but seeing him walk home with Naomi last year had disenchanted me.

The hours went by quickly. I couldn't wait to see my sisters after school. The public schoolkids on the bus were very rowdy. The bus driver stood up and announced, "If you want to get home you need to settle down." They were excited about their first football game on Friday.

It looked like my sisters had also had a good day.

"Sister Alquin was very pleasant," Priscilla said.

Mary Ann said, "I love Sister Devota."

Bessie said, "It looks like I will be getting a lot of homework, but Sister Mary Joseph is very sweet. I miss seeing Leo in class, though."

Mary Grace did not have very much to say. She needed her afternoon nap as soon as we walked in the door. Leo also had a very good day; he didn't have to deal with school at all!

We changed our clothes, and went out to play. Leo rode up on his bike and handed Mary Ann a roll of Necco assorted wafers. The candy wafers were the size of a nickel, and the package held about forty. Five were white. We decided to play Sunday morning Mass, in which we dressed like nuns, and the one holding the hard candy played the part of the priest giving Communion. The package held only five white wafers, so we were soon done with that.

Next we played baseball. When Joe drove up, he took off his work apron and asked Priscilla to hand him the bat.

"Can I hit some balls for you to catch?"

We were happy to oblige. We had fun until he hit a fly toward Bessie. She looked up; the sun blinded her; and the ball came down hard. It hit her left eye. Joe laughed, not realizing how hard the ball had hit. Bessie's pride made her act as though it were nothing. Joe saw her eyes water and realized that she was too embarrassed to cry. He knew that asking if she was all right would hurt her pride, so he pretended not to notice. Joe handed Priscilla the bat and promised to play with us another time.

As we all went inside, Mother and Father returned from work. Mary Grace had peeled and sliced potatoes, and now she made tortillas. Joe leaned against the kitchen counter, expressing his joy that a new hall had opened in Alamosa for Friday night dances. He and Mary Grace loved dancing. Mother wasn't too keen on the idea of their driving out of town for the dances. The country roads were very dark. She forbade Mary Grace to go and tried to talk Joe out of driving so far at night.

Mother made a delicious "bumpy gravy"—steamed mild Ortega green chili peppers with ground beef in beef gravy. It tasted so good with fried potatoes and flour tortillas. We took turns during dinner telling about our first day at school.

Joe came into the kitchen and stopped in front of the mirror over the sink to admire himself. Not one hair out of place on his head, he sang a catchy tune. Everyone stopped talking to listen as he sang "Cherry Pink and Apple Blossom White."

He winked and smiled at us, and then began singing the same lyrics again.

"I like that new song too, Joe," said Mary Grace. "And the 'Tequila' one is the best to dance to!"

Joe nodded and continued to sing as he walked out the door.

"It's still early, Mother. I think I'll ride my bike over to see Jimmy. I'll be home before it gets dark."

"Okay, Leo. See that you do. I don't want to worry."

After he went out, she continued, "Leo is so happy these days, but it breaks my heart that he is not in school. Only time will tell how it will affect his future."

Mother helped Bessie and me with the dishes. Father came into the kitchen with his accordion, and Mother sat at the table to clean beans.

I worked on a math assignment, and Bessie did English homework. We heard a knock at the door. I could guess who was standing on the other side by looking at Father. He sat with his accordion on his lap and a big smile on his face. So it had to be Primo Catalino.

Mother opened the door, and we saw Father's compadre holding a bag of oranges and his guitar. We were entertained with renditions of "Good Night, Irene," "You Are My Sunshine," and "I'm Walking the Floor Over You."

Now that the weather was cooling, we knew we would have frequent visits from Father's good friend. He told Father that coming over made his evening hours not seem so long.

Chapter Fifteen

The wind was rising; October was near. Fall had finally taken over summer. The absence of the greening agent in leaves had revealed the autumn colors of coral, auburn and gold. I loved to go with Father when he picked Mother up from Mrs. Roth's house, because I could look at the hardwood trees in her yard with their brightly-colored leaves.

Autumn is truly my favorite season, I thought. And when I grow up and have a house, I will plant trees that have color-changing leaves all around. I will, I will! And my sisters will say, "Oh Pauline! You have the most beautiful trees! May we sit under them?" And I will say, "Why of course! Come help me rake heaps of leaves from the ground in November. I imagined how beautiful Aunt Victoria's place looked at this time of year, with the aspens' light bark and golden leaves.

Tuesday was a very upsetting day for us, and most especially for Joe. On his lunch hour, he couldn't get his car to start. Luckily there was an automotive shop across the street from the Boy's Market, so Father and Mother met him there after work. The mechanic checked the car out and found a plugged fuel system caused by crystallized sugar in the gas line. Joe was very upset. Who could dislike him so much that he would put sugar in his gas tank? He always took pride in his car and took good care of it.

That evening at the dinner table, talk of Joe's car dominated the conversation.

Mary Grace said, "It has to be someone that is jealous because Joe's car is the hottest car in town."

Cousin Phil stopped by when he heard the bad news. He thought it had to be an ex-boyfriend of Dolly's.

Bessie, Priscilla, Mary Ann and I had discussed it at length earlier. Our opinion was that it was because Joe was the best looking guy in town, dating the most beautiful gal in town. According to a girl in our comic book, "It was just a matter of time before jealousy reared its ugly head."

The car was in the shop for a couple of weeks. Dolly's brother Corny dropped her off at our house to visit. My sisters and I got an eyeful watching the young lovers. They kissed and hugged right in front of Mary Grace while she did the ironing.

Cousin Phil spent a lot of time at our house with Joe. One day, Joe was chopping wood while Phil helped stack it.

"Man, it's a bummer to be without wheels. But the waiting will be worth it; I've saved enough to get a new paint job after the fuel lines are replaced."

"Wow! What color?"

"Metallic green."

Joe wasn't aware that we were playing close by. They went on talking and laughing. The girls and I overheard Phil say to Joe, "Hey Joe, have you heard this one?"

"Down by the willows where nobody goes, there sat Miss Rita without any clothes."

Joe just laughed. Phil always had a way of cheering him up. Bessie and I looked at each other. Priscilla and Mary Ann did not pay much attention; they were too busy playing with our play dishes.

I whispered to Bessie, "So...that is what she does at the willows, but why!?"

Bessie shrugged her shoulders.

"I have no idea, but I do know that it isn't very nice of her, and she will catch her death of cold."

"I know, how...sad."

Chapter Sixteen

The next few weeks went by quickly; Joe got his car back from the shop. He had an idea about who had damaged his car, but no proof.

Father and Leo spent a lot of time chopping and stacking wood for the winter months.

Mother baked sandwich bread for the next two weeks. It was potato harvest time; she would need to pack lunches for herself, Mary Grace, Bessie and me. The schools were closed for the two weeks. Leo stayed at home so that he could take Priscilla and Mary Ann over to Aunt Raquel each morning, and Father picked them up after work.

Mother had taught us, "Thanks to ideal growing conditions, Monte Vista developed into a thriving potato raising and marketing center. This allows many families to earn extra money for coal and other needs for winter months. Not all families can go up to the mountains to get wood. Irrigation canals made it all possible, because without water, Colorado is a desert. But with water, it is a garden."

Mother promised Priscilla and Mary Ann that they could go to the field with us at the end of the week. They were too little to go every day, and it was much too cold.

"Priscilla, you and Mary Ann have to be very good for your Aunt Raquel. I realize there won't be a lot for you to do at her house on Sunny Side, but it will only be for two weeks. You girls will not be allowed to go outside unless your cousin Estrellita goes out with you. You can also watch your aunt roll her own cigarettes or help Estrellita clean house or brush her pretty long hair. You can also ask cousin

Willy to read out loud when he reads his Bible, and we know for sure you will enjoy listening to him play his electric guitar. I believe he purchased it right when they came out, and he knows how to play.

"Mother, how come Willy and his sister have green eyes and not blue like their mother's?"

"Well, Priscilla, I don't know the answer to that. Maybe they just took after their Aunt Vittoria and their uncle, your father. None of our children got the green eyes, but maybe our grandchildren or our great-grandchildren will. Only time will tell."

"Mother, maybe if we roll our own cigarettes we can have long, long hair like Aunt Raquel; it comes down past her waist and maybe we can be real small like her," said Mary Ann.

"Mother," asked Pauline, "why does Aunt Raquel look so sad all the time?"

"Oh, it could be that she had a very hard life. Her husband, may he rest in peace, had a drinking problem. Now, Girls, no more questions. By the way, rolling and smoking cigarettes will not make your hair grow, but it may stunt your growth."

We were lucky that our house was the first that the foreman came upon, so we were the first to be picked up. Mother, Mary Grace, Bessie and I got to sit up front in the truck cab. The other pickers climbed into the bed of the truck to be driven to the fields.

A tractor-drawn digger was used to harvest the potatoes. The digger unearthed the potatoes and separated them from the vines and roots of the plants. The land could be cultivated every year because the area was humid.

The first day was fun, and although it was very hard work, Bessie and I were fast. We kept up with all the other young adults. The digger dug eight rows from one end of the field to the other, and since Bessie and I were so young, we shared a row. After a couple of days, we got so good at keeping up that we chose to pick the potatoes that the digger driver had unearthed for the return trip.

Mother's job was to walk behind the sorter that filled the gunny sacks; then she would sew the sacks closed with a huge needle. She had to be quick; she couldn't get too far behind. About a hundred feet behind her, a man drove a truck with a flatbed about five miles per hour. Another man with big, strong muscles walked behind this truck and hoisted the sacks of potatoes onto the truck. A man just had to be brawny to do this work.

We got home exhausted each day. Priscilla and Mary Ann played Susie Homemakers; they made the beds as well as they could and helped Father and Leo get dinner going. We'd wash up, eat dinner, and get to bed. We rose at five in the morning to be picked up for another day of work. We were excited when the foreman Averillio made a stop at the market on the way. Mother bought garden gloves, Royal Crown soda pop and cupcakes, to go with our homemade lunch.

On Friday, Father picked up Priscilla and Mary Ann and drove to the Potato Ranch.

Priscilla wanted to help. The foreman's father put her up on the tractor that pulled the sorter. He showed her how to shift the gear forward to make the tractor move up very slowly behind the pickers. The speedometer must have been set to "coast," because it barely moved.

I looked forward to the weekend. Thank goodness Father McDevitt only gave the students two weeks off from school, and Mrs. Roth could spare Mother no more than two weeks.

Mother asked Father to stop at the bank so that she could cash our paycheck.

"The girls worked hard, and I'm sure they'd like their pay today!"

Mother winked at Father as she got out of the car. When she returned, she handed each of us two rolls of nickels.

"Why is it payday for Mary Ann and me?" asked Priscilla. "We don't pick potatoes."

"You two helped Daddy and Leo start dinner and make the beds, so it is payday for you also."

"Oh, thank you, Mommy!"

On the way home, Father stopped to put gas in Joe's car. Father had borrowed it to pick us up, and Joe had ridden home with Phil.

Mother thanked Leo for having the house nice and toasty. I could see the red flames through the small window in the door of the coal burning furnace in the front room. I could hear the crackle of the wood popping in the kitchen stove too.

On Saturday morning, Mother served us cornflakes with half and half in her special cereal bowls from Mrs. Roth. The bowls were tangerine in color and we handled them with care. When I saw the cereal box on the table with the rooster on it, I guessed we would be using Mother's special bowls, because we only had cornflakes maybe two or three times a year. With the extra money earned from the potato harvest, Mother could afford to buy cornflakes and bananas.

I thought how wonderful it was to be alive. Words couldn't explain how happy I felt to be sitting at the kitchen table with my sisters, my brothers, and Mother and Father there with us. I quietly enjoyed my breakfast and watched Mother and Father making plans for the day.

"Mother, Phyllis called to say that her parents are coming to visit sometime after lunch. They would like to bring the boys if it's all right with you? Phyllis told me that two of her brothers still live in Durango with her grandparents, and they've come to Monte Vista for two weeks before school starts for them. They are very close to their dad's parents and prefer to live with them."

"I didn't realize she had two more brothers. You may tell Phyllis that it's fine for them to visit; we will be home all afternoon."

My sisters and I couldn't understand how Junior and Manuel could choose to live with their grandparents. We love Grandmother Genevieve, but we couldn't go one day without Mother and Father.

That afternoon, Mother and Father visited with Phyllis' parents, while the boys stayed outdoors with Leo.

"Have you noticed how very quiet Raymond is in comparison with his brothers?" I asked Bessie.

"Yes. Albert, Raymond, and J.C. look so much like Phyllis too."

We sat on the bed of the truck eating roasted pine nuts. Priscilla and Mary Ann discussed how they would spend their rolls of nickels.

"Pauline, did you notice that Albert just walked into the house?"

"No, he didn't, Bessie. They are all watching Leo chop wood!"

"Okay, don't take my word for it."

I couldn't resist. I wanted to talk to him. I jumped off the truck and walked toward the house. Sure enough, he was standing in front of the kitchen sink with a glass of water. I looked at him and smiled.

He was so cute and I was so shy. I have to get out of here before he says something to me, I thought.

I started walking toward the front room, but he followed me.

"Pauline, what's that in your hand?"

I turned to face him and looked down at my hands. My goodness, it's my two rolls of nickels! I hadn't given them much thought since their visit, but he had noticed them.

"How about we go outside and play?"

I smiled and walked toward the front door. As I moved to take the first step down, he put his hand on my arm.

"Careful, these steps are very steep."

I was flattered at his attention, but felt foolish. He was only ten years old and already a gentleman. I sure hadn't noticed this trait in his father, so where was this coming from? He must go to the movies a lot. I smiled again, but pulled my arm away.

"Hey, how about if we go to the side of the house and dig a hole in the ground with our eyes closed, then kneel down and bury one of these rolls of nickels?"

"Then what?" I asked.

"Well, we can come back in an hour and dig for it, and the one that finds it is the winner. It's just a game. Come on!"

Reluctantly I said, "Okay, let's do that, but I've never heard of this game."

"It's called 'treasure hunt.'"

We found a spot on the ground with soft dirt and began to dig.

"Do you want to bury both rolls?"

"One is plenty! I worked hard for these nickels; what if we can't find them again?"

"Of course we will. I'm a good hunter. We are done now. You can go back to the truck with your sisters, and I'll go back to the woodpile with my brothers. See you in an hour—okay?"

I walked toward the truck; my sisters were still eating pine nuts. Manuel was talking to them. I walked up and smiled at them.

I noticed that his hair was very black, not at all like his brothers' burnt blond. I guess one of them had to look like their mother; the rest looked like their father Wedo.

"And just where have you been, Pauline Montoya?" asked Priscilla.

"She was with my brother Albert. Where were you two?"

I was not going to tell until I had my roll of nickels safely back in my hand.

"Don't you want to live in Monte Vista with your other brothers?" asked Bessie.

"Nope, Junior and I have lived with our grandparents since the day we were born."

"Pauline, Albert is walking toward the house again."

"My brother drinks a lot of water."

"Oh, really?" said Bessie.

I started to walk toward the house as well.

"Pauline likes Albert…Pauline loves Albert," my sisters teased.

I walked into the kitchen. I noticed Albert was absent.

"Mother, have you seen Albert?"

"Yes, Honey; he drank some water then went out the front door. Where are your sisters? Please stay together."

"We will," I said. I entered the front room and looked out the front window. Albert was walking around the corner of the house.

As quietly as I could, I went out the door and down the steps to spy on Albert. I was not surprised when I caught him digging in the spot where we'd buried my nickels. A little voice in my head had told me earlier that he might try to pull a fast one.

I walked up to him and stood there looking. He looked up and grinned at me.

"I know what you are thinking, but really—I got scared that we might not be able to locate the coins we buried. Then I would go away feeling bad because it was my idea! Here, let me wipe the dirt off the wrapper."

I put my hand out and he dropped the roll into it. I walked away feeling like I had just lost my best friend. I didn't believe him.

Soon Wedo and Tiofila said goodbye to Mother and Father. Phyllis was going to spend the night again. Albert was looking at me. He smiled and said, "Goodbye, Pauline."

I smiled back at him, but thought, I'll never forget that you tried to steal from me, and it really hurt my feelings.

My sisters and I had consumed a pound of pine nuts. We could have continued with another pound, but Mother was home and we knew we must not be greedy. The rest of the family also liked them as a snack food.

"It looks like I have two to pick from," announced Priscilla.

"What do you mean?" asked Bessie. "Pick of what?"

"The Sanchez boys! You like Raymond; Pauline likes Albert; Mary Ann likes J.C.; so there are two more boys available for the picking. Since I'm without a Sanchez, I get to pick between Junior and Manuel."

"So which one are you leaning toward?" asked Mary Ann.

"Let me think for a minute; then I'll tell you."

Bessie leaned toward me and whispered, "This is the biggest decision she'll make in her life, and she needs one whole minute!"

We giggled. Priscilla stared at us.

"What are you two giggling about? Are you laughing at me?"

Bessie tried to reassure her.

"No, Honey. I was just thinking that you might take more time to decide on your choice. Junior is fifteen years old, but Manuel is eleven, closer in age to you."

"Oh Priscilla! They are much too old for you! I will share J.C. with you; we can both like him!"

"That's a good idea, Mary Ann. After all, we are not going to marry them."

She had that right; I could never marry someone who tried to steal from me, no matter how much I like him.

"We are too young to be talking marriage anyway. What would Father think if he heard our conversation?" said Bessie.

"She does have a point," I agreed. "I wouldn't want Father to hear me."

"Well neither would we!"

Mother came out with her handbag and Father followed.

"We have some errands to run; your sister and Phyllis are in the house," she said. "Be good. I'll be back soon to start dinner."

Bessie went into the house. We waved as our parents pulled out of the driveway.

"What do you girls want to do?"

"What do you suggest, Pauline?"

"Mother's gone, so we could sit around and eat more pine nuts, or we could go into the house and ask Phyllis about her brothers the Sanchez boys!"

"Why do you and Priscilla always call them the 'Sanchez boys'? They do have names," Mary Ann scolded.

"Because there are so many of them."

"There are only five boys!"

"We have only two; so five seems a lot to name."

"Then don't call them by name. Just say Phyllis' brothers."

"Okay, okay. We will drop using 'Sanchez' when we talk about them. Are you happy now?"

Mary Ann smiled and pointed toward Bessie, approaching with her hands behind her back.

"Can you guess what I have in my hand?"

"Pine nuts?" asked Priscilla.

"'Love' comic books?" I guessed.

Mary Ann ran behind Bessie to see for herself.

"Boy, are you the impatient little one!" said Bessie as she brought forward a box of cherry Jell-O.

"Come on! We need to take our turn going up the ladder to the garret. We need to start thinking about Christmas now, because soon it will be too cold to go up to the attic!"

Bessie went up the ladder first, followed by Mary Ann, then Priscilla, and then me.

We sat on the two-by-fours, close to the entrance. A flat board ran crosswise, and we rested our feet on it. We sat patiently and watched as Bessie very carefully opened the small box of Jell-O.

She broke open the bag inside. We were ready to begin our yearly ritual. We reached across, and Bessie poured Jell-O on the palm of each of our hands, youngest to oldest.

We waited for Bessie to get the Words catalog resting on a two-by-four. Bessie flipped the pages looking for the toy section and then poured Jell-O for herself. Finally, we could begin. I dipped my index finger into my mouth, then into the Jell-O powder, and back onto my tongue.

"Now, Girls," Bessie instructed, "Take time before expressing your wishes for Santa Claus." She raised her head to look at us, and began to laugh. "You have red tongues and black lips! Didn't you notice your fingers before you put them in your mouth?"

"Look who's talking! Your lips are black also!"

"It's from the charred wood up here that was not replaced after the fire," I suggested.

"No, it's from all the smoke that settled up here," said Bessie. "We'd better go down and get washed up before Mother and Father get back. We can come back up another day to make our choices. Let's hurry and finish this cherry Jell-O."

"You promise we can come back up soon?" begged Mary Ann.

"Yes, as long as Mother and Father are not home, and I can snatch another box of Jell-O."

I added, "We don't have much time to make our Christmas lists."

"We must come back very soon," said Priscilla.

"That's right! Now we really must head for the ladder."

We brushed ourselves off, but we couldn't tell how badly we'd stained the seats of our pants with soot. Bessie reminded us to change our clothes; Mother would be very unhappy if we sat on the furniture with dirty clothes. After that, we sat around listening to school talk from Mary Grace and Phyllis.

For dinner, Mother fixed peas in white gravy, buttered biscuits, and ham that she had baked earlier in the afternoon. We were still at the dinner table when Joe walked in with a tall nice-looking fellow. We all took note when he introduced him to Father and Mother as Lester, an old friend from school. He wasn't shy; he soon circled around and engaged in conversation with Mary Grace and Phyllis. Shortly after that, Joe asked Phyllis if she'd like to go for a Coke and invited Lester and Mary Grace too.

After they left, Mary Ann asked, "Mother, is Dolly not Joe's girl anymore?"

"I think she still is, Honey; I haven't heard anything to the contrary. Joe and Phyllis are just friends. He will bring the girls back in a little while, and then he and Lester will be on their way."

Mother was right; before long, the girls were back.

"Mother, Lester seems very nice," said Mary Grace. "He asked if he could call on me tomorrow."

"Yes, he was very polite, although you should ask Joe about him. I got the impression that they have been friends for some time."

"We plan to corner Joe when he comes in."

Leo popped his head in for a moment.

"Mother, I'm back. Jimmy and I will be out by the woodpile; I need to skin a couple of muskrats and clean my traps."

"That's fine, Son. When you are done, wash your hands good. We have ham, biscuits, and white gravy on the stove."

"Thank you! Is it ok if Jimmy spends the night with us?"

"Yes, he may, but have him call his parents for an okay."

"Are we going to Mass in the morning?" Priscilla wanted to know.

"Now you sound like Pauline when she had Sister Alquin. Yes, I will attend Mass with you girls, but your father and brothers will go up the mountain for firewood."

Mary Ann and Priscilla followed Father into the front room, while Bessie and I started on the dinner dishes. Mother sat at the table with her needle. Holding the small, slender piece of steel with its sharp point, she began to stitch her papalina. A papalina is Spanish for a colonial bonnet with a brim that extends out about six inches; just like the ones worn on the "Little House on the Prairie" television show.

Mary Grace and Phyllis came back for a drink of water, still talking about Lester.

"Joe said that Lester lives on Sunny Side, very close to where we used to live and where my parents bought some property," said Phyllis.

"By the way, did I ever tell you that we used to live in the same house that you're now renting?"

"No, you didn't tell me. That's interesting," said Phyllis as they walked back into the bedroom.

"Now we know exactly where the boys live!" said Bessie. "Why, what is the matter with you, Pauline? You don't seem at all excited to know where Raymond and Albert live."

I told Bessie about my nickels, and she understood my disillusionment with Albert.

"Mother, will you take us to the show tomorrow afternoon? I'd like to use my pay for that!"

"Yes, I suppose I could do that for my hard-working potato-picking girls," said Mother with a smile. "What movie do you want to see?"

"'Seven Brides for Seven Brothers'!" said Bessie excitedly.

Priscilla and Mary Ann came back into the kitchen and heard us telling Mother about the movie.

"Oh Mother, you will like this movie! It has snow, singing, long dresses and even a baby!" said Priscilla. "We saw picture previews for the movie on the Marquis."

"Yes," said Mary Ann, "They even sing while they chop wood!"

Her appreciative expression made us laugh.

"Well, they do! I've never heard Father, Leo or Joe sing while they chop!"

"Father does whistle, though," said Priscilla.

"Your father and I would like to see 'The Yellow Rose of Texas'; maybe the week after the potato harvest is over. It should be coming to our theater soon."

"Mother, may we also go with you to see 'The Rose'?" asked Priscilla.

"Gee, Priscilla, it didn't take you long to change the name of the movie! You could at least say, 'The Yellow Rose,'" said Mary Ann.

"Well, excuse me, Darling! I'll be sure to say 'The Yellow Rose of Texas' next time. And I'll be sure not to say 'the Sanchez boys' either."

"Don't call me 'Darling'; you always call me 'Baby.'"

"Mary Ann, please stop now!" begged Priscilla.

"Okay, let's go out and play."

"Only for a little bit, Girls," said Mother. "It's getting windy out there; the wind is cool and crisp."

Chapter Seventeen

It was a new experience on Sunday to climb into Joe's car and see Mother behind the wheel. On the way home from the theater, I began to sing "Bless Your Beautiful Hide."

"Oh no, Mother! Now we are going to have to listen to Pauline sing those songs from the movie for the next six months!"

"Mary Ann, I saw you smile all through that movie."

"I didn't say I didn't like the movie; it's just that Pauline was not born to sing."

"Thanks a lot, Baby! All this time I was under the impression that you just lived for my singing."

Mary Ann rolled her eyes and we all had to laugh.

When we got home, we told Mary Grace all about the movie.

"Your father and the boys have not returned yet?" asked Mother. "I hope they're okay. I expected them to be home by now."

"Don't worry, Mother. It's getting close to supper time; they'll be home shortly."

"You're right. Please come help me start dinner."

With the strike of a match, Mother lit the newspaper under the wood in the stove, and soon the wood was crackling. We played jacks since it was too chilly to be outdoors.

I watched Mother lay lamb chops in a pan, side by side. She sprinkled salt and pepper on them and placed pieces of garlic and some sweet-smelling leaves in the pan.

"Why do we have lamb so often for our meals? I can almost smell the wool when it starts to cook; can't you?"

"I serve it often because it's affordable. Mister Corlett gives it to us at a very good price. After your father butchers a lamb, we are able to keep it in a rented freezer downtown. We also keep the chickens there that we raise for food.

"You want to hear something funny? When I shine the silverware for Mrs. Roth, she usually sits at her kitchen table and either helps me or reads out loud to me from a book or newspaper. One time, she read from a Colorado paper that, 'Every man in the San Luis Valley is fired up by the growing of peas and sheep. Some men are so enthused that they greet each other with a 'ba-a-a-a' instead of 'hello'!"

"That would be funny, for grown men to bleat like sheep!"

"We are also having baked potatoes, Pauline: your favorite with green beans. As far as the smell of wool, it might just be in your head."

"Yes, Mother. It is in my head, because your chops taste so good."

We sat down for supper the minute Father and the boys came back. Mother wanted us to go to bed early. We had another week of picking potatoes ahead of us, and five a.m. comes very early.

"Girls, don't worry about the dinner dishes. I will do them tonight. I want Mary Grace to braid your hair; we won't have time in the morning."

Mother was right. Five a.m. does come too soon. I felt like I had just closed my eyes when I was told to get up. We worked fast and hard; and thank the good Lord, the week finally came to an end. We were able to return to school, and Mother bought some sacks of potatoes for a good price.

Aunt Raquel and
Aunt Victoria,
father Ignacio's sisters

Our home in Colorado

San Luis Valley

Aspen turning gold

Chapter Eighteen

The first hint of frost always came in October. The holidays seem close, and the wind rattles anything in its path. At night, one can hear the sound of the wind knocking about the trees.

We spent Thanksgiving with Aunt Rosa Bella and her family, and I'm almost sure it was one of their big pet turkeys on the table. But it was delicious with candied yams and Mother's cornbread stuffing. *Next time we'll probably be eating one of the kid goats that she raises on her property!* I thought. But I wasn't complaining; she was a good cook.

After Thanksgiving, the nuns began preparations for the Christmas programs. I don't recall Sister Alquin ever having her class participate in the programs, but Sister Amelia did.

Sister Devota had her class perform one year for Easter, and Bessie was one of three girls on stage singing "I'm A Little Teapot." Mother recalled, "Bessie looked so pretty and so confident with her right hand on her hip and her left arm out; just like a teapot!"

This year, my friend Julia and I were very excited, for Sister Amelia had put us in the front row of our class to sing "Up on the Housetop" and "Silent Night."

We loved December and everything it brings. The Christmas season was a very joyous time for us. The town's theater owner donates treats, a movie, and popcorn to all the classes of Saint Joseph's School. Words couldn't describe the happiness it brought to all the students when each class marched downtown for their annual free treats.

Finally, the very special day arrived, two weeks before Christmas, when Father pulled into the backyard with our Christmas tree in tow. Mother plugged in the lights on the tree, and my sisters and I smiled ear to ear. There was something about the multi-colored lights on the tree that brought so much joy to us.

It was truly a very happy time of year. Even the snow falling outside looked much whiter and brighter during the holidays. If I closed my eyes, I could even hear sleigh bells ring if I really listened.

As Mother hung ornaments on the tree, she looked at us girls sitting together on the sofa, so content to watch her. She picked another bulb from a box, then turned to say, "Times are tough this year."

It almost sounded like an apology, but why? She and Father always made Christmas special for us. In any case, our home was ready for that special Holyday when Jesus Christ was born in Bethlehem.

On Friday after school, my sisters and I stayed in the front room for the rest of the day. It was as if we felt we mustn't leave the tree alone, and in the evening it would be a waste to have no one looking at the lights.

Mother called Leo inside for supper. After Father said grace, Mary Grace spoke first.

"Mother, Phyllis and I will need a ride tomorrow to Saint Joseph's. We are helping to spruce up the church and the grounds in preparation for the Christmas season!"

"I'll also be gone tomorrow, Mother," said Leo. "Jimmy wants me to go along with him, his brother Danny and Uncle Jim to bring down their Christmas tree from the mountain."

"Saturday will be a very busy day for the Boy's Market," said Joe. "I will be out on deliveries all day. If you'd like, you may use the car, Mother."

"Thank you, Joe; I'll let you know in the morning if your father and I need to go out. Most likely it will snow all night. I plan to bake bread and cinnamon rolls most of the day, and your Uncle Manuel and family are visiting in the afternoon, if the ranch roads are open on that end of town."

"I'll be up early tomorrow morning to help you if the car is snowed in," said Father. "Most likely I'll be shoveling snow all day, if we get another three feet of snow like we did last weekend. Making a path to the outhouse isn't something I want to do at the last minute. And the wind also blew the tarp off our firewood; I may need some more rope."

"Oh boy, Daddy! May we go out with you and build a snowman?"

"Yes, Priscilla, you and your sisters may play outside if it's not too cold."

Right after dinner, Bessie and I did the dishes so Mother could have her work area for mixing the baking dough. We also needed to get back to our Christmas tree watching.

Father fed the ironstone furnace with coal. The room was nice and warm, and Mother left the front-room drapes open so we could watch the snow come down.

Priscilla and Mary Ann lay in front of the tree with coloring book and crayons. Bessie and I curled up on the couch. I read from my catechism book. Bessie had her writing tablet and pencil with her although she just sat quietly.

Joe stayed in for the evening. He picked up his guitar and handed Father his accordion. Mary Grace ironed her clothes for tomorrow, and Mother mixed ingredients for her bread.

Leo was talking with Jimmy in his room.

We loved watching and listening to Father and Joe play, but we couldn't pull ourselves away from the tree, so we listened from the front room. Joe was in a country mood tonight; he was singing "Honky-Tonk Man."

Joe went from one country song to another for about twenty minutes. Then Mary Grace suggested he sing some Christmas music, so he did. It was a perfect family Christmas evening; and the best part was that we would have more like it. What else was there to do on cold snowy evenings but gather around the kitchen?

Phyllis called to say her dad would take them tomorrow to Saint Joseph's to help the nuns and Father McDevitt. Mary Grace went to bed early. My sisters and I stayed up late with Mother after Father and the boys went to bed.

On Saturday morning, Father placed four chairs in front of the ironstone furnace, and called us to come sit while he fixed us each a half cup of black coffee. Priscilla and Mary Ann waited in bed for Father to come carry them into the front room.

Joe had left for work; Mary Grace had gone with Phyllis and her father. Leo and Jimmy went out right after breakfast.

Mother came into the front room where we were curled up on the chairs in front of the furnace. She carried a plate of biscochitos to go with our coffee.

"We won't be leaving the house today; it's much too cold," she said. "It's windy and snowing hard out there. Your father is making oatmeal, and the kitchen is now nice and warm."

The aroma of baking bread was already coming from the kitchen stove; Mother must have gotten up with the chickens.

Joe called to say that most of the roads had been cleared by the snow plow, but that it was still very cold. He wasn't coming home for lunch.

"If the roads are cleared, your brother Manuel will be able to come this afternoon," said Father.

"He'll call either way, I'm sure. I'm going to bake bread all day, and I'll put on a nice pot of stew to go with it for dinner."

Uncle Manuel, Aunt Elsie and the kids came in the early afternoon. After dinner, Uncle Manuel opened his Bible and read a little. He had studied to become a minister of the Pentecostal religion. Mother and Father enjoyed listening to the stories in the Bible, but made it very clear to Uncle Manuel that they would never leave the Catholic Church.

"Ignacio and I were born and raised Catholic, as you were, Manuel. We are raising our children by the teachings of the Catholic religion, just as our parents did."

Uncle Manuel accepted and respected Mother and Father's feelings on this matter and did not push the issue. He and Mother were very close. It saddened Mother that Uncle Manuel would be moving his family to Idaho in the spring. All of Aunt Elsie's family had moved there except for two sisters in Colorado. Mother was grateful that she would still have Uncle Louie and Uncle Jim nearby, and that she was close to Father's family too.

On Sunday morning, Mother explained to Priscilla that we could not attend Mass because of the snow.

"The snow plow will probably not be out on the country roads early. I will have Mary Grace write a note to Sister Alquin for you." Mother didn't read or write. She only went up to about the third grade.

We spent most of the day playing grownup sisters; only this time, we had husbands from the movie "Seven Brides for Seven Brothers." I chose to be Millie, married to Adam; Bessie wanted to be Dorcas, married to Benjamin; and Priscilla wanted to be the one married to Gideon, the youngest brother.

"Mary Ann, which one of the girls would you like to be?" asked Bessie. "For a husband, you can choose Frank, Daniel, Caleb, and Ethan."

"None, thank you!"

"I don't want to marry a rugged frontiersman that expects his wife to cook, clean, and milk the cow! I want to be the baby born to Millie and Adam."

"Well, I like Gideon," said Priscilla. "It's so funny when he tells Millie what he would say to a girl when he is 'Goin' Courtin.'"

"I forgot; what did he say?" asked Bessie.

Priscilla was proud that she remembered this part of the movie.

"Gideon would say, 'Nice night for a coon hunt!'"

We all laughed. That was a funny thing to say to a girl.

On Christmas Eve, Mother and Father arranged to meet Primo Catalino and his wife Star at church for Midnight Mass. They would take us to Mass on Christmas morning if the roads were open and safe to drive. Leo got to go along with them, and Joe attended Mass with Dolly.

Father promised, "If you girls go to bed early and do as Mary Grace tells you, we will wake you and let you know that Christ has been born, the minute we return from Mass. Then we can open presents."

Mary Ann asked, "Mary Grace, will you read to us the story of the birth of Jesus?"

My sisters and I knew the story by heart, but we never tired of hearing it. It helped us to relax and fall asleep. As I drifted off, I wondered, Is Bessie going to sleep too, or will Mary Grace allow her to stay up? What will we find under the tree when we wake?

Chapter Nineteen

"Merry Christmas, Girls! It's Christmas Day, and Christ is born in Bethlehem!"

We jumped out of bed and rushed into the front room, where we found a wrapped gift for each of us, and a brown lunch bag for each, filled with peanuts, candy, an apple and an orange.

We put on our new nightgowns and started to eat. Our peanuts and colorful ribbon candy sometimes stuck to each other, but we didn't care. It was snowing hard. It was about two in the morning when we looked out the window. By the glow of the porch lights, we could see that the tires on the car and the truck were buried in snow.

"Christmas won't be Christmas if we can't attend Mass," I sighed.

"I know, Pauline," said Mother, "but thank goodness you girls go to Catholic school. You get to celebrate Christmas for a long time, with the nuns having the students prepare for all the Christmas programs! You get to sing all the Christmas carols, and you receive Holy Communion once a week! We need to be grateful for that!"

"Yes, Mother. We also can be happy that Baby Jesus is safe from that bad man called Herod! It's a good thing an angel appeared to Joseph in a dream and told him to take Baby Jesus and Mother Mary and escape into Egypt, because Herod was going to search for the Child to kill him! And the three Magi returned to their country by another route, and didn't go back to Herod to tell where the Child was!"

"That is right, Pauline. Jesus, Mary and Joseph ended up living in Nazareth, and that is why Jesus is called the Nazarene."

We spent the last week of our winter break in the house. Joe and Phil talked a lot about the dances they attended, but were even more excited about the upcoming New Year's dance. Mary Grace and Phyllis were disappointed because Mother and Father wouldn't allow Mary Grace to go out of town to attend it.

On December 31, more and more snow fell, but nothing was going to keep Joe from the dance of the year. He came in from work, grabbed a quick bite, brushed his teeth, and disappeared into his bedroom to bathe and get ready to go out. Before he left, Joe knelt in front of Mother and Father and asked for "La Bendición." Mother and Father made the Sign of the Cross over his head and told him to be very careful driving in the snow.

Joe grabbed his winter jacket and assured Father that he and Phil would most likely be home right after the dance. Dolly was out of town visiting family.

Mother told us girls to get into our nightgowns and retire into the front room; she would take care of cleaning up after dinner. We were happy to do as we were told. We got our Christmas coloring books and curled up on the chairs and sofa. We began our yearly ritual of discussing the adventures we'd been on and what we had gone through during the past year that had left an impression on us.

"Bessie, you're older, so you need to go first."

"Well, I have to say that Leo is my hero. I never realized how strong he is; it's probably because of all the wood chopping he does year round. Do you remember the day we were out in the front yard, and we saw the new neighbor Felix walking home on our country road? Remember we spotted Leo riding fast on his bike with his BB gun in one hand? He came to a fast stop in front of Felix, jumping off his bike without dropping his BB gun. He grabbed Felix by the collar and swung him around with just one arm. He looked down at Felix on the ground, and shouted, 'Don't you ever talk about my sister Bessie, or any of my other sisters! Do you hear me?' Felix looked scared when Leo was yelling at him."

Leo had explained to us afterward that Felix had told Gilbert Gold that he hadn't been in this town long and had already taken a girl to the willows: a very pretty new neighbor of his.

"Leo is definitely my hero!" finished Bessie. "Okay, Pauline it's your turn. Do tell."

I had to think for a minute. "I was with Cousin Della at Monte Vista's ice skating rink one time without you girls. I needed help just to stand on skates, but I saw this girl standing there talking for the longest time without falling. This girl could talk, skate, and chew gum all at the same time! She was nice too, because she saw me staring at her, and she just smiled at me and went on talking. I think she is my hero on ice! Now it's your turn, Priscilla. Do tell."

"I'm remembering many, many years ago when we were very, very young and we lived on Sunny Side."

Bessie leaned over and whispered, "Isn't it cute how she repeats a word when she is telling a memory?"

Priscilla stopped for a moment to look at Bessie.

"Go ahead, Priscilla; we are all listening."

"This took place sometime in the summer of 1952; I remember because I was just six years old: very, very young. I happened to find a dime on the school playground, and when we got home from school, I begged Pauline to walk with me to the little one-room candy store at the end of the block.

"I asked the little old lady to please put the candy in two little bags. On the way home, two nasty boys stopped us. 'Hey you girls, what do you have there?' asked one. Pauline and I just stood there looking at them. 'Give me your bag!' he said. 'Is there candy in it?'

"I was so proud of Pauline! She handed him her bag, grabbed my bag out of my hand, grabbed me by the hand and told me, 'Let's run!' We ran as fast as we could, and never looked back until we were in front of our house! Pauline was my hero that day! Okay, Mary Ann, it's your turn."

"I have a hero every single day, and it's Bessie. She helps take care of me every day."

"That is very sweet, but you did not have very much to say."

"I know, but right now that is what I want to share. Besides, Priscilla talked about something that happened two years ago and you did not stop her."

"I forgot I was supposed to share something from this past year," said Priscilla.

"That's okay, Girls; Jesus was born a very, very long time ago and the whole world still talks about it every day during the Christmas season," said Mother as she walked through the room.

Father came in and sat on the sofa. "My heroes are Mr. and Mrs. Roth because they went to their cabin, and your mother has another four days off work to spend with you girls!"

"Really, Daddy? And you too?"

"No, Baby, the animals have to be fed and cared for every day, especially the baby lambs. But I will be home early in the evenings now that I have your cousin Faustino to help."

Chapter Twenty

On Saturday morning, I woke up and got into bed with Bessie, Priscilla and Mary Ann. Mary Grace had left our bed, and I was cold. We lay talking for a little bit until Mary Grace came into the room and asked us to go into the kitchen so she could use the bedpan. She seemed deep in thought.

When we walked into the kitchen, something was not right. Mother was not at her usual place in front of the stove. She, Father, Joe, Phil and Leo were all sitting at the table. Joe had a strange look on his face; he was obviously upset.

Leo motioned to us to keep quiet. It sounded like Joe was repeating himself. He and Phil were taking turns telling about a horrible accident they had witnessed.

"Father, I was horrified at the sight of the injured women lying on the road. There wasn't a thing we could do to help, except to throw jackets on them to keep them warm and keep their body heat until help came."

"It makes me shudder just thinking about the blood; so much blood!" said Phil. "When the dance was over, some guy came up to Joe and asked if he wanted to race home. Joe told him he had just put a new motor in his car after someone had put sugar in his gas tank. This guy argued that speeding would not hurt the new motor and called angrily to Joe as he walked away, 'You're yellow! Joe banana!'

"I was mad, but Joe said, 'Let it go. We'll probably never run into this guy again.' But we did. We came upon the accident about fifteen minutes later. It looked like this guy got someone to race him!"

Joe just sat at the table for a long time. He looked like he was in shock. Mother made breakfast and tried to get Joe to eat something, but he wasn't interested in food this morning. Father said a prayer and asked us girls to pray for the families of these young folks.

Around noon, the phone started ringing nonstop. Cars pulled into the driveway. Some of Joe's friends and our Cousin Mitch came over. Monte Vista was in shock.

Mary Grace cleaned the bedrooms and then did her makeup, hair and nails, while Mary Ann and Priscilla watched. Bessie and I went into the front room to listen to more accounts of the horrid accident. The more we listened, the worse it got. Two women from Monte Vista in two different cars had died at the hospital. Another woman, who was not well known in town, was also killed. It was thought that three cars were involved.

Mary Grace came into the front room and said hello to Cousin Mitch's girlfriend Maggie. We were happy to see Cousin Mitch, who was an aunt's son from her first marriage. Mitch claimed that as a little boy people would address him as Indio, Spanish for Indian. His real father was a Ute Indian. He states, "It hurt my feelings at that time."

He never failed to mention though that Uncle Charley was very good to him. Today he was happy to see us, but sad about the lives lost. I guess in a small town everyone knows one another.

Maggie was introduced to some of Joe's other friends that had never been to the house before. One fellow caught our eye. He was tall, dark and handsome, and leaned quietly against the wall, looking shy. After they left, we asked about him.

"That guy's name is Josito Montoya. No relation to us, but a very decent fellow. His brother worked with Mother and the girls this year at the potato harvest. He was the big brawny fellow bucking the sacks of potatoes onto the trucks."

"I remember him," said Mother. "I remember his good manners and his respectful way."

"The brother's name is Tony. I call Josito 'Jo`so' (Bear) because of his build. Man, those guys are big."

Bessie and I went into the bedroom to ask Mary Grace if she had taken notice of the nice-looking guy.

"No, I didn't, but he sure took notice of me!"

"How would you know, if you didn't notice him?" asked Bessie.

Mary Grace threw her hair back with a shake of her head and walked out of the room.

"She is not fooling me," said Bessie. "She noticed him as much as we did."

The year 1955 was off to a bad start. The next day, we learned that the accident had been closer to home than anyone thought. Felix came over and knocked at our door, and Father asked him to come in. He stood looking at the floor.

"Leo is in his room. I'll get him for you," said Father.

Felix shook his head and looked up at Father. "I came over to talk to you and Mrs. Montoya."

Bessie and I half expected an apology for what he had said to Gilbert Gold. Tears rolled down his cheeks as spoke. He looked up as Leo walked into the kitchen.

"My mother is in the hospital, and my sister Beatrice was killed in a car crash last night!"

His mother and sister had gone to the New Year's dance in Alamosa, and his mother had been drinking at the dance. On the way home, she had her daughter stop the car on a dark country road, so she could get out to relieve herself.

"My sister got out of the car and started to go around to the passenger side to help Mother out. A car hit them from behind, killing my sister instantly. My mother is at the hospital in traction!"

Mother stepped over and put her arms around him as he cried hard. Father signaled to the rest of us to go to him. Mary Grace and Leo told him how bad they felt for him, and Bessie said, "I'm sorry about your sister and mother."

Felix left before Joe got up. Joe was having a bad time; he had not slept well. Mother let him sleep in and called his work to let them know he would not be coming. She fixed him a cup of coffee, fried eggs, fried potatoes, and roasted green peppers.

Joe ate a little. Father told him what we had learned from Felix.

"So, that was the other lady that was being covered up by a policeman! I never saw who was in the other car. I'll be darned! It was our very own neighbors. That is so sad for Mr. Maes. The police never questioned me and Phil because other cars had come up on the crashed cars before we did."

When we returned to school, a lot of kids talked about the accident. On our way home, we debated whether to go to the mortuary and pay our respects. We decided not to; it would be too sad to see Beatrice lying there lifeless. The two other girls lay in state with her.

There were three of them, I thought, just like when Ernest Pollock and his two brothers drowned. When Jesus died on the cross, He had a man to His right and a man to the left. I guess no one dies alone.

Chapter Twenty-one

January went by quickly, and February arrived. Little did I know that it would be a terrible few weeks for me, of my own making. It started on a Friday after school. We walked to the public school to get on the bus. It was not like any other Friday. Every seat on the bus was taken but the one in front of Mary Grace that she'd saved for us. The bus driver stood up and asked some older boys, juniors and seniors, to settle down. Some girls were leading a cheer: "We've got the team and there's no doubt about it; and if you don't believe it, we'll yell a little louder!"

The bus started to move, and the students finally settled down. As the bus approached our house, Mary Grace told us, "Don't forget your jackets."

She had just finished her sentence when this brawny guy sitting behind her stood up and yelled, "We won our football game against Alamosa!" Then he leaned over, grabbed Mary Grace, tilted her face up and back, and kissed her right on the lips! The bus driver told him to sit down and not get up again, as he opened the door to let us out.

Everything was fine until Mother got home from work.

"Some boy kissed Mary Grace on the lips on the bus," I began, but I never got to finish my thoughts.

Mother took Mary Grace by the shoulders and gave her a single shake. She had a fierce look on her face and it frightened me.

"I will not have you behave that way! Is that what you learn in public school? Why do you think I sent you to Catholic school all those years? I thought I taught you to behave like a lady! What example have you just set for your sisters?"

"Mother, it wasn't the way it sounded! Listen to me!" cried Mary Grace.

Mary Ann started to cry. Mother stopped scolding Mary Grace and ordered her to the kitchen to start dinner. Then she went into her bedroom to change.

I followed Mary Grace into the kitchen. I did not know what to say, but I wanted to say something to her.

"You brat! You tattle-tale! How could you tell Mother? You just couldn't wait to tell, could you? I'll never forget how you got me into trouble with Mother!"

Bessie and Priscilla stood by the doorway into the kitchen.

"Now get out of here, you tattle-tale!"

There was no one to help me. Even Bessie didn't try to pacify Mary Grace. Why would she? She, Priscilla, and Mary Ann had seen the wrong I had done.

The storm cleared when Mother came into the kitchen. She sensed the wrong she had done.

"I'm sorry, Honey. I should not have reacted the way I did. Mary Ann told me how it happened." Mother looked grieved.

"Okay, Mother, but I will never forgive Pauline. She just couldn't wait to tell!"

I went into the bedroom. I regretted ever opening my mouth. I fell asleep. Later that evening, I got up hungry. I got a piece of bread with butter and went back to bed. A little while later, I heard someone coming toward the bedroom. I closed my eyes and pretended to be asleep. It was Mother. She put her hand on my forehead, pulled the blanket over me, and left the room.

I was relieved on Saturday morning to find that Mary Grace had left with Joe. She was spending more and more time at Dolly's house. Ramona, Dolly's sister, also invited Mary Grace over a lot. I sat down to breakfast, but my sisters were nowhere to be seen.

"Finish your breakfast and go join your sisters," said Mother. "They are out back with your father, helping to gather boards. He is going to build a swing set with an overhang for you girls."

I went outside; the girls were on the other side of the fence pulling on some old abandoned boards. Mrs. McCoy had let Leo have them; she had no use for them.

As I approached, Priscilla looked up at me and whispered, "Go away from us, you tattle-tale."

I wanted to die. I should have kept my mouth shut. Why did I not discuss it with Bessie before I said anything? I wanted to talk to Bessie now, but she wouldn't even look at me when I called her.

"She is a big, big tattle-tale, huh, Bessie? Huh, Mary Ann?" said Priscilla.

I got a knot in my stomach when they nodded their heads in agreement. Priscilla was especially upset with me, because she was very close to Mary Grace.

I decided to stay close to Father and give the girls their time to be mad at me. Just don't let it be too long, Jesus, because I can't stand the silent treatment from my sisters!

Snow covered some of the boards that I stepped on, and suddenly pain shot through my foot. I cried out, and Father picked me up. He knew right away that I'd stepped on a nail. He carried me into the house, and the girls followed.

Mother looked up from her sewing.

"Pauline just stepped on a nail out back."

Mother grabbed a little wash pan with hot water, took my shoe off and washed my foot. She put some kind of tape on it. The girls watched for a little bit, and then went back out with Father. Tears rolled down my cheeks. My sisters had no sympathy for me; they had abandoned me in my hour of pain.

"Does it hurt a lot, Pauline? I can call Dr. Roth. He is not in his office today but we can go to his house."

Mother was not aware of the trouble between me and my sisters.

"No, Mother. It does not hurt at all anymore. I'm going to go lie down and read my catechism book; I need to study for my Confirmation."

"Tomorrow morning, I will have Leo stay with you while we attend Mass. I will also go to the drug store and pick up some Epson salt to soak your foot. It will soothe it so it can begin to heal."

"Okay, Mother, thank you."

I slept the whole afternoon. When Father came in for the day, I sat next to him and we listened to the radio. I was so unhappy that I was glad it would be bedtime soon.

Eddie Fisher's voice came through the speakers on the radio. Father had dozed off. I was alone with my thoughts, and I heard Eddie singing: "Any time you're feeling lonely, any time you're feeling blue..."

Oh, nice going, Mr. Fisher! That is all I need right now: some 'feel sorry for yourself' song!

I got up, turned off the radio, and read my catechism book.

I went to bed early, with my foot still aching. I was glad that sleep came quickly. The snow covered everything: even the little twigs on the trees looked like tiny icicles.

Chapter Twenty-two

On Sunday morning after breakfast, the girls went out to play. It hadn't snowed in a couple of days. I just sat there again; there was no invitation coming my way. The girls continued to ignore me. I came to the conclusion that Mary Grace was the only one who could fix the trouble between me and the girls. It would have to be her judgment call. If she forgave me, hopefully the rest would too.

I was limping a little but I had to go outdoors for a while. I walked toward the little shed to play on the piano. Father had taught us a tune and we were all good at it. As I approached, I couldn't believe my eyes. On the outside walls, there were initials all over it: "P+F, P+F," meaning "Pauline likes Felix."

Okay, that does it! Father doesn't call me "Apache" for nothing. I did not see the girls anywhere. Priscilla and Mary Ann were probably playing with Jenny. I walked back to the house and got a grocery marking pen.

I proceeded to add a loop to every P, thus changing it to a B. Now the initials read "B+F"—"Bessie likes Felix."

When I was done, I heard the girls giggling behind Father's truck. I giggled too, but the girls ran off without me. It was a start. Maybe the girls were warming up to me. Maybe they too missed my company.

It started to snow and I went into the house. I told Mother that my foot was aching. She gave me some baby aspirin and told me to stay off my foot.

Chapter Twenty-three

On Monday morning, we returned to school. I had missed seeing Sister Amelia; she had a way of making everyone cheerful. She was good for me. After a couple of days, my foot began to ache again. At school on Wednesday, I got sick to my stomach. Sister asked if there was anyone that could pick me up from school. I said no, but that my aunt and uncle lived a block away, and I could stay there until my older sister got home from public school. Sister let me leave.

I whispered to Julia, "Please let my sister Bessie know that I will be at Uncle Jim's house until I see the bus go toward our house. Then I will walk home from there."

After a few hours, Aunt Louise woke me up. I had fallen asleep on her sofa.

"Pauline, your sister Mary Grace just called. She is home from school and does not want you walking home alone. Your Uncle Jim will give you a ride home; he will be back from the flour mill in about fifteen minutes."

"Thank you, Aunt Louise."

I could hardly wait to be with Mary Grace. I did not feel good at all; I wanted to go home.

Aunt Louise met Uncle Jim at the door as he drove up, and said, "Jim, you need to take your niece Pauline home. She came here from school; she is really sick."

Uncle Jim walked me to my door where Mary Grace met us; she was on the phone with Mother. She thanked Uncle Jim and began to tend to me.

Mother had told her to soak my foot in Epson salt again, but when Mary Grace had me take off my snow pants, she looked concerned. She put my foot in warm water and had Bessie call Mother on the phone.

"Tell Mother that Pauline has a very high fever, and she has a red line on her leg leading from the bottom of her foot to her upper thigh!"

Mother told Bessie to put Mary Grace on the phone. When Mary Grace came back, she dried my foot and put clean socks on me.

"Dr. Roth is taking Mother to get Joe's car at the market. Then she will pick you up and meet Dr. Roth at the hospital. He is afraid you have blood poisoning from what may have been a rusty nail that you stepped on!"

"Am I going to die, Mary Grace?"

She kissed me on the cheek and said, "No, Pauline, you are not going to die. Who would tattle on me if you did?"

She smiled at me, but I couldn't bring myself to smile back.

"Mary Grace, I'm so sorry I got Mother so upset with you!"

I was admitted to the hospital. Doctor Roth was very nice; he patted me on the head and reassured me.

"Pauline, you are going to be our guest here for a couple of days. We need to get the infection out of your foot so you can get back to the business of running around the farm with your sisters. I have ordered hot compresses for your foot; do try to take the heat from the towels as much as possible. I'll be in to see you tomorrow morning."

I smiled at him, but was too shy to talk to him.

Mother stayed till visiting hours were over. "Pauline, I'm going home now, but I will be here first thing in the morning. A very good friend of mine is working the night shift and she will watch over you for me, okay, Baby?"

Mother bent down to kiss me and whispered, "In the morning, a couple of gals are coming to work the day shift that have a crush on your brother Joe, so you will be in good hands. Cheer up, Honey. It will just be a couple of days, then you will be home."

She left and then peeked back in and waved goodbye. But the only thing that could cheer me up would be to see Bessie, Priscilla, and Mary Ann in the empty bed to my right. I had never been separated from them before.

I slept pretty well, though, and did not wake until the nurse woke me to go to the rest room to wash my hands.

"Your breakfast will be brought to you in a few minutes."

Mother stopped in to see me before she went to work. "I'll come by after work, Sweetheart, and at lunchtime, I'll call you on the phone."

I fell back to sleep, but woke up when the nurse came in to put more hot compresses on my leg. I heard voices behind the curtain; someone was now in the empty bed next to me. When the nurse opened the curtain, I couldn't believe my eyes.

My "hero on ice" was in the next bed! Her family was all around her. She had a cast on her arm. I soon learned that she had broken her arm, and that her name was Roxana.

On Saturday morning, Mother and Father came to take me home. The infection had cleared. It was a very nice day. The girls were playing outside when we drove up. They ran up to the truck and smiled at me.

After Mother and Father went into the house, Priscilla announced, "Guess what, Pauline! Mr. Corlett's house is empty again; the neighbors moved away the day after you went to the hospital!"

"Oh, and you will never guess what!" said Bessie.

"What? Tell me!"

"Mary Grace is dating Joe's friend Josito!"

"And Phyllis and her family moved back to Durango; it was very sudden. We will never see the Sanchez boys again," said Priscilla.

"My goodness, I was gone only four days. What other news do you have for me?"

"Oh yes," said Priscilla, "and Mother's brother Uncle Frank called from California to let us know that he and Mother's sister Mary and a friend of theirs are coming for a visit next month."

"Also, Joe and Dolly are cooling their relationship; Mary Grace says that they don't see each other as much anymore."

"But why? He is in love with her—we all love her!"

Boy, a lot has changed in the New Year! I thought, as I walked into the house that I had missed so. The house hadn't changed, thank the good Lord for that.

I went into the bedroom and lay on the bed I shared with Mary Grace. I was alone with my thoughts. Beatrice had passed away, and her family had moved away. Priscilla wouldn't have her little playmate "Jenny" any longer. Bessie and I couldn't tease each other about Felix any more. The Sanchez family would not be around either, and we'd sure miss Phyllis and the boys. Uncle Manuel would be moving to Idaho as soon as the cold weather ended.

Why must everything change? I want everything to stay the same. I love my life just as it is; I don't want to accept changes.

Mary Grace came into the bedroom and sat on the bed. "Does your foot still hurt? Do you still have pain?"

"No, it does not hurt at all." I took my shoe and sock off and showed her that the wound had completely closed.

"Why are you in here? Go outside with the girls."

"I will, but I want to tell you that I didn't mean to tell Mother that you kissed a boy. What I meant to say that dreadful day was that the football player got in trouble with the bus driver, because he just helped himself to your lips without your permission! It all came out wrong and I got Mother so upset with you; I am so sorry!"

"It's okay, Pauline, but next time something happens, hold your horses and let the person it happens to, do the telling."

"The girls told me that Mother is letting you date this boy Josito."

"Well, I am seventeen, or will be on March 12. Mother had always wanted me to wait until I turned eighteen before I start dating boys, but because Josito is Joe's friend and is such a respectful boy, Mother and Father gave in and let me go out for Coke, and to the show, and double date to the drive-in with Joe! Life is very good for me right now, and everyone, including Bessie, says that he treats me like a queen. I have to admit; he treats me just like Father treats Mother. I couldn't ask for more. You are going to fall in love with him too, just like Bessie and I have!"

Mary Grace left the room and I lay there and wondered if the girls would love me again. I hoped they wouldn't always ignore me and call me a tattle-tale, which really hurt my feelings.

I was very ready to go back to school. Things had to be the same there. Yes, school would be the same. The nuns would never stop teaching the word of the Lord. That is where I want to be, back in school. I want to be a nun when I grow up, and I just hope that the nuns never abandon their distinctive traditional habits in favor of a simple dress or suit.

The month of March arrived with some sunshine, not much, but some. On Monday morning, Sister had us spend more time on our catechism books; she wanted her class to be very prepared to receive the holy sacrament of Confirmation.

The day arrived when I stood in front of the bishop with my white and royal-blue striped beanie on my head. I received a certificate with my Confirmation name, Teresa, written on it. Aunt Louise was my sponsor. She sat with Mother, Father, Cousin Della and my sisters.

Uncle Frank, Aunt Mary and their friend Coron arrived as planned, but I don't think my parents had any idea what their trip entailed.

This man Coron was a "medium," a psychic. He believed in spiritualism: the belief that human spirits continued to exist after death and that they could communicate with him and other psychics. This was a very grave matter, and a great sin against God, because the Church has always condemned spiritualism. The First Commandment reads, "Thou shalt not have strange gods before me." But at the time Mother and Father did not seem to fully consider this.

Father and Mother were skeptics, Mary Grace told us. They were certainly skeptical of this one man.

Mother was pleased, however, to see her sister Mary and one of her younger brothers. She had not seen Mary since she moved to California with her three children, Louie, Freddy and the baby girl, Georgia. Uncle Frank's wife Aunt Vickie and their two children, Frankie and Aurora, couldn't make the trip.

I spent most of my time listening to the grownup conversation. I learned a lot about our family in California.

Uncle Frank told Mother and Father that they should think of moving to California.

"Our sister Dolores' husband Johnny works for a paper factory, where they make paper towels, napkins, toilet paper, foil paper, and many other things. Oh, and by the way, Linda, Rebecca, John Howard, and Andrew send their love to their Aunt Della and Uncle Ignacio.

"Yes, Brother Ignacio, you could work with Johnny at the paper mill! You wouldn't have to work out in this cold weather. I don't know how your fingers don't fall off; I couldn't do this kind of work that you and our father Manuel Ortega did, before he was killed by that evil man.

"The bullet that hit my father Manuel did not cause a mortal wound, but because Pat Maes ran out of bullets, that wicked man finished my dad off by hitting him with the butt of his rifle while he sat in his truck. One can't get more evil than that, and he is still living! One day he will have to stand in front of God, and be judged!"

"We will all be judged one day."

Priscilla came into the kitchen and sat next to me. She whispered, "I don't like that man Coron even if he can do magic!"

"He does magic?"

"Yes, he can pull money out of your ear! But I stay clear of him and his coins. He keeps trying to catch me; he tells me, 'You are a pretty little thing.'"

"Don't worry; he will never catch you. You are just too fast; no one can twirl as fast as you can. You always manage to get away. And remember to call Jesus three times if you are ever scared. Just say, 'My Jesus, my Jesus, my Jesus.' That is what I do when I'm scared. Another thing you can say is what we hear Father McDevitt say in Mass: 'Dominus vobiscum.' It means, 'The Lord be with you.' And 'Et cum spiritu tuo'—'And with thy spirit'."

"Is that what you do when you are scared?"

"Yes I do, and also I say 'Kyrie, eleison'—'Lord, have mercy on me.'"

"Boy, Pauline, we should be nuns when we grow up!"

"We really should."

By the next evening, our company had convinced Mother and Father to have a séance. This was also grave matter and very clearly a mortal sin against the First Commandment, which places us under the care of God alone.

"Here we go again," said Father. "This man heard that my grandfather is Guillermo LeBlanc, who had the map of the treasure!"

"Ignacio, if you don't want to go through with it, we can just let him know how we feel. We can still stop."

"No, let's do it, so we can finally put it to rest once and for all!"

Mary Grace told us that we needed to stay in the bedroom out of sight.

Bessie asked her, "What is a séance?"

"The way Coron explained it, because he's a psychic, he is sensitive to the spirit messages and he can relate them to others. At the gathering tonight, Mother, Father, Uncle Frank, Aunt Mary, and Joe and I, if we choose, will join Coron in intense concentration to make contact with the spirit of our great-grandfather LeBlanc! The messages will come mentally and be transmitted during the séance."

"Just how does Coron know that Father's grandfather has a message for him?" I asked.

"That is a good question, Pauline. The whole reason for the séance is that by our concentration, his spirit will know that we want to know where the treasure was buried by the men of the French expedition when they had to make a run from the Indians."

"But just think about it, Mary Grace. How would our great-grandfather know where the treasure was buried? He was never a part of the expedition; it was his grandfather! According to Mama Vincentia LeBlanc, her father came from Nova Scotia with only a copy of the treasure map; and then his wife threw the copy in the fire!"

"Boy, Bessie, you girls sure have done your homework. Your questions are really good!"

"That's because we listen, and listen good, whenever the subject comes up. And we have long discussions about it, because when we grow up we plan to help Father find it and dig it up! We are all descendants of the man LeBlanc! The treasure belongs to us girls, and Leo and Joe."

"I bet those questions are the same ones going through Father's mind, and that is why he is skeptical. I'd better go see what preparations are being made for the gathering; you girls stay put."

Later in the evening, my sisters and I stayed in our bedroom while the adults went into Joe and Leo's room. We didn't like being separated from Mother and Father, especially at a time like this. But we sure did not want to be in the room with that man Coron!

We were very, very quiet, and we only whispered to each other. We were sure that we heard rapping and tapping in the room on the other side of the wall and even noises coming from the kitchen. We were so spooked; it seemed like forever before Mary Grace came in and told us we could join her and Josito in the front room. We laughed and acted silly around Josito. He was such a nice person, and we liked him a lot.

We went to bed that night still somewhat spooked. Nothing ever came of the séance, just as Father had predicted. Coron claimed that there were not enough believers at the gathering; so that was that.

In two days, they were packed and ready to return to California. Uncle Frank took a few family pictures, and shed a few tears, and held Mother very tightly. I guess it was hard to say goodbye to his older sister.

"Thank you, Della, for all the baking lessons you gave me as a little boy. You must move to California so you can come to my bakery every day for donuts."

Mother kissed him and her sister Mary goodbye.

Brother Joe and father Ignacio entertaining

Grandfather Manuel Ortega

Milkweed

Josito, a very close
friend of the family

Chapter Twenty-four

In March, Mary Grace celebrated her birthday with Josito, Joe and some of her friends. By the end of March, Mr. Corlett's family told Mother that they had new tenants for the house. A couple was moving in, with their four grandchildren.

I was bewildered, puzzled, and confused, when I learned that the new neighbors were none other than my hero on ice and her family! I had seen them all around her bed at the hospital a few weeks before! I remembered her name was Roxana. She was not shy at all; she ran over to say hello.

"Hey, I remember you! I heard the nurse call you Pauline! I'm Roxana Munford, and this is my brother Jack. We are only ten months apart in age. I'm ten and he's eleven. This is my little brother Toby, and my sister over there helping my grandparents is Peggy. She is eighteen years old; her boyfriend rides a motorcycle and my grandparents are not very happy about that! Hey, do you and your sister want to come over and play at our place?"

"This is my little sister Priscilla, and I have three other sisters and two brothers in the house. We live with our mother and father."

I could feel Priscilla's eyes on me. It was as if she had never heard me talk before. I surprised myself too, by just rattling all that off to an almost-stranger. I wanted to stop in the middle of my sentence and laugh because of the way Priscilla stared at me with her untidy hair and cute freckles and the smudge on her nose. Her eyes were so clearly saying, "What the heck got into Pauline?" But I kept talking. I don't know what had gotten into me, but I felt like I'd always known Roxana and her family. I was instantly happy for our new neighbors.

"Come on, let's go and play!" she said.

"We can't, our mother won't allow us. Not just yet, maybe in a couple of days."

"Okay, we have plenty of time! We should go help our grandparents; there is a lot to do, moving into a house. See you later!"

"Pauline, what do you mean 'in a couple of days'? You should have said 'in a couple of weeks'! What the heck got into you? I thought you would never stop talking, just like her!"

"I don't know what got into me, but isn't her brother Jack so cute? Freckles and all."

It wasn't long before we began to spend every afternoon after school with the Munfords. We got to know them very well. They shared and didn't hold anything back about their lives. Their parents had gotten a divorce and their mother thought it best that her parents raise the four children. They loved that they got to live with their grandparents.

Priscilla and I loved Roxana; she exposed us to the big, big world out there. She invited us to all her Brownie meetings, where we got to eat at rich people's homes with two-story houses. They barbecued meat that they called hot dogs. She took us to her school one Saturday and we met her and Jack's teacher. She was a lady, not a nun. Priscilla and I had thought all teachers were nuns. Her school had a lot more than just swings and a teeter-totter. She took us to the city park one day and introduced us to four-leaf clovers. She was a very good friend and never ignored us when her other friends were around. Her grandparents didn't talk much to us, but we were always welcome in their home.

Spring had arrived, and the fragrance of the lilac bushes made it official. Pansies and sweet peas bloomed over our property. Mother and Father worked the ground for the vegetable garden.

Josito dubbed the farm "El Rancho De Las Linda's Flowers." In Spanish, 'linda' is also used to describe a pretty face. Father asked Josito, "Are you talking about the flowers we've planted, or my daughters?"

Josito responded, "Both, Mr. Montoya!"

Needless to say, Father was in agreement with him. But spring brought more than blooming flowers and sunshine. The Ratenias reappeared, and so it was a time for running shoes and detours.

It also brought unhappiness for Roxana and her family. On a beautiful spring morning, Peggy's boyfriend picked her up on his motorcycle. On a country road, he lost control of the cycle going over a bridge. Peggy hit the embankment headfirst and was killed instantly. Her boyfriend died at the hospital later in the day.

This weighed heavily on us. My sisters and I had gotten close to this family, and two bad accidents in one year were a bit much to handle.

Priscilla asked, "Will they also move away, like Jennie and her family?"

We all hoped that they wouldn't. Moving wouldn't bring Peggy back. For the next few days, we spent a lot of time at Strohmayer's Mortuary.

That whole week, we took a detour down Gun Barrel Road to avoid meeting up with the Lariat gang, but the Ratenias got wise to us. They decided to wait for us in front of the bus. As we approached, we spotted them before they saw us. We decided to go back into the mortuary and pay our respects to Peggy. We took turns looking to see if they'd tire of waiting for us and leave. We were thankful that they gave up before the bus left without us. Peggy was gone by the third day, but other caskets were filled and although we did not know the people, the girls and I decided to do an unorthodox viewing till the Ratenias left. To put it mildly, we would rather view the dead than get our butts kicked.

I had hoped they would think we had moved to another town and would stop looking for us, but it didn't happen that way. On Thursday, when the bell rang, I started down the steps, but Bessie and Mary Ann were coming back up.

"Pauline! Hurry! Let's go find Priscilla before she goes down the steps. We just spotted the Ratenias approaching the church! Public school must have let out early!"

"What do we do now?"

"We must hurry and go out through the back doors of the school and walk home!"

"Good plan! There's Priscilla! I'll get her!"

I grabbed Priscilla by the hand; Bessie took Mary Ann; and we rushed down the stairs. We walked as fast as we could toward home, hoping they hadn't spotted us.

No such luck. We looked back, and Bessie yelled, "Run, Girls, run! Faster!"

Without meaning to, Priscilla let go of my hand. I knew that I could run faster than she could, but she was falling behind me. I slowed down to wait for her and saw that the five Ratenias were gaining on us. Priscilla ran a few steps ahead of me, and I suddenly felt hands on my hair. Before I knew it, I was on the ground being kicked.

But the kicking stopped as fast as it had begun. I got up, shaken, and saw ahead of me Bessie, Mary Ann, Priscilla, and a lady.

My sisters had knocked on a door and asked this lady to help. The Ratenias let go of me when they saw her come out. The lady asked if we'd like a glass of milk and a cookie. I don't remember if I had any, but I remember feeling humiliated.

We walked home the rest of the way. The bus was pulling away from Billy McCoy's house. Roxana and Jack waved as they drove by; they probably figured we had missed the bus. I asked the girls to promise that they would not talk to anyone about the beating I had gotten.

"But we can tell Mother and Father, right, Pauline?"

"Yes, we can tell them. I just meant Billy, Jack, and Roxana."

When Mary Grace heard about it, she promised to take care of it, once and for all. She couldn't understand why we had never mentioned the trouble we'd been having. She made us promise always to tell her if anyone tried to hurt us.

"Mary Grace," said Priscilla. "That man Coron tried to catch me, and I ran and got into Joe's car. I hurt his arm when he tried to reach for me, and I rolled the window up!"

"Where were we when this happened? We never left you girls alone!"

"Everyone was on the side of the house. Uncle Frank was taking pictures. I was the only one in the front yard. I saw Priscilla run and jump in the car," I said.

"Why didn't you say anything?"

"Well, Priscilla took care of him good, and they left the same day."

"Always, always tell someone if anyone is bothering you. Even if you are told not to tell! Tomorrow I will pick you girls up from school, and you will point these girls out to me! These Ratenias will never bother you again. I just hate knowing that they hurt Pauline!"

I didn't tell anyone, but after hearing what Mary Grace said, I thought the beating I got was worth it. It made Mary Grace open up; it let me know that she loved me again, and that she hated to hear that anyone had hurt me—the tattle-tale.

After school on Friday, we saw Mary Grace parked right in front when we came out. We got in Joe's car and waited. Within fifteen minutes, we spotted the five girls coming and pointed them out to Mary Grace.

Our big sister got out of the car and had words with them. Finally, she got back into the car.

"What did they say? What did they say?"

"I asked them, 'What is up with you girls acting like bullies to girls that you don't even know?'" Mary Grace started the car. "We are going to stop at Uncle Jim's house on the way home. They claimed that Grace Ortega, our cousin, told them that you four had said that they are so ugly and dark, that they look like wild Indians. They said it hurt their feelings, and that was why they wanted to beat you up. 'That is why we pulled little Pauline's hair and kicked her,' they said. 'She is the only one we could catch, so we gave it to her good!'

"I told them that if they ever bother you girls again, I will come looking for them with a policeman! They promised to never do it again."

Uncle Jim and Aunt Louisa were not at home, but we were greeted by Cousin Grace. After Mary Grace questioned her, she began to laugh.

"I'm so sorry! I did tell that lie a long time ago. One day, my sisters and I wanted to go play at your house, and Aunt Della wouldn't allow us to come that particular day. The next day at the bus stop, I spotted my cousins, and being still upset at Aunt Della, I lied to those five girls. I'm so sorry! I love my Aunt Della and Uncle Ignacio; they won't hate me, will they?"

"I'm not going to tell your mom and dad, but you need to talk to those girls and tell them what you did," said Mary Grace.

Chapter Twenty-five

The weekend went by quickly. The girls and I discussed the events of the last few weeks: Uncle Frank's visit, our new neighbors, Peggy's unexpected death, the reappearance of the Ratenias, the break-up of Joe and Dolly, and Josito being welcomed into our lives by every single person in our family. We had had a lot of ups and downs, but we decided that we needed to put it all behind us. Spring was here, and our wonderful flowers were blooming again. We decided to sing together again; it's what we did best.

On Monday morning during recess, Priscilla came to me crying because Sister Alquin had taken her quarter from her.

"She said, 'Priscilla, you do not need to be buying candy when this quarter can go toward your tuition. I'll put a credit next to your name on the blackboard.'"

My heart ached when I saw the tears roll down her cheeks. I took her by the hand.

"Come with me; we need to have a talk with the good Sister."

I smiled at her, and I could tell she was thinking, "What the heck is she going to do? Get us kicked out of school?"

We walked into the candy room. Sister Alquin sat waiting for students to come in and make their purchases. Sister looked up at us, and I started to talk quickly before I lost my nerve.

"Sister Alquin, you really need to return the quarter you took from my little sister, because our mother Della Montoya told us that if our names ever go up on the blackboard next to the word 'tuition,' that we need to let that nun know that our parents have made arrangements with Father McDevitt concerning the tuition fees."

The good Sister looked at Priscilla and asked, "Would you like to make a purchase?"

Priscilla just pointed. Sister handed her some candy and gave her change. We both said, "Thank you, Sister," at the same time, and we walked out together.

Priscilla said, "I never expected that you would find the words to say to her!"

"I didn't, either! But if one shows respect, that respect will be returned."

Priscilla put her arms around my waist and gave me a long hug. "I'll see you at lunch time. I'm going to find Julia."

I walked away thinking, Priscilla loves me again.

After school, Mary Ann sat next to me.

"Pauline, how do you do that thing with your hands that you say, 'Here is the church, and here is the steeple. Open the door and look at the people.'"

I was on top of the world; Mary Ann loved me again too. I had scored three out of four.

I needed to see if Bessie would come around too.

As we were getting off the bus, Bessie whispered, "When we get into the house, please don't take off to go to Roxana's house. We haven't played grownup sisters in a very long time; let's do it today."

Bessie loved me again!

In April, I sensed that life as we knew it was coming to an end. Mother and Father got the news that Mr. Corlett, whom Father had once worked for, had passed away in February. We also heard Cousin Phil tell Leo that since he was turning fifteen in April and had already "sown some wild oats," that he was not a boy any more. Now he was a man.

I didn't understand what Phil meant by the phrase "wild oats," but I knew it was the beginning of more change.

Priscilla also turned nine in April, and Mary Ann was excited that she would turn seven in May. The two of them felt that they would no longer have to stay with Aunt Raquel during the potato harvest. Little did they know what hard work it was.

Mary Grace overheard their conversation. "Girls, Mother will not be able to go to the fields this year."

I sensed some excitement in her voice. If Mother couldn't go to the fields this year, that meant that we would not pick potatoes this year either. As far as Bessie and I were concerned, this was a good thing. But why was there more change in our lives? Mary Grace left with Josito, so I didn't get a chance to ask why.

In June, Bessie turned thirteen, and more change came. Leo and Bessie were teasing each other. Leo pushed Bessie gently, but she lost her balance and fell down. Father walked in at that moment and said, "Son, there is to be no more rough-housing; your sister Bessie is no longer a little girl. She is a young lady now."

I didn't have a clue what that meant, but Bessie left the kitchen quickly, embarrassed.

July was one of my favorite months of the year. It was summer time: a time for us to pick flowers to arrange in our hair, walk barefoot in the creek every day, and spend time in the vegetable garden with Mother and Father.

I thought about how I would turn eleven in July and decided that it didn't matter. I hadn't changed. I didn't want to bring any more change to our lives. I loved my life just as it was. I had a mother and father that loved me; I had Joe and Leo's love, and my sisters loved me again. Their love was very special to me. Most importantly, I loved that the nuns taught us how much Jesus loves us.

Love was what brought the biggest and best change to our lives: a change that I had no problem accepting. So I guess change can be a good thing sometimes. When Mother and Father dropped the news, we were never the same again.

Mother emptied a can of pine nuts into a flat pan to roast, put the pan in the oven, and came to sit next to Father at the table.

"Come, Girls, your father and I have something to tell you."

"Your mother and I have decided to ask Our Lord to bless us with another baby! We feel that in order to receive this blessing, we need your help."

I think this was the first time we ever just sat and listened until Father had nothing more to say before we began to speak.

"Joe, Leo and Mary Grace have already been asked."

Mother went on, "What we need from you is a lot, a lot of prayers! If the whole family prays every single day that God will grant us this wish, He will, because He will know our sincerity."

"We know how to pray, and we can do this!" said Bessie. "We visit Jesus in church every day!"

"Your father and I thought you might feel this way! We have asked God to grant us this blessing around the end of the year, in December or January."

Needless to say, my sisters and I were very excited. We never tired of praying and talking about the baby. In early August, we got the good news. The whole family was out in the garden when we noticed that Mother had a hard time getting up and down. Father had to give her a hand. It looked like she was walking more slowly, and being careful not to lose her balance.

At supper time, Father began to speak and we were all very, very quiet. We looked at Mother and she smiled at us.

"Our Lord has answered all our prayers! We are going to get a baby. Doctor Roth tells us the baby may come sometime in January of 1956. Joe and Mary Grace get to be the godparents and they also get to pick the baby's name. Because there are so many girls in this family, your sister Mary Grace has picked the name for a girl! Debra May Montoya."

In the first week of September, the leaves on the trees were flaming with color. Once again, I admired the beautiful changing colors before they fell to the ground. The breezes cooled and rattled the trees. We loved playing in the heap of fallen leaves on the ground at Mrs. Roth's, when we went with Father to get Mother.

October came and brought with it "The Wayward Wind," as the song goes, "A restless wind that yearns to wander." The clothes on the line were brought in soon after they dried, or we'd find the cows clothed and warm. We were excited that there would be no potato picking for us this year. We had a few dust storms, but when they settled, we got to play with the tumbleweeds.

On the last day of October, we picked Mother up at work and Mother announced that she would not be returning to work for three months. The arrival of the baby was nearing.

Words can't explain the feeling we had that something strange and remarkable was about to happen.

On our way home, Father said, "I love Colorado, the way the snow covers the mountaintops all year long, and the aspen trees stand tall in the valley. It is said that the canyons and the water turn deep red in the late afternoon. And the columbines grow in the Rocky Mountains. The blue spruce decorated in homes at Christmas time— who would ever want to live anywhere else in the world, but here in beautiful, beautiful Colorado?"

Chapter Twenty-six

On a cold winter evening in November, we lost Blacky.

Blacky was loved by the whole family. He would stay close to Leo when Father and Mother were not at home. He was not a fat dog, as Father's nickname for him would indicate. Father also had a dog when he was a young boy, and it was a chubby dog. Father also nicknamed that one "Ma Gros' Chien." Blacky was good; he never chased our cat Goldie and he would nap next to her.

Poor Blacky only got into trouble with Mother one time that I can recall. Mother was helping Aunt Raquel by giving her daughter Estrellita a wedding reception here in our home. Mother wanted it to be very special for her. Mother had baked half a dozen cakes, and on the day of the wedding, we all went out to the yard to take pictures. When Mother came back in, she found that a cake had been knocked off the table. At first we couldn't figure out how it happened, but it was Blacky who had white frosting all over his snout.

Blacky's death was a great loss and left us sorrowful. I believe this was the first time we ever saw Father cry. Seeing the tears roll down from Father's eyes was much worse than seeing Blacky's lifeless little body. For the first time, I think Mother was at a loss for words. Would we ever want to replace Blacky?

Chapter Twenty-seven

The holiday season was upon us, starting with Thanksgiving. There was not a lot of pretense in the way Mother took on the task of preparing to celebrate the holiday. She put together the best cornbread stuffing, turkey, gravy, mashed potatoes, and mixed vegetables. For dessert she made the very best glazed yams and fruit pies, not the typical pumpkin pies, but the most wonderful fruit pies, filled with cooked prunes, apples and apricots. She also made green and red Jell-O. I didn't know if Mother realized that we were watching, and that she was making memories for us which would become holiday traditions.

The time had arrived for us to dream of Christmas and everything wonderful it brings with it. Bessie dared us to aim high in our wishes for Christmas Eve. We couldn't go up to the garret because Mother was home and there was no going up that ladder. But Bessie asked us, "Wouldn't you girls like to have a doll and buggy under the tree this year? Wouldn't it be wonderful to play and pretend we too have babies to care for, the way Mother is going to care for the baby God is blessing us with?"

So we wished for dolls and baby buggies, although I missed our eager dash up to the garret with giddy expectation to browse through the toy catalogs.

The holiday spirit began when Primo Catalino showed up at the front door with a bag of oranges in one hand, and his guitar in the other.

The finest words in the dictionary couldn't express the joy that filled our home. We were in a place full of wonder, and I knew that we treasured every moment. It was like no other time in our lives. It had everything to do with the baby, and Mother.

It began with Mother not being expected to go to work, at least for the time being. Thank you, Mrs. Roth, thank you, Doctor Roth. Getting ready for school in the morning was totally easy; Mother had a hand in every step we took.

She waved goodbye as we climbed on to the bus in the mornings, and she waited with the door open as it pulled in to bring us back in the afternoons. I had the urge to applaud when I saw her. Usually, she had already poured milk in small glasses, with a cookie beside each. It was much too cold for Leo to be out and about on his bike, so he also loved having Mother home all day.

At school, all the classes participated in Christmas plays. We sang every Christmas song ever written. We sang "Silent Night" in front of the manger. The nuns had a way of bringing to life the story of Christ's birth.

Friday finally arrived, the last day of school. We took the most exciting walk of the year, marching downtown again for our free treats and movie. This year, we didn't see a typical cowboy movie; instead they played an old 1952 movie.

A beautiful young lady, played by Ann Blyth, is shanghaied by her man, Jonathan Clark "the Boston Man," played by Gregory Peck. They fall in love, and he calls her "The World in His Arms." As we left the theater, we were given bags of candy.

Afterwards, we made a dash for the house. Mother was ironing and listening to the radio.

"Mother, we saw the best movie today!" said Priscilla. "It was a little scary, though."

"You don't say," said Mother. "Why was that?"

"It was about a ship and pirates, but it had a good ending. And now when we play, 'Let's Pretend We're Sisters,' I get to be 'The World in His Arms'!"

Leo laughed. "And all this time, I thought you were real sisters."

"It's just a game that we like to play!" said Priscilla.

"And I'm sure one day, you will have a girl in your arms!" said Mary Ann.

Leo pretended not to hear Mary Ann's comment.

Mother was humming a lullaby, and it reminded me of ones the nuns had taught us. They were my very favorites.

"Mother, do you know this one?" I sang,

> When Irish eyes are smiling,
> Sure 'tis like a morn in spring.
> In the lilt of Irish laughter,
> You can hear the angels sing.
> When Irish hearts are happy,
> All the world seems light and gay,
> And when Irish eyes are smiling,
> Sure they'll steal your heart away!

Then I started singing another one,

> Too-ra-loo-ra-loo-ral, Too-ra-loo-ra-li,
> Too-ra-loo-ra-loo-ral, hush now, don't you cry!
> Too-ra-loo-ra-loo-ral, Too-ra-loo-ra-li,
> Too-ra-loo-ra-loo-ral, that's an Irish lullaby.

"No, I don't know those, but Honey, when the baby comes, I want you to sing them to her or him. They are very nice."

"Do you think it might be a baby boy?"

"Only God knows. I just pray for a healthy baby. Now go into the front room; I have a surprise for you there."

We went quickly and found the Christmas tree all decorated and lit. Mary Grace was throwing the last of the silver icicles onto it. It was the most beautiful tree I'd ever seen. Mother decorated it the same every year, but each year it felt like we were looking at it for the first time.

Christmas! Christmas! It truly is the very best birthday ever celebrated in the whole world, I thought. I'm sure Our Blessed Mother would agree; it's her little Boy's birthday.

Christmas Eve arrived, and I realized that each year the gifts under the tree got better and better. When I was eight, my sisters and I each found a small paper bag filled with fruit, candy and peanuts under the tree. When I was nine, we each found those again as well as a new nightgown for each of us. When I was ten, we found the brown paper bags, a nightgown, and our very own rubber dolls.

This year I was eleven, and we dashed for our beautifully lit tree. We found the paper bags, nightgowns, dolls, and sitting out in plain view were four doll buggies. Seeing the joy on my sisters' faces just added to my excitement and happiness. It truly was our very best Christmas.

January 1956 arrived, and although we didn't know it, plans were being made for this country family to move to Sunny California.

We returned to school right after the New Year. When we met up with the Ratenias now, the experience was totally different. We had our dignity back. We walked with self-confidence, our heads held high.

The Sanchez boys had moved back to Durango, and it was just as well; I really was too young to be having boy problems like the gals in the comic books. But I received attention from Billy McCoy and Jack Munford, who turned out to be very good friends. I told myself I'd never forget how fond I had been of Master Albert Sanchez. I had my sisters, now and forever. They would always be there; would I ever need anything more?

On a very cold and snowy night in January, Mary Grace woke us from our sleep.

"Get up, Girls; there is so much to do! Father and the boys have taken Mother to the hospital! The baby is coming; the baby wants to be born!"

Debra May was born that January 31 at 3:30 a.m. The name was perfect for the precious little girl Mother and Father brought home three days later.

The images of the day Father brought them home from the hospital are deposited forever in my memory bank. I thought it so romantic when Father carried Mother into the house, even though she did hit her head lightly on the door frame. Mary Grace explained to us that Mother was a little weak, and that Dr. Roth ordered a blood transfusion to be given to her after the baby was delivered. We were astonished as Father talked about the great efforts needed to give Mother pints of blood to replace what she had lost.

Father explained how Mother's RH negative blood type is very hard to find because only 15% of the white race has this type. Doctor Roth researched his medical records and found that a man in Monte Vista with this blood type could be brought in and sobered up so that he could donate blood for Mother. He was referred to around town as "the wino," but he was willing to do this for Dr. Roth. Bless his heart.

It was hard to leave for school knowing that Mother was at home, with this little bundle of joy. After school, we never failed to make a dash for the house the second the bus driver opened the bus doors. Mother always had the house nice and toasty, and the aroma of baked bread and cinnamon rolls filled the house. The image of Mother sitting on the sofa in the front room nursing the baby will stay with me the rest of my days, as well as the lullaby that Father sang to Debbie in Spanish. The English translation was,

Go to sleep, my baby. What shall Mother do?
Wash your little diapers, make a dress for you.
Lady Montoya, why does baby cry?
She has lost her apple and there is no money to buy!
Go on to my cottage. I will give you two:
One for little Debbie, another one for you.

Debra May might never recall the joy her birth brought to our family, but nevertheless, she was born a country bumpkin. She will see snow fall, and see tall beautiful blue spruce trees and wonderful purple lilac bushes, I thought. She'll smell the sweet fragrances of pansies, sweet peas and lilacs. In the spring, she'll be carried out to the vegetable garden by Mother and Father.

We will take her to the creek so she can feel the wonderful spring water running between her toes. When Debra May is older, we will tell her about the lost treasure, and how Grandfather lost his life. She will not recall much of her first months of life, but she will always be a part of this Rocky Mountain state: beautiful, beautiful Colorado, her birthplace.

The radio introduced us to more wonderful songs. In those very cold wintry months, we stayed indoors, sang, and learned the words to songs like: "Star Dust," "Hey There" by Rosemary Clooney, "Half as Much," "Don't Let the Stars Get in Your Eyes," "If I Give My Heart to You" by Doris Day, "Sincerely" by the McGuire Sisters, "Hearts of Stone" by the Fontaine Sisters, "Because of You" by Tony Bennett, and last but not least, "Goodnight Irene" and "Sixteen Tons."

We took turns singing or sometimes sang together. But it was music to my ears when I heard someone suggest, "Let's pretend we're sisters."

"Let's play, Sis!"

"Okay, Sis!"

These three remembered statements take me to a safe place where I am at my happiest. We are sisters, my sisters and I.

~ My sisters, mother, and I ~

Mary Ann, Pauline, mother Della, Debbie, Bessie, and Priscilla

Mother Della, father Ignacio, and sister Debra May

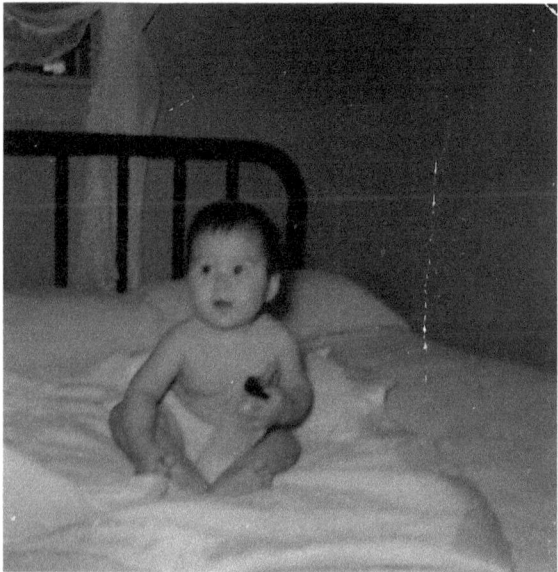

Debbie as a toddler (Debra May)

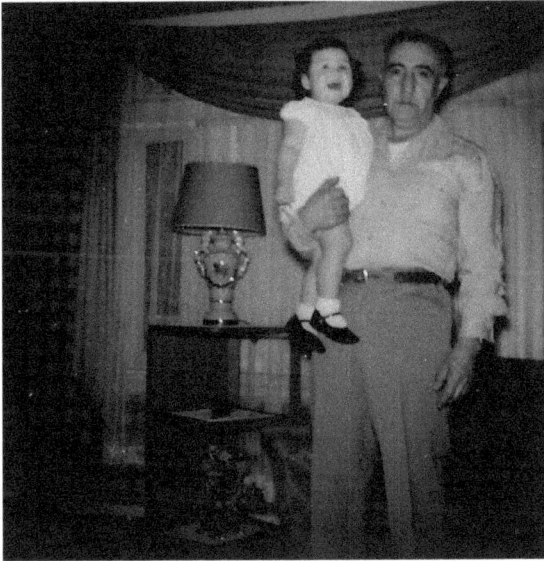

Father Ignacio and sister Debbie (Debra May)

Debbie (Debra May)

Brother Joe

Brother Leo

Sister Mary Grace

Joe, Debbie, and Leo

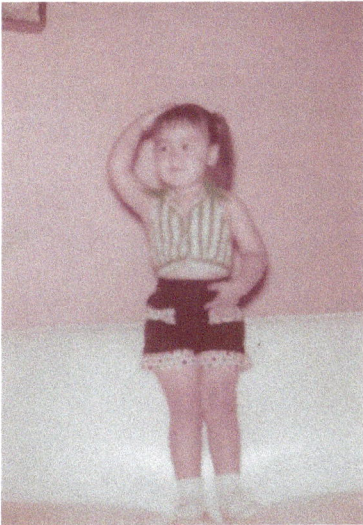

Debbie (Debra May) being
her silly self

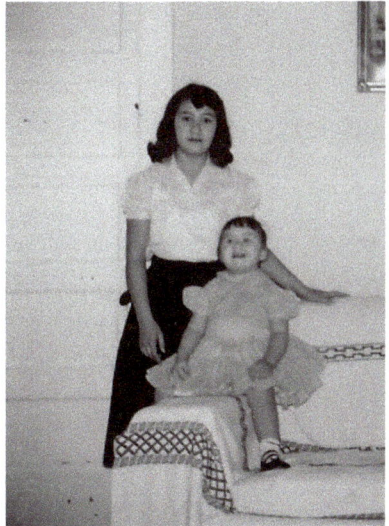

Pauline and Debbie

Leo, mother Della, father Ignacio,
and Debbie (Debra May)

Acknowledgments

My greatest appreciation and love goes to my daughter, Veronica, for patiently giving me a crash course in word processing. Time and time again, she gave of her free time to run over to my home and help when I was stuck at the keyboard.

Veronica very sweetly told me, "Mother, I will not read the story in your manuscript; I will read it after it is published, when it is in book form."

With her help, this book is now complete, and I may begin on my next narrative.

Thank you, my sweetheart.

My love and appreciation also goes out to my grandmother, Genevieve. She helped to nurse, nurture, protect, and indulge all her grandchildren with a love so pure and warm.

A very special "thank you" is in order to the Saint Joseph's Dominican nuns, for fulfilling their vocation in teaching children to know, love, and obey Jesus.

~ My brothers, sisters, mother, and I ~
Leo, Pauline, Priscilla, Joe, Debbie, Mary Grace,
mother Della,
Bessie, and Mary Ann

Brothers Joe and Leo

~ My sisters, mother, and I ~

Debbie, Bessie, Priscilla, Mary Ann, mother Della, and Pauline

About Leonine Publishers

Leonine Publishers LLC makes fine Catholic literature available to Catholics throughout the English-speaking world. Leonine Publishers offers an innovative "hybrid" approach to book publication that helps authors as well as readers. Please visit our web site at www.leoninepublishers.com to learn more about us. Browse our online bookstore to find more solid Catholic titles to uplift, challenge, and inspire.

Our patron and namesake is Pope Leo XIII, a prudent, yet uncompromising pope during the stormy years at the close of the 19th century. Please join us as we ask his intercession for our family of readers and authors.

Do you have a book inside you? Visit our web site today. Leonine Publishers accepts manuscripts from Catholic authors like you. If your book is selected for publication, you will have an active part in the production process. This book is an example of our growing selection of literature for the busy Catholic reader of the 21st century.

www.leoninepublishers.com